GW00372043

New York NOW

Published by
Dorling Kindersley Limited
80 Strand, London WC2R 0RL
www.dk.com

Editor-in-chief
Douglas Amrine

Project manager
Nigel Duffield

Editorial
*Julie Ferris, Donna Dailey,
Ellen Dupont, Fay Franklin,
Esther Labi, Fiona Morgan*

Design
*David McDonald, Steve Bere,
Tony Foo, Louise Parsons,
Mark Stevens*

Contributors
*Lester Brooks, Patricia Brooks,
Dahlia Devkota, Susan
Farewell, Rachel F Freeman,
Jonathan Schultz*

Photographers
*Mark Alexander, Andrew
Holigan, Dave King,
Michael Moran*

Illustrators
*Richard Draper, Robbie Polley,
Hamish Simpson*

Production
Chris Avgherinos

Advertising
Caroline Gibson

Marketing
Liz Statham

© 2005 Dorling Kindersley Limited

All rights reserved. No part of this work
may be reproduced or utilized in any
form or by any means, electronic or
mechanical, including photocopying,
recording or by any information
storage and retrieval system, without
the prior written permission of the
publisher. Content taken from *DK
e guide New York* and *DK Eyewitness
Travel Guide New York.*

Printed in England by Butler & Tanner.

Welcome!

New York is one of the most exciting and vibrant cities on the planet. The consummate city that never sleeps, it is both a cultural and architectural mecca.

In this magazine, we cover all the famous sights, such as the Statue of Liberty and the Empire State Building, but we also dig deeper to uncover the city New Yorkers know and love. From boutique-browsing in SoHo and poetry slams in the East Village, to concerts at Carnegie Hall and strolls through Central Park, this guide is packed with ideas to suit all tastes and budgets. There are also plenty of useful tips to help you make the most of your visit, such as when to visit the Guggenheim for free, what bars offer the best views, and which hotels are the best romantic hideaways.

This magazine has been written by the team behind the award-winning DK Eyewitness Travel Guides, which are filled with detailed illustrations, floor plans of key sights, 3D maps, and guided walks that whet the appetite whilst giving you all the information you need for the perfect holiday. Our new e»guides have been designed for savvy travellers who want to experience city life like a local and come with their own exclusive websites. And our pocket-sized Eyewitness Top 10 Travel Guides are perfect for time-strapped city-breakers. Wherever you are going on holiday, let DK be your guide.

Editor-in-chief

Contents

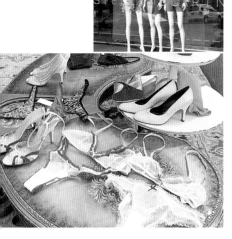

Performance 130

As well as the Broadway big sellers, New York has a host of other artistic venues devoted to music, theatre, dance, cinema, poetry, comedy, and literature.

Bars and Clubs 152

From super-cool cocktail lounges and lively DJ clubs to neighbourhood joints with jukeboxes and pool tables, New York has bars to suit everyone.

Shopping 66

Nowhere beats New York when it comes to shopping, from the designer flagships of Fifth Avenue to the funky boutiques of Brooklyn and Harlem.

Art and Architecture 104

From its soaring skyscrapers and art deco architectural triumphs to its impressive collections at the Guggenheim, Whitney, and The Met, this is a city for the serious art lover.

Hotels   200

Alongside the usual international chains, New York has a wide range of independent hotels offering individuality, character, and style.

Streetlife   180

To experience the variety of New York life, you need to visit neighbourhoods away from the well-known tourist destinations.

Havens   190

There's no need to leave the city limits in order to find a peaceful retreat. There are a plethora of parks and gardens, spas and tea rooms.

top choices

Against a backdrop of thrusting skyscrapers, New York is a city that buzzes with energy, its adrenaline-fueled, 24-hour lifestyle always charged with excitement. This is also a city of diverse cultures, which come together to offer some of the most talked-about shops, bars, restaurants, and clubs in the world. This guide leads you to New York's latest and best, opening with the top choices of what to do through the year and 24/7.

Whatever the season, there's always something going on in New York. Spring's arrival recharges New Yorkers, sending everyone outdoors to explore their city. Many venture to Brooklyn's Botanic Garden to witness the brief, energizing display of cherry blossoms. Summer, hot and sultry, offers the greatest number of cultural events for visitors, with outdoor concerts, parades, and neighborhood festivals, and the famous Museum Mile celebration. The metamorphosis of Central Park into a sea of bright yellow, rusty red, and mellow orange foliage heralds the Fall, when the Marathon snakes through the city's five boroughs. Winter might bring record snows one month and mild days the next. Yet not even the weather's mercurial nature can detract from the pageantry and fairytale spirit of the holidays.

SPRING

Cherry Blossoms at Brooklyn Botanic Garden
www.bbg.org; first weekend in May
Blooming on 220 trees adjacent to the world-renowned Japanese Hill and Pond Garden, the cherry blossoms are celebrated for one precious weekend. Traditional Japanese dances are performed, music is played, and there are origami workshops, Japanese animated films ("anime"), and samurai sword demonstrations. **May**

Tribeca Film Festival
www.tribecafilmfestival.org; late Apr–early May
Since it began in 2002, the Tribeca Film Festival has attracted hundreds of thousands of cineastes eager to view, debut, and discuss films of all scales and styles. Every year the festival attracts more attention, so check the website's booking page as early as possible if you want tickets to the hottest premieres. Everything from one of the *Star Wars* prequels to 10-minute, student-produced animated shorts have featured. The festival box office is at 20 Harrison Street (Map 1 C1), and events take place in venues as diverse as the Tribeca Film Center and Prada's SoHo store. **Apr–May**

SUMMER

Outdoor Concerts
www.summerstage.org; www.celebratebrooklyn.org/celebrate
Central Park's eclectic SummerStage outdoor concert series might host superstar DJ Paul Van Dyke one night and the New York Philharmonic the next. Meanwhile, across the East River in Prospect Park, Celebrate Brooklyn has more of a neighborhood flavor, with jazz, indie pop, and plenty of Latin salsa. **Jun–Aug**

Museum Mile Festival
www.museummilefestival.org; 6–9pm second Tue in Jun
For one June evening, the stretch of Fifth Avenue known as the Museum Mile (82nd to 105th streets) closes to traffic, and its venerable art museums waive admission charges. However, three hours to rush around the Met or the Guggenheim is a little tight, and it's better to

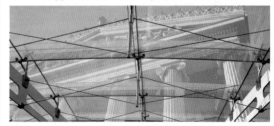

simply soak up the vibrant street scene on Fifth Avenue. Noted local artists lead art workshops, while musicians, dancers, and jugglers perform. **Jun**

Parades

Puerto Rican Day: 2nd Sun in Jun;
Gay Pride (www.hopinc.org): last Sun in Jun

The Puerto Rican Day Parade takes over Fifth Avenue from 42nd to 86th streets, and ranks among the city's largest and most festive celebrations, with over 100,000 marchers and 3 million spectators. The Gay Pride March (check website for current route) commemorates the 1969 Stonewall riots in West Village, a galvanizing moment in the Gay Pride movement. The parties and club nights built around Gay Pride are legendary. **Jun**

FALL

Feast of San Gennaro

www.sangennaro.org

Get a taste of old Little Italy during the grandest festival on the calendar for Italian New Yorkers. For 11 days, the spiritual heart of the neighborhood – Mulberry Street between Canal and East Houston streets – teems with vendors selling sausage-and-pepper, fruit ice, and Italian pastries. Processions featuring effigies of San Gennaro take place throughout the festivities. **Mid-Sep**

New York Marathon

www.ingnycmarathon.org; first Sunday of November

Attracting 35,000 athletes and over two million spectators, the marathon weaves through all five boroughs before a victor crosses the finish line. Celebrity competitors have recently included local hip-hop impresario Sean "P. Diddy" Combs, who ran modeling a mohawk – and a pack of bodyguards. Check the website for the race route map. Most spectators congregate along Central Park; head to an outer borough to get a closer look at the action. **Nov**

WINTER

Carnegie Hall & Lincoln Center Holiday Performances

www.carnegiehall.org; www.lincolncenter.org; www.nycballet.com

Come December, Carnegie Hall turns its attention to seasonal favorites, with performances by the Vienna Boys Choir and Musica Sacra. The New York City Ballet's staging of George Balanchine's *The Nutcracker* at Lincoln Center is a hallowed holiday tradition. Evening and weekend performances sell out quickly, but off-peak tickets are far more readily available. **Dec/Jan**

Restaurant Weeks

Check www.restaurantweek.com for dates

What began as an effort to attract local diners to their neighborhood restaurants has evolved into one of the city's most hotly anticipated events. For selected weeks in winter (and also in summer), Manhattan's most acclaimed restaurants offer three-course, prix-fixe lunch and dinner menus that rarely venture above $20 and $35 respectively. **Jan/Feb; Jun**

Hot Chocolate Festival at City Bakery

www.hot-chocolate-festival.com, throughout Feb

As if the original hot chocolate at City Bakery *(see p47)* were not cause enough for celebration, more than 20 novel varieties join the menu during February to melt away the city's winter doldrums. Visitors can perk up with a regular or espresso hot chocolate until 11am, after which the day's specially prepared flavor is featured. Some unlikely successes include chili pepper, beer, and banana peel varieties. **Feb**

TOP CHOICES – *morning*

The start to any day in the city-that-never-sleeps is filled with anticipation. Take a stroll around Manhattan in the early morning light and you may see fruit vendors setting out produce on a midtown corner, oblivious to suited professionals hustling by, or Upper East Side dog-walkers, with four leashes to a hand, shepherding overeager purebreds through Central Park. Though the subways are thronged with commuters, there is a less harried side to New York mornings, offering pleasures that even many locals are oblivious to. Workers in Herald Square may never know the simple enjoyment of watching chess in Chinatown, or of sampling fresh-baked muffins at the Union Square Farmer's Market. So, take advantage of the early hours to best experience snippets of the city as it rouses itself for the day ahead.

Jog or Walk on Brooklyn Bridge

For the virtuous early riser, no activity in New York suggests "morning" so emphatically as a jog across Brooklyn Bridge. To best appreciate the early rays, take the A or C train to High Street/Brooklyn Bridge, and walk or run with the commuter traffic toward Lower Manhattan. The sun glows pink against the bridge's arches and gradually illuminates the city's towering columns of glass, steel, and stone. Below, the East River shimmers gold.

Wall Street at the Start of Trading

The New York Stock Exchange, founded in 1792, is America's most hallowed temple of money-making. At around 9:15am, just before the opening bell tolls at 11 Wall Street, glimpse traders scurrying between the granite columns of the Broad Street entrance. Watching their hustle might give you an appetite, so grab a fortifying gourmet muffin and coffee from Dean & DeLuca Café at Borders (100 Broadway). *(See also p182.)*

Sunday Mass at St. Patrick's Cathedral
50th Street and 5th Avenue (Map 6 E1)

Even for travelers who have seen Europe's most dazzling Gothic cathedrals, St. Patrick's is still an awesome spectacle. It is the country's largest Gothic church – at 405 ft (123 m) long and with spires reaching skyward some 330 ft (100 m). Every Sunday, the cathedral fills with hundreds of parishioners and visitors for Mass. Should you not wish to participate directly in the service, watch proceedings from a pew near the Fifth Avenue entrance.

The Early Boat to Liberty Island
Ferry: www.statueoflibertyferry.com
Statue of Liberty: www.statuereservations.com

After nearly three years of closure following the 9/11 terrorist attacks, the Statue of Liberty reopened to the public. Once again, visitors can experience the sweeping panorama of New York Harbor from the feet of Lady Liberty. It is, of course, a perennially popular attraction, but you can avoid the heaviest crowds by catching the 8.30am Circle Line ferry from Battery Park's Castle Clinton (ticket windows open at 8:30am).

Union Square Farmer's Market
E. 17th St. and Bdwy (Map 3 D1), 8am–6pm Mon, Wed, Fri & Sat

For four days each week, the lot adjoining Union Square West fills with farmers from all over the region, eager to show off and sell the season's bounty. Besides the unmatched quality of the produce, the market provides a direct link between growers and consumers. Drink a little cider, and chat to the farmer about the orchards where his apples grow.

Brunch in the West Village
Paris Commune, 411 Bleecker Street (Map 3 A3); Deborah, 43 Carmine Street (Map 3 C4); Florent *(see p46)*

Around 10am, on virtually every West Village block, slate signs spring up outside the neighborhood's bistros, proclaiming "Brunch!" in bright pastel chalk. At the most popular restaurants, you may have to queue

for a table, but with mimosas, juices, and Bloody Marys often included free of charge, the value and quality of a West Village brunch is worth the wait. Try the French toast at Paris Commune, the fluffy, vegetable-studded omelets at cozy Deborah, or the old favorite Florent.

Dress Racks in the Garment District
The grit and pace of workaday New York is on vibrant display in this historic district. Roughly bounded north and south by 34th and 40th streets, and east and west by 9th and 7th avenues, the Garment District hosts a colorful fashion show every morning as clothing and fabric wholesalers of Hasidic Jewish, West Indian, Pakistani, Chinese, and Indian backgrounds push bulging dress racks from delivery trucks to storefronts. Buy a bagel and coffee from a vendor's cart, and try to avoid encounters between dress-rack wheels and your toes.

Pastries at Dean & DeLuca
560 Broadway *(see p65)*

The nation's pre-eminent purveyor of gourmet groceries traces its origin to the corner of Broadway and Prince Street, in the heart of SoHo. Morning customers can find formidable temptations among Dean & DeLuca's renowned pastries and cakes, as well as superior coffee and fine teas. The in-house grocer selects muffins, Danishes, doughnuts, and scones from the city's top bakeries, so customers can choose from a cross-section of the best baked goods leaving New York ovens. The coffee counter is designed with commuters in mind – drinks are sold to go.

A Stroll through Columbus Park
Mei Lai Wah Coffeeshop, 64 Bayard Street (Map 2 E1)

Over 100 years ago, this pleasant Chinatown park was the heart of the violent Little Five Points neighborhood, dramatically depicted in Martin Scorcese's film *Gangs of New York*. Though times have clearly changed, tempers do still flare when elderly Chinese men battle it out over chessboards at the park's many picnic tables. Close to the park's gates, palm readers and cobblers solicit business from Chinese-speaking passersby. Buy a roast pork bun and coffee from the Mei Lai Wah Coffeeshop, and take in the charming scene.

Dim Sum in Chinatown
Golden Unicorn *(see p33)*; HSF, 46 Bowery (Map 2 E1)

Be it a fishmonger tying crab claws shut or a woman weighing a sack of lychee nuts, Chinatown offers a feast for the eyes. And during late morning, the feast moves into the neighborhood's grand dim sum dining rooms. Steaming carts filled with roast pork buns, lotus leaf-wrapped rice, vegetable dumplings, and dessert custards circulate between communal tables. Indicate to the server which plates intrigue you (note that most servers speak very little English, so pointing is the accepted vocabulary), and start eating. Two of the best dim-sum restaurants are Golden Unicorn and HSF.

New York hits its stride in the afternoon. Save for the nightclubs and a few bars and restaurants, the entire city is open for business and the shopping streets are at their most bustling. Of course, even commerce takes a lunch break, and, when it does, there is no better place to be on a sunny day than midtown's picturesque Bryant Park. Here, in one of the city's most treasured green spaces, you can enjoy unrivaled people-watching. If you're feeling energetic after lunch, you might opt for a walk or bike ride through Central Park, art gallery browsing in Chelsea, or some retail therapy in SoHo's chic boutiques. Afternoons are for taking things at your own pace, even if that means simply sipping an espresso and reading a first-edition classic in a cozy armchair.

Boutique-Browsing in SoHo
Moss *(see p74)*; Chanel, 139 Spring St. (Map 3 D5); Helmut Lang *(see p72)*; Dolce & Gabbana, 434 West Broadway (Map 3 D4)
Shoppers who stray from the big, brash emporiums on Broadway's SoHo stretch are duly rewarded on the neighborhood's quaint side streets, where designer boutiques abound. Fans of sleek, modernist furnishings should stop at Moss. European-fashion mavens can take their pick from Chanel, Helmut Lang, and Dolce & Gabbana.

Gallery-Hopping in Chelsea
Pace Wildenstein, 534 W. 25th St.; Mary Boone Gallery, 541 W. 24th St.; Gagosian Chelsea, 555 W. 24th St. (All Map 5 D5)
Chelsea has some of the world's most prestigious commercial art galleries, including Pace Wildenstein and Mary Boone, who has built on her success with 1980s art stars Julian Schnabel and Jean-Michel Basquiat. Larry Gagosian is one of the biggest international dealers, with galleries in the Upper East Side, Beverly Hills, and London. Exhibitions at his Chelsea outpost are among the most hotly anticipated in New York. *(See also p108.)*

Open-Air Swimming
Astoria, 19th Street & 23rd Drive, Queens; Hamilton Fish Pool, 128 Pitt Street, Manhattan (Map 4 G4); www.nycgovparks.org
Many New Yorkers themselves are not aware that the city's park service maintains over 20 outdoor swimming pools, let alone that the facilities are free of charge. This inexplicable oversight by the locals is the visitor's gain, however. Of all the city's pools, the jewel in the crown is the Astoria in Queens (use the Astoria Boulevard stop on the N or W subway trains). This giant of a pool hosted the U.S. team's swimming trials for the 1936 Olympics. Portions are sectioned off and designated for lap swimming or for general use. In Manhattan, check out the Hamilton Fish Pool in Alphabet City, which has pleasant shady areas around the pool. Note that there is no admittance without proper bathing attire, and you need to take a padlock for your locker.

An Invigorating Massage
Graceful Services, 2nd Floor, 1047 2nd Avenue (Map 8 G5), 212 593 9904, www.gracefulservices.com
Should sightseeing leave your muscles tight and achy, Graceful Services holds the remedy: deep tissue massage, practised according to the age-old techniques of the East. Refreshingly bereft of rose petals, scented candles, and other frivolous spa accoutrements, the private rooms at Graceful Services appear somewhat clinical. But as your blocked chi, or life energy, is released by the deft hands and fingers of a licensed masseur, you will not want for anything more. It's popular with midtown workers and diplomats from the nearby U.N. headquarters, so you'll need to book.

Biking & Boating in Central Park

Loeb Boat House, between 74th & 75th streets (Map 8 E2), 212 517 2233; open 10am–5:30pm; roads closed to vehicular traffic 10am–3pm Mon–Fri, 7–10pm Sat & Sun

Comprising 843 acres of ponds, meadows, hills, and forest, Central Park is an urban oasis like no other, but its sheer scale presents a challenge for those with limited time. Luckily, you can hire a bicycle and helmet by the hour at the Loeb Boat House. Note that cycling teams practice in the park, and etiquette requires recreational riders to move toward the curb to let them pass. Alternatively, take to the water in a rowing boat or gondola.

Picnicking at Bryant Park

42nd Street (Map 6 E2), www.bryantpark.org

At the first sign of fair weather, beautifully maintained Bryant Park transforms into the alfresco lunch room for

hundreds of midtown professionals. Garden furniture is plentiful, and the public restrooms are uncommonly clean. There's also a "reading room," where visitors can borrow current issues of popular magazines, while music and dance performances take place on the sprawling lawn. Above all, the park is a prime spot for people-watching. Buy a sandwich at Pret a Manger (11 W. 42nd St.), take a seat, and indulge.

Reading a Book

Housing Works Used Book Café, 126 Crosby Street (Map 3 D4), 212 334 3324, www.housingworksubc.com

Browse books, sip cappuccino, nibble cookies, and support a good cause – all at the same time. Housing Works provides job training, health care, and housing advocacy for the city's homeless who have HIV and AIDS, via profits from its used books and coffee. This bookstore-café, housed in a former warehouse, has high ceilings, mahogany paneling, and spiral staircases that impart an airy richness to the ambience. Make your purchases, find a comfortable armchair, and while away the afternoon with an out-of-print classic.

Markets and Shops of East Harlem

East 116th Street between Park & 3rd avenues (Map 12 F5)

Spanish Harlem was populated almost entirely by Puerto Rican New Yorkers until the 1980s, but now it also has many Mexican, Chinese, and other Caribbean residents. On East 116th Street, the waft from a Mexican bakery is just as likely to seize your attention as the candles burning inside a Haitian *santería* (shop selling mystical goods), or the elderly Dominican gentleman pushing his tropical fruit ice cart and shouting out the day's flavors in Spanish. Score authentic Mexican sweets and restorative *horchata* drinks at Don Paco López Panadería (2129 3rd Ave.).

A Tour of Penn Station

4th Mon of every month; meet at 34th St. Tourist Info Kiosk, Penn Station Rotunda (Map 5 D4), 212 719 3434

New York lost a treasure when this Neo-Classical station was destroyed by thoughtless planners in 1964. However, traces of the 1910 structure do survive, and well-informed guides illuminate these details, and describe the grandeur that was lost.

TOP CHOICES – *evening*

Evening's arrival might signal the end of the working day, but to board the homebound train immediately after leaving the office is an alien concept for most New Yorkers. With so many happy-hour specials at the city's myriad bars, a dining scene unmatched in its diversity and quality, free cultural events, and top-quality sports games, it is not difficult to understand the reluctance to go straight home. Such choice can be overwhelming, even for locals – should you be racked with indecision, concentrate on the area below 14th Street, where Manhattan's restaurants and bars are most densely packed. It never hurts to call ahead and reserve a table for dinner, especially on weekends. But, unless you plan to dine at the most exclusive restaurants *(see pp30 & 46)*, getting a table on the day is usually easy.

"Vicious" Cocktails at the Algonquin
59 W. 44th Street (Map 6 E2), www.algonquinhotel.com
In the 1920s, when the acerbic Dorothy Parker wrote for *Vanity Fair*, she would meet with other writers (including novelist F. Scott Fitzgerald) for cocktails and gossip at the Algonquin Hotel. Their group was known as the Vicious Circle, as no celebrity was spared their sharp-tongued critiques. Soak up the sophisticated atmosphere in the hotel's Blue Bar, where witty cartoons by *New Yorker* veteran Al Hirschfeld adorn the walls.

Museum Deals
**Museum of Modern Art *(see p113)*; Jewish Museum *(see p117)*; Guggenheim *(see p116)*; Whitney *(see p113)*; BMA *(see p120)*
Several museums operate a "pay what you wish" policy in the evening: the Museum of Modern Art (4–8pm Fri); the Jewish Museum (5–9pm Thu); the Guggenheim

(6–8pm Fri); and the Whitney (6–9pm Fri). At the Brooklyn Museum of Art, admissions are waived all day (until 11pm) on the first Saturday of the month, when bands, dance troupes, and a cash bar create a party atmosphere.

Latin American and Yiddish Theater Peformances
El Repertorio Español, 138 E. 27th St. (Map 6 F4), www.repertorio.org; Folksbiene Yiddish Theater at the Manhattan JCC, 334 Amsterdam Avenue (Map 7 B1), www.folksbiene.org
El Repertorio Español stages productions adapted from Spanish literature as well as original pieces from emerging Latin playwrights. Performances are in Spanish, with simultaneous translation through headphones. The Folksbiene's repertory recalls early 20th-century New York, when scores of Yiddish theaters dotted the downtown area. Productions (in Yiddish, with English supertitles) are heavy on songs and slapstick humor.

A Sunset Ferry to Staten Island
Whitehall Ferry Terminal (Map 2 E5), www.siferry.com
Sunset adds immeasurable ambience to an already spectacular ferry trip across the Hudson River. The free 25-minute journey offers views of Lower Manhattan's skyscrapers and bridges, plus Liberty, Ellis and Governor's islands. Ferries depart every 15 to 20 minutes between 5 and 8pm.

Shooting Pool
SoHo Billiards, 298 Mulberry Street (Map 4 E4); Fat Cat Billiards, 75 Christopher Street (Map 3 B3)
A pool player's pool hall, SoHo Billiards dispenses with

the brass fixtures and high polish of uptown parlors and simply provides 20 pool tables in excellent condition, and reasonable hourly rates. It doesn't have a bar though – if you want a beer with your Eight-ball, head over to the subterranean world of Fat Cat.

Happy Hour at McSorley's
15 East 7th Street *(see p142)*
Around 5pm on weekday evenings, a mix of intellectuals, edgy East Village types, and hard-drinking regulars congregate at this old bar for discounted rounds of ales. More convivial than on busy weekends, weeknight happy hours allow you to relax at a communal wood table, or press the bartender for obscure McSorley's history.

Catch the Knicks at Madison Square Garden
2 Pennsylvania Plaza (Map 6 E5), 212 465 5867, www.nba.com
Although the Knicks are one of the most popular basketball teams, visitors to Madison Square Garden can nearly always obtain tickets – even when the game is officially sold out. The Garden box office withholds the release of hundreds of tickets until game day, so spontaneous travelers with a sudden desire to scream in unison with a 20,000-strong crowd should phone the ticket line or go down to the box office. Check the team's website for occasional discount-ticket promotions.

Poetry Slams in the East Village
Nuyorican Poets Café, 236 East 3rd Street *(see p119)*
The Nuyorican Poets Café was founded in 1973 with the specific aim of providing a forum for Puerto Rican-New Yorker writers – a group that included poet and award-winning playwright Miguel Piñero. The intimate space has a much wider remit these days, and is renowned for its raucous, informal poetry-recital competitions – known as

"slams" – and collaborations between musicians and vocal artists. Performances often blur the line between hip-hop lyricism and spoken-word poetry. Respected hip-hop personalities Mos Def, Company Flow, and Rahzel occasionally stop by for impromptu sessions.

Outdoor Movies in Bryant Park
Map 6 E2, www.bryantpark.org
Enchanting at any time of the day *(see also p21)*, Bryant Park acquires a communal, festive mood on warm summer evenings. Every Monday throughout July and August, the Park organizes free screenings of classic movies on the lawn, which begin as soon as the sun sets – with luck, you might see it dip below the horizon while gazing down West 40th Street. Go early, take a picnic meal, and enjoy the show. Also during summer, jazz musicians play free concerts by the park's terrace; most performances have a groovy, Latin flair.

The View from Top of the Tower
Top of the Tower @ Beekman Tower Hotel *(see p194)*
This cocktail lounge and restaurant offers some of the best seating in New York to watch the spectacle of the city's buildings lighting up at night. Book a window terrace table (off the main room), and ideally arrive at dusk to enjoy the subtle transformation of the skyline. Once night has fallen, you can turn your attention to the well-mixed cocktails and menu of American cuisine.

On weekends in Chelsea and the East and West Villages, and spilling over into adjacent neighborhoods, sidewalks teem with as many pedestrians at 2am as at 8pm. New York, in this regard, feels more akin to European cultural capitals than to any other American urban center. The pulsing nightclubs of New York attract the world's top DJs, lured instinctively to the city that nurtured jazz in its infancy and gave birth to hip-hop and rap. The city is also famous for producing sharp-witted comedians, who supply laughs nightly in the many comedy clubs. It is difficult not to love such a place, even if you prefer more subdued diversions, such as ogling New York's incomparable skyline from the top of its most fabled building, or swapping stories with friends over a few glasses of wine at Rhône.

Stargazing at the Hayden Sphere

Rose Center for Earth and Space, American Museum of Natural History (Map 7 C1), 212 769 5200, www.amnh.org/rose
Housed in a glass box, the 87-ft (27-m) diameter Hayden Sphere is the world's largest virtual reality simulator. Its striking form, luminescent at night, has endeared it to New Yorkers since the Rose Center opened in 2000. Come on a Friday, when it stays open until 8:45pm, for a mesmeric journey through the cosmos.

Improv at the Upright Citizens Brigade Theatre

307 W. 26th St. (Map 5 C5), www.ucbtheatre.com New York's boldest, most irreverent comedians ply their trade on this Chelsea stage. Any given night sees performances by sketch and improvisational comedy troupes, plus stand-up comics. Tuesday's "Harold Night," which generally offers the most reliable laughs of the week, pits the city's best long-form improv comedy troupes against each other.

Nighttime Views from the Roof of New York

Empire State Building Observatory (Map 6 E3), 212 736 3100, www.esbnyc.com (last elevator up at 11:15pm)
On a clear night, the scene from the 86th floor of the Empire State Building is breathtakingly beautiful. Southward views show the Flatiron Building cleaving downtown traffic into two luminous veins: one bound for further travel down Fifth Avenue, the other for Broadway. Surrounding you are the twinkling icons of the Art Deco era *(see p111)*, including the Chrysler, Chanin, and General Electric buildings. No visit to the city is complete without this experience.

Bar-Hopping in East Village

If you're in the mood for a sleek, intimate wine bar, an authentic Irish pub, a hard-rocking dive, or any combination thereof, make the East Village your destination. Second Avenue has the neighborhood's greatest concentration of bars, and high-quality drinks and diversions abound off this principal nightlife thoroughfare. The scene below St. Mark's Place is fun, but can become rowdy after midnight. Try Swift *(see p162)* for traditional Irish cheer and well-drawn pints. Bar Veloce *(see p164)* is good for reasonably priced Italian wines. Should you find yourself craving cheap beer, loud rock and 1970s living-room kitsch, then put Welcome to the Johnson's *(see p160)* on your itinerary.

Wine-Sipping at Rhône
63 Gansevoort Street *(see p168)*
Following a long day at the office, New York's stylish set migrates to this cavernous wine bar in the Meatpacking District. Rhône is a reflection of everything the area has become: pricey, chic, and trend-setting. It has a lofty ceiling, painstakingly modern furnishings, and mammoth windows. The knowledgeable bartenders can assist you in choosing one of the 30 reds available by the glass.

A Midnight Movie at the Sunshine Cinema
143 East Houston Street (Map 4 E4), 212 330 8182, www.landmarktheatres.com
Each weekend brings a different cult classic for a midnight screening at this immaculately restored, late 19th-century former vaudeville theater. Favorites include Mel Brooks's *Blazing Saddles* (1974), while Steven Spielberg's *The Goonies* (1985) is popular with NYU students hooked on 80s nostalgia. The screenings are social events; some audience members even arrive in costume and shout out classic lines along with film.

Music on the River
Barge Music, Fulton Ferry Landing, Brooklyn *(see p150)*
Ships on the East River, when sounding their baritone airhorns, impart a salty maritime character to the city. But could they share the river air with, of all things, the dulcet harmonies of chamber music? Barge Music, docked at the eastern end of Brooklyn Bridge, believes so. This gorgeously renovated barge provides the city's most rarified environment for hearing classical music. And for a backdrop, the 125-seat auditorium has the entire glittering spectacle of nighttime Manhattan.

Club-Hopping in Chelsea
Style is paramount in Chelsea – a neighborhood of design studios, art galleries, and architecture firms. And where aesthetically minded people work, nightclubs tend to follow. Witness Avalon *(see p169)*, a world-class dance club housed in a former church. Spirit *(p170)* is unrelenting in its pursuit of sensory stimulation: multiple rooms offer a panoply of sounds, light shows, and performance arts. Hiro *(p170)* feels like a modern speakeasy hiding in the bowels of an exclusive Tokyo hotel, while Roxy *(p169)* caters to the most colorful clubbers in the city.

Jazz at the Village Vanguard
Village Vanguard, 178 7th Avenue South *(see p136)*
The Vanguard inspires almost religious levels of veneration, and a glance at the roster since it was founded in 1935 explains why. Miles Davis, John Coltrane, Dizzy Gillespie, and Wynton Marsalis have all performed (and sometimes recorded albums) in this intimate West Village space. The award-winning Vanguard Jazz Orchestra plays on Mondays; saxophone master Joe Lovano and jazz-rock fusion artists The Bad Plus are other regulars.

Late-Night Quick Bites
New York caters well to nocturnal appetites. Wherever there is a large concentration of bars, there is also a choice of eateries that are open late. The East Village has the Turkish cafeteria Bereket *(see p35)*, the inexpensive Yaffa Cafe *(p38)*, and the bright, historic Ukrainian café Veselka *(see p275)*, which prepares a wondrous borscht. West Village night owls congregate outside Joe's Pizza *(see p274)* for some of the best slices in Manhattan.

The Food Doctor, Ian Marber, as seen on *Richard & Judy*

EAT WELL
LOOK
GREAT
LOSE WEIGHT
FOR GOOD

No hunger, no calorie counting – the plan that will change your life

GI BALANCED

"...what you really want
to know is does it work?
The answer is yes"
HEAT

Available now from **WHSmith**

discover more at www.dk.com/fooddoctor

restaurants

New York is one of the world's finest cities for dining out, whether you aspire to a table at one of the most fashionable restaurants, or simply want to pick up something cheap and tasty from a café or from a street vendor. Myriad restaurants cover every cuisine imaginable, the food served up on anything from banana leaves to porcelain plates. The following pages provide a snapshot of NY's dining scene.

HOT TABLES	ROMANTIC SETTINGS	WORLD CUISINES

Babbo
110 Waverly Place
One of celebrated Italian chef Mario Batali's first restaurants – tables here need to be booked two weeks in advance. *(See p42)*

Aquavit
13 West 54th Street
Succulent herrings, seafood stews, and other Scandinavian delectables are served in an atrium with its own running waterfall. *(See p53)*

66
241 Church Street
The combination of Chinese fusion cuisine, sleek furnishings, killer cocktails, and a fashionable crowd makes 66 a hot Tribeca ticket. *(See p32)*

Tomoe Sushi
172 Thompson Street
New Yorkers are prepared to line up outside this small, simple space in order to sample ultra-fresh and tender sushi. *(See p41)*

Atlantic Grill
1341 3rd Avenue
This seafood restaurant is a perennial favorite with discerning Upper East Siders. Book in advance or be prepared to wait. *(See p56)*

New Leaf Café
Fort Tryon Park
Beautiful Fort Tryon Park provides a delightful backdrop – take a stroll before settling into the café. *(See p59)*

Tamarind
41–3 East 22nd Street
Here you'll find spices and Indian flavors with an individual twist, as in Tamarind's signature tandoori scallops. *(See p49)*

» *If you register on the www.iseatz.com website, you can do your restaurant booking online, using a credit card.*

Sobaya
229 East 9th Street
Noodles in broth never tasted so good as at this hip East Village Japanese dining room. There's a great range of sake too. *(See p40)*

i Trulli
122 East 27th Street
Excellent Italian cuisine enhanced by first-rate Chianti. Cozy up by the fire in winter; enjoy the garden in summer. *(See p50)*

The River Café
1 Water Street
The ultimate mix of top-quality cuisine and divine views of the Manhattan skyline, rising up from the East River. *(See p60)*

SWEET TOOTH

Mezzaluna
1295 3rd Avenue
The pasta and brick-oven-baked pizza may be delicious, but the tiramisu is *divine* in this Upper East Side Italian joint. *(See p55)*

Ouest
2315 Broadway
Ouest's generous helpings of panna cotta are heavenly – so long as you have room after meat loaf or braised lamb shank. *(See p57)*

Balthazar
80 Spring Street
Balthazar is known throughout town for brunches and sweet pastries. The home-made donuts are perfect for dipping into a coffee. *(See p33)*

>> *Remember that tipping the waitstaff is de rigueur in New York, regardless of whether the service is great or indifferent – the accepted rate is 15–20%.*

Tartine
253 West 11th Street
This bijoux West Village bistro has a tempting array of fresh fruit tarts and mousses. It also does a wonderful crème brûlée. *(See p46)*

DINERS

Paul's Palace
131 2nd Avenue
Monstrous hamburgers, fries, and milkshakes team up well with the salty personalities of Paul's endearingly gruff waitresses. *(See p39)*

Relish
225 Wythe Avenue, Brooklyn
This Williamsburg destination serves robust, inventive American bistro cuisine in a classic diner setting. *(See p63)*

2nd Avenue Deli
156 2nd Avenue
More than 50 years of tradition go into huge sandwiches, thick soups, smoked fish, and other Jewish classics. *(See p41)*

BARGAIN BITES

NY Dosas
West 4th Street & Sullivan Street
A vendor cart in Washington Square is renowned for sublime South Indian crêpes filled with finely spiced vegetables. *(See p45)*

Daily Chow
2 East 2nd Street
Creative pan-Asian bites include marinated chicken skewers, Mongolian barbecue bowls, and luscious, exotic fruit juices. *(See p38)*

Joya
215 Court Street, Brooklyn
Joya's ultra-modern, hip dining room belies a menu rich in absurdly affordable, delicious Thai standards. *(See p60)*

Sandwich Planet
534 9th Avenue
A tiny shop that scores with almost limitless combinations of fillings, and fresh breads. *(See p51)*

66 *Chinese with a twist* `1 D1`

241 Church Street • 212 925 0202
>> www.jean-georges.com
Open lunch & dinner daily (to midnight Mon–Thu,
to 1am Fri & Sat, to 10:30pm Sun)

A restaurant in the empire of prestigiously gifted chef
Jean-Georges Vongerichten, 66 has a chic, minimalist
interior, immersed in shades of white, silver grays,
and black. The lofty space, with a view to the kitchen
above a row of fish tanks, attracts style slaves and
foodies alike. Dishes draw on Chinese influences,
and are produced with the customary Jean-Georges
flair – specialties include Peking duck, the 66 sesame
noodles, sweet and sour two-flavored shrimp,
steamed cod, Vietnamese coffee-flavored sorbet, and
five-spice vanilla ice cream. The evening is when 66
is at its liveliest best – if you haven't reserved,
imaginative cocktails ease the wait for a table. Lunch
is cheaper, with a reasonable prix-fixe menu. The
check is accompanied by light, green-tea fortune
cookies. **Expensive**

Montrachet *quality food and wine* `1 C1`

239 West Broadway • 212 219 2777
Open lunch & dinner Mon–Fri, dinner only Sat

With one of the best cellars in the country,
Montrachet has a wine selection to match its *haute
cuisine*. A sommelier will provide information and
advice without a trace of condescension, should the
list seem daunting. The three-room dining space is
relaxed and comfortable. **Expensive**

Acappella *gourmets and grappa* `1 C2`

1 Hudson Street • 212 240 0163
>> www.acappella-restaurant.com
Open lunch & dinner Mon–Fri, dinner only Sat

This ever-popular New York haunt produces
deliciously authentic northern Italian food. Along
with seasonal variations, the menu boasts well-
prepared lamb and fish as well as superb pasta and
pesto. And the indulgent waitstaff provide free
grappa. **Expensive**

Peking Duck House *perfect poultry* `2 E1`
28 Mott Street • 212 227 1810
Open all day from 11:30am daily

Chinatown's bustle carries into this restaurant on busy nights, and the Peking duck leaves little wonder why: crisp skin and succulent meat are served with sliced cucumber, scallions, and tangy-sweet sauce. Service can be brusque, and other dishes are fairly standard, but the bird is transcendent. **Moderate**

Golden Unicorn *a beacon in Chinatown* `2 F1`
18 East Broadway • 212 941 0911
Open all day from 9am daily; dim sum 9am–3:30pm

Deep in Chinatown lies this shrine to the indulgent Cantonese tradition of dim sum. Late on Sunday mornings, the 1,000 seats of a pleasantly appointed dining room fill with families eager to sample petite plates of shrimp dumplings, roast pork buns, and sweet egg custards. Dinner is a quieter affair. **Cheap**

Balthazar *timeless brasserie* `3 D5`
80 Spring Street • 212 965 1785
>> www.balthazarny.com Open from 7:30am daily (to 1am Mon–Thu, to 2am Fri & Sat, to midnight Sun)

Parisian in style, Balthazar has retained its popularity through consistently good bistro fare. The menu changes throughout the day, catering for breakfast, lunch, dinner, and through to after hours. Sublime desserts, and weekend brunch is a winner. **Moderate**

Mercer Kitchen *hip French/American* `3 D5`
99 Prince Street • 212 966 5454
>> www.jean-georges.com Open breakfast: 7–11am; lunch: noon–2:45pm; dinner: from 6pm daily

The Mercer is all about keeping things simple and chic. The SoHo location attracts the trendsetters; the menu attracts the foodies. Its setting is casual, with tables, banquettes, and bar seating surrounding an open-plan kitchen. **Moderate**

L'Ecole *gastronomy defined* `3 D5`

462 Broadway • 212 219 3300

>> www.frenchculinary.com/lecole

Open lunch & dinner Mon–Fri, dinner only Sat

A restaurant that ticks all the right boxes: set in a prime location, it has a bright, airy interior with huge windows, serves excellent food, and offers bargain prices. L'Ecole is indeed a school, and the students of the French Culinary Institute use the patrons as their willing and hungry guinea pigs. It's a wonderful arrangement – diners indulge on three- and five-course meals without having to sell off the family silver, while students have a chance to hone their skills. You can order à la carte, but the prix fixe is excellent value.

These students are potentially star chefs, and the menu reflects that ambition by offering dishes rooted in both traditional and contemporary French cuisine. Creations such as poached sole with shrimp and mussels in a cider cream sauce, eggplant and red pepper terrine, and tea flan served with madeleines demonstrate the challenging nature of the cooking. If you prefer simpler fare, omelet with shoestring potatoes won't disappoint. Even the delectable bread is made on the premises. The menu changes every six weeks.

You'll be hard-pressed elsewhere to find such a winning combination of bright atmosphere and first-rate cooking at these prices. **Cheap**

Jane *creative American fare* `3 D4`

100 West Houston Street • 212 254 7000

>> www.janerestaurant.com

Open all day from 11.30am daily

Jane takes the food you may already know and adds special touches, subtly reinventing but not disguising the main ingredients. Meat and salmon burgers reign supreme, though the juicy fruit-purée cocktails give them a run for their money. **Moderate**

Cafe Gitane *North African spices* `4 E4`
242 Mott Street • 212 334 9552
Open all day from 9am daily

French/North African offerings such as fragrant cous cous and spicy mergüez sausages draw the area's fashionable youth. In summer, the sidewalk tables are hotter commodities than the designer sandals in the neighboring boutiques, but the cozy dining room holds plenty of charm too. **Cheap**

Cafe Habana *Cuban/Mexican café* `4 E4`
229 Elizabeth Street • 212 625 2001
Open all day from 9am daily

Flavorful specialties from this bustling corner café inspire devotion among Nolita's beautiful people, who eye one another over delicious Cuban pork sandwiches, huevos rancheros, and corn on the cob. Quench your thirst with a *chelada*: Mexican lager with lime juice and salt. **Cheap**

Bereket *late-night Turkish belly-filler* `4 F4`
187 East Houston Street • 212 475 7700
Open 24 hours daily

Rare is the downtown resident who, after a night of barhopping, hasn't relished the succulent lamb shawarma sandwich, fresh hummus or tangy, stuffed vine leaves at this East Houston institution. For what is essentially a Turkish fast-food restaurant, Bereket offers surprisingly subtle, authentic eats. **Cheap**

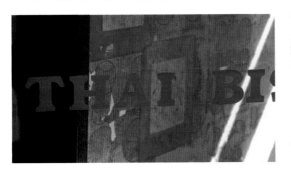

The Elephant *French/Thai fusion* `4 F4`
58 East 1st Street • 212 505 7739
>> www.elephantrestaurant.com
Open lunch & dinner daily

Reds and golds dominate the whimsical, evocatively lit dining room, where couples sip luscious Elephant Martinis – vodka, cassis, and pineapple. Don't miss Sticky Rice – chicken and pork steamed with rice and vegetables in lotus leaf wrapping. **Moderate**

'inoteca *great small plates* `4 F4`

98 Rivington Street • 212 614 0473
Open noon–3am daily

A happening corner wine bar/restaurant, 'inoteca is perfect for a few glasses while you munch on a selection of snacks, known as "small plates." These include cheeses, a generous helping of sliced meats, panini, and salads. Weather permitting, you can sit outside for high-caliber people-watching. **Moderate**

WD-50 *adventurous American* `4 G4`

50 Clinton Street • 212 477 2900
>> www.wd-50.com   Open dinner daily

Chef Wylie Dufresne built his reputation on taking risks in the kitchen, and you can try some of his daring and delicious experiments in this simple, clean restaurant. Rabbit sausage with avocado, snapper with juniper berries, or lamb with hibiscus-date purée are typical attention-grabbers. **Expensive**

Cube 63 *unique sushi in a stylish setting* `4 G4`

63 Clinton Street • 212 228 6751
Open lunch & dinner Mon–Fri, dinner only Sat & Sun

Having worked in New York's top sushi kitchens, brothers Ken and Ben Lau carry priceless expertise into their sleek restaurant. Mellow green light illuminates the sushi counter, while votives cast sexy shadows on young professionals sharing *omakase*: a sampler platter of the Laus' wildly creative rolls. **Moderate**

Alias *deceiving appearance; convincing menu* `4 G4`

76 Clinton Street • 212 505 5011
Mon–Thu 6–11pm, Fri & Sat 6–11:30pm, Sun 5–10pm

Don't let the kitsch signage mislead you; there's no spam on the menu. Alias serves imaginative dishes, including lamb spare ribs, duck confit, and candied avocado. It's one of the places that has made the Lower East Side a destination for eclectic dining. The prix-fixe Sunday menu is a bargain. **Moderate**

Le Souk *North African dining* `4 G3`
47 Avenue B • 212 777 5454
>> www.lesoukny.com Open dinner daily

With the arrival of trendy restaurants, boutiques, and bars in recent years, Alphabet City (easternmost part of the East Village) has seen its profile rise considerably. But the neighborhood conceals some of its best assets behind a gritty urban cloak. Le Souk is a fine example of this – a fantastic North African restaurant that, externally, does little to distinguish itself from the surrounding neighborhood grocers and bars. An unassuming shell, however, belies a sultan's treasure trove of African textures, tones, and delicacies within. Fashionable groups dine shoulder to shoulder on plush banquettes, while the adjacent bar area has low, Moorish tables, floor pillows, and softly lit iron lanterns. Meze plates serve as a prelude to the arrival of ceramic tajines filled with aromatic cous cous, tangy mergüez sausages, and garlicky mussels. After 9pm, belly dancers gyrate between the tables. **Moderate**

Bao 111 *modern design meets Vietnamese food* `4 G3`
111 Avenue C • 212 254 7773
>> www.bao111.com Open dinner daily

Architect/chef Michael Huynh prepares brilliant Vietnamese cuisine in this sleek space of his own design. Diners – many of them artists and fashion models – rest on crimson banquettes sipping fragrant *pho* soup or browsing Bao's eclectic dessert menu. Black sesame ice cream, anyone? **Cheap**

Le Tableau *French/Mediterranean cuisine* `4 F3`
511 East 5th Street • 212 260 1333
>> www.letableaunyc.com Open dinner daily

Wonderful French food in a button-sized hot spot. The menu changes often, but the produce is consistently flavorful, with dishes such as pork loin with maple yam purée, gorgonzola, and porto reduction. Try the early evening prix-fixe three-course menu for super savings. **Moderate**

Pylos *taverna in Alphabet City* `4 F3`
128 East 7th Street • 212 473 0220
>> www.pylosrestaurant.com
Open dinner Mon–Sun, brunch Wed–Sun

Many worlds lie within eight blocks of the 2nd Avenue subway station: the Orthodox Jewish Lower East Side, Ukrainian East Village, and Chinatown, for example. Most surprising of all, however, is the spirit of the Aegean that hides amid Alphabet City's hard-rocking bars. Pylos is a handsome Greek taverna, with stucco walls, blue shutters, and earthenware jugs hanging from the beams. Gastronomes from all over the city worship the *dolmathes* (stuffed vine leaves) here. Another popular dish is *arnaki yiovetsi* – stewed lamb chunks redolent of clove, oregano, and tomato, served on toothsome *orzo* grains. Knowledgeable staff help you navigate the encyclopedic Greek wine list. Save room for the *galaktobaureko* – these flaky, custard-filled phyllo triangles covered in warm honey are perhaps Pylos's greatest temptation. **Moderate**

Yaffa Cafe *pita stop* `4 F3`
97 St. Mark's Place • 212 674 9302
Open 24 hours daily

Day and night, punk rockers and poets flock to this offbeat eatery on St. Mark's. After last call at the neighborhood's bars, Yaffa's leafy, festively lit back patio fills with hungry revelers eager to curb their impending hangovers with home-made pita, hummus, and other tasty Middle Eastern fare. **Cheap**

Daily Chow *casual pan-Asian dining* `4 E3`
2 East 2nd Street • 212 254 7887
Open dinner daily

Smart dining areas and huge windows overlooking the Bowery ensure that there's not a bad seat in the house. The decor has a subtle Polynesian theme, while the menu stretches from the Pacific to mainland Asia. Luscious coconut-flecked chicken skewers and creamy Thai iced coffee make fantastic starters. **Cheap**

Paul's Palace *huge hamburgers* `4 E3`

131 2nd Avenue • 212 529 3033
Open all day daily

The quintessential American hamburger experience. From the linoleum countertop and checkerboard tablecloths, to the cheeky burger descriptions posted above the well-seasoned grill, Paul's is a greasy charmer. Go in for peerless 1/2 pound burgers and extra thick milkshakes. **Cheap**

Mermaid Inn *seafood, New England style* `4 E3`

96 2nd Avenue • 212 674 5870
»**www.themermaidnyc.com** Open dinner daily

With its framed nautical charts, ship diagrams, cabin lamps, and rustic tables, this classic fish house would seem more suited to the Maine Coast. But the modern rock soundtrack and style-conscious local clientele anchor the proceedings in urban bohemia. When restaurant mogul Jimmy Bradley unveiled this oddity on edgy Second Avenue in 2003, it was an instant hit.

The inn is extremely popular, and you'll generally have to wait for your table at the weekend. This is when the seafood bar comes into its own, providing Nova Scotia oysters on the half shell. Once seated, you can continue with roasted mussels or feather-light clam fritters before considering the mains. Depending on the season, these might range from classic grilled salmon through tender pan-fried skate wing to the popular lobster salad sandwich. Complimentary cups of lemon pudding cap the meal. **Moderate**

Morning Coffee and Afternoon Tea

New York's plentiful "coffee shops" are great for cheap food and people-watching, but, ironically, not for coffee. For a real, European-style coffee, you need to seek out the city's best cafés. For excellent cappuccinos, go to **Via Quadronno** *(see p273)*, and if you want to pick up a quick espresso, stop at the orange mobile **Mud Truck** (on Union Square) or the **Mud Spot** (permanently parked on 9th St.). **Joe** *(see p272)*, in the West Village, also does great coffee.

The **Palm Court at the Plaza Hotel** serves a formal afternoon tea. **Tea & Sympathy** is cozy and casual, offering freshly made scones and perfectly brewed tea in mismatched china. **Lady Mendl's Tea Room** is rather upmarket, but their scones are divine. *(For all, see p274.)* For something funkier, try **Teany** *(see p80)*.

Angelica Kitchen *incredible vegetables* `4 E2`

300 East 12th Street • 212 228 2909
Open all day daily

A vegan pioneer since 1976, Angelica earns high marks for cooking with extremely fresh ingredients grown using sustainable methods. This would be reason enough to lure environmentally aware citizens to the charming, Tuscan farmhouse-inspired dining room. Yet Angelica's greatest asset is perhaps the chef's ability to coax dazzling flavors out of the most basic ingredients. Omnivores will be hard pressed to note the absence of cream in a rich butternut squash soup, or bemoan the missing corned beef in a warm tempeh (a soybean preparation) Reuben sandwich.

Vegan approximations of American classics are on the menu alongside such exotica as *hiziki* and *kombu* (Japanese seaweeds), and *daikon* (a radish), which bolster the Kinpira salad. Service is friendly and, should you be ignorant of the virtues of *edame* (salted soybeans), refreshingly non-condescending. **Cheap**

Sobaya *noodle seduction* `4 E2`

229 East 9th Street • 212 533 6966
» www.ticakean.com/restaurant.html
Open lunch & dinner daily

The menu explains that soba buckwheat noodles contain vitamins and protein, and are especially good to eat after drinking alcohol. Well, if that doesn't explain the crowds, then it must be the authentic Japanese flavors. Big bowls of stomach-pleasing noodle soup are the main focus, served with fresh scallions and your choice of extras, such as vegetables, duck, tempura, and yam. Appetizers include fried mushroom with shrimp paste, spinach with sesame sauce, and selected sushi-style dishes. A comprehensive sake menu offers a guide to the level of fullness and flavor of each type.

The decor is typically Japanese in its simplicity and sense of order. The friendly waitstaff are generally hip Japanese transplants sporting navy samurai bandanas on their heads. **Cheap–Moderate**

2nd Avenue Deli *kosher delicatessen* `4 E2`
156 2nd Avenue • 212 677 0606
>> www.2ndavedeli.com Open 7am–midnight
King of Manhattan's Jewish-style delis, 2nd Avenue
has been stuffing New York bellies with towering
pastrami sandwiches, hearty matzo ball soup, and
complimentary pickled vegetables since 1954. It's
always crowded, but lines move surprisingly fast.
Tables are communal. **Moderate**

Blue Ribbon Sushi *the freshest fish* `3 C4`
119 Sullivan Street • 212 343 0404
Open noon–2am daily
Like its West Village brother *(see below)*, the SoHo
outpost of Blue Ribbon obsesses over the freshness
of ingredients. Here, the main ingredient is raw fish. Try
sitting at the sushi counter rather than the popular
back room, where waits can seem interminable. And
don't overlook the vast sake selection. **Moderate**

Blue Ribbon Bakery *Old World delights* `3 C4`
33 Downing Street • 212 337 0404
Open lunchtime to 2am daily (to midnight Sun)
Inside this cozy space, Village sophisticates crowd
windowside tables for European indulgences such as
foie gras, antipasti, and crusty home-made breads.
Ask to be seated downstairs in the wine cellar-like
space where diners can watch freshly baked breads
come out of the oven. **Moderate**

Tomoe Sushi *Japanese-style delectables* `3 C4`
172 Thompson Street • 212 777 9346
Open all day Wed–Sat, dinner Mon (cash or Amex only)
Tomoe presents New Yorkers with some of the
freshest fish available in the city. That is why,
despite a lack of atmosphere in this small sushi
joint, people will line up for as much as an hour, just
to get a taste of the "real thing." If the weather's
nice, the wait is worth it. **Moderate**

Otto Enoteca & Pizzeria *huge snacks* `3 D3`
No. 1 5th Avenue • 212 995 9559
≫ www.ottopizzeria.com Open all day daily
Throngs gather nightly to taste celebrity chef Mario Batali's hearty Italian snack foods. The thin pizzas are grilled (not baked) and topped with a diverse range of ingredients – anything from meatballs to fried duck eggs. Save room for the unique, savory *gelati* (ice creams). **Moderate**

La Palapa Rockola *authentic Mexican* `3 C3`
359 6th Avenue • 212 243 6870
≫ www.lapalapa.com Open all day daily
This place debunks the myth that New York lacks credible Mexican cuisine. The interior evokes Mexico's colonial heartland and cinematic Golden Age, providing a festive backdrop for the robust dishes. Pair fish tacos with a frosty Negra Modelo beer and say "Hola" to heaven. **Moderate**

Babbo *the sophistication of northern Italy* `3 C3`
110 Waverly Place • 212 777 0303
≫ www.babbonyc.com Open dinner daily
Babbo's reputation as one of New York's top Italian restaurants is due to the quality of its menu, devised by Mario Batali *(see also Otto, above)*. You will need to reserve early or ask about last-minute cancellations.

If your party agrees on a pricier meal, try the culinary adventure of either the traditional or pasta tasting menus. However, the main menu, offering dishes such as beef cheek ravioli and fennel-dusted sweetbreads, is also daring and justly lauded. Take time to peruse the wine menu or discuss the options with the knowledgable sommelier. The Italian selections are extensive and expertly chosen.

Despite the price tag, there's no need to dress up – the bi-level converted carriage house, with a skylight and elegant floral arrangements, provides the panache. Your only responsibility is to leave just enough room for a dessert and *digestivo*. **Expensive**

John's of
Bleecker Street *profound pizza*

3 C3

278 Bleecker Street • 212 243 1680
≫ www.johnsofbleeckerstreet.com
Open daily, to 1am Fri & Sat (cash only)

In this city, pizzeria comparisons are a hot topic and frequently dissolve into shouting matches. Even politicians dare not state their position on pizza, for fear of alienating potential voters. Out of the din, however, one name emerges that inspires more emotion than any other: John's of Bleecker Street.

John's likes to shout about its time-honored credentials: "Est. 1929" is writ large in white letters on its burgundy awning, and rapturous restaurant reviews are plastered to the window. For some New Yorkers, who believe a great pizzeria should be unknown to all but the savviest subway riders, John's very accessibility and fame are sufficient reasons to eliminate it from any discussion of the city's best.

Yet free from that illogical mindset, visitors to John's are in for a supremely satisfying meal.

The restaurant's popularity means that weekend lunch and dinner lines extend to the next storefront, but they move quickly. Once you're inside and seated at a weathered wooden booth, your olfactory nerves will soon react to the unmistakable, heady waft of garlic and romano cheese. To quiet your stomach, start with fresh antipasti and a frosty Peroni lager.

Purists should then opt for the basic cheese and tomato pie, fresh from John's coal-fired oven. What they will be presented with is a thin, smoky, lightly charred crust covered with a bright, slightly acidic sauce, full-cream mozzarella and vibrant spices. Non-purists can choose from garlicky meatballs and other tempting home-made toppings. Once you've chomped your way through a pie, you'll be able to establish your own position in a debate on New York's explosive topic. **Cheap**

Cones *superior ices* `3 C3`

272 Bleecker Street • 212 414 1795
Open 1–11pm Sun–Thu, 1pm–1am Fri & Sat (cash only)
What compels a man to drive two hours from Upstate New York to the Village with an empty portable freezer plugged into his car's dash, only to drive straight home again after filling it? Simply this: hand-packed quarts of the best ice cream in the state. True story.

Looking at Cones, there is little to indicate what might stir such passion. It's a tidy parlor, with a few tables and photos of unremarkable sundaes on the walls. But the real show is in the freezer: 32 steel bins brimming with kaleidoscopically colored creams and sorbets, in the tradition of authentic Italian *gelaterias*. *Dulce de leche* and coffee mocha are deliciously rich, whereas tangy fruit sorbets and dairy-free ices present a lighter antidote to the summer swelter. This is why Cones' acclaim stretches from New York to its owners' native Argentina. Still undecided? Brothers Raul and Oscar readily offer tastings. **Cheap**

BB Sandwich Bar *cheesesteak perfected* `3 C3`

120 West 3rd Street • 212 473 7500
Open 10.30am–10pm daily
Gary Thompson claims he prepares the best cheese-steak in the city, and the length of the lunch line at his small, upstairs sandwich counter confirms this is no mere boast. Thinly sliced steak is placed on a puffy Kaiser roll, then topped with marinated onions, spicy tomato relish and white American cheese. **Cheap**

Food on the Hoof

Many downtown snack stops cater to people with bite-sized budgets and a desire to keep moving. Irresistible pork and vegetarian wontons can be had in the Lower East Side's **Fried Dumpling**. West Villagers swear by **Mamoun's** fresh, crispy falafel and tangy hummus, and **Pepe Rosso's** bright, delicious Italian specialties. Eat them while watching life's rich pageant in Washington Square Park. For late-night barhoppers, **Crif Dogs** offers sustenance in the form of Chihuahua hot dogs (wrapped in bacon and topped with avocado and sour cream). Or draw a barrage of envious glances on Second Avenue with a paper funnel full of fries from **Pommes Frites**, topped with any of their 25 tasty sauces. For all addresses, *see pp260–61*.

NY Dosas *cheap veggie manna* `3 C3`
West 4th Street & Sullivan Street • 917 710 2092
Open 11am–5pm Mon–Sat

Even on blustery winter days, NYU students line up at this vending cart at the southwest corner of Washington Square for heavenly vegetarian dosas. The south Indian crêpes are filled with root vegetables, chickpeas, and spices, resulting in something far too delicate to be classified merely as "street food."
Cheap

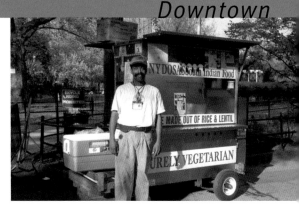

Mary's Fish Camp *chowder heaven* `3 B3`
64 Charles Street • 646 486 2185
»www.marysfishcamp.com
Open lunch & dinner Mon–Sat

Mary's seafood chowder, and lobster and clam rolls are equal to the best of any New England oceanside restaurant. Add to this the atmosphere of rustic charm, and you see why customers are lured to this tiny space, if necessary waiting outside for tables.
Moderate

Wallsé *august Austrian fare* `3 A3`
344 West 11th Street • 212 352 2300
»www.wallse.com Open dinner Mon–Sun, brunch Sat & Sun

Opened by chef Kurt Gutenbrunner in 2000, Wallse has developed a devoted following. The two-room restaurant has a restful feel, with white linen table-cloths, pale walls, and carefully chosen art work. Many of the clientele are regulars, giving the place an easy-going West Village vibe.

In accordance with Austria's gastronomic traditions, Gutenbrunner produces richly flavored dishes. Besides his famed Wiener schnitzel, other notable dishes include beef goulash with herbed *spaetzle* (a noodle side dish), apple strudel, and *rosti* (a potato and onion side dish) with lobster.

Wallsé also attracts a die-hard band of smokers too, due to its policy of lending all puffing customers beautifully tailored, bright red capes to wear during their stint outside in the cool night air. **Expensive**

Florent *24/7 camp* `3 A2`

69 Gansevoort Street • 212 989 5779
» **www.restaurantflorent.com** Open 24 hours daily
There's no better place than this for *moules frites* at
3am. In addition, Florent offers great home-made
soups and a superb weekend brunch. The clientele
ranges from daytime workers to outrageously dressed
clubbers. Regularly changing messages placed over
the bar provide an amusing distraction. **Moderate**

Sumile *great fish – raw and cooked* `3 C2`

154 West 13th Street • 212 989 7699
» **www.sumile.com**
Open dinner daily
A chic Japanese joint. Chef Josh DeChellis creates
innovative dishes, such as tea-smoked eel and black
sesame paste with raspberries. The cocktails are
fruity and fun, and the menu changes seasonally.
There's not a grain of rice in the house! **Expensive**

Tartine *bijou bistro* `3 B2`

253 West 11th Street • 212 229 2611
Open lunch & dinner Tue–Sat, dinner only Sun,
brunch Sat & Sun (cash only)
On a prime corner location that's great for people-
watching, Tartine serves consistently delicious light
French fare. Croissants are super-buttery, the savory
tarts are divine, and the weekend brunch is one of the
best deals in town. There's a BYOB policy. **Moderate**

Dining Institutions

Whether for food, tradition, location, or ambience,
some classic restaurants in New York just can't be
ignored. **Nobu** is renowned for celebrity-spotting and
the chef's tasting menu of creative sushi. **The Four
Seasons** has been serving Continental cuisine to those
with deep pockets since 1959. The space was designed
by Mies van der Rohe and Philip Johnson and features
Lichtenstein lithographs. **Chanterelle** in Tribeca has
been offering classic French and innovative Franco-
American cuisine since 1979. For a more casual feel,
with first-rate food to boot, **Gramercy Tavern** is another
favorite, serving New American cuisine in relaxed
surroundings. Finally, **Tavern on the Green** does
great brunches. For individual restaurant details,
see pp272-74.

City Bakery *pastries & chocolate* `3 C1`
3 West 18th Street • 212 366 1414
Open 7am–7:30pm Mon–Sat, 9am–5.30pm Sun
City Bakery leaves every customer contented. Its salad bar is arguably New York's best, and it also has a huge selection of flaky breakfast pastries, tarts, and decadent tortes. Linger over one of their superb hot chocolates – irresistible with a big home-made marshmallow floating in the froth. **Cheap**

Union Square Café *NY favorite* `3 D1`
21 East 16th Street • 212 243 4020
Open lunch and dinner daily
Perennially rated as one of New York's favorite restaurants, USC delivers New American cuisine in a relaxed atmosphere. The crowds never seem to abate, so reserve a table early or try for a space at the bar. Fresh flowers and a spacious feel give the café a relaxed air. Go for the daily specials. **Expensive**

Red Cat *creative cuisine in a funky place* `5 B5`
227 10th Avenue • 212 242 1122
>> **www.theredcat.com**
Open dinner daily
Red Cat's funky decor, fabulous food, and seamless service round off perfectly an afternoon spent gallery-hopping. Creative dishes might include chicken with sugarplum and sweet onion sauce, or risotto fritters with blueberry compote. **Moderate**

Grand Sichuan `5 C5`
International *bad decor, great food*
229 9th Avenue • 212 620 5200
Open all day daily
In style-obsessed Chelsea, this rarity attracts a loyal crowd on the merits of its food alone. For while the decor is stark, the Chinese cuisine is excellent. Try whole fried fish, garlicky sautéed spinach, and addictive pork and vegetable dumplings. **Cheap**

Biltmore Room *plush atmosphere* `5 C5`

290 8th Avenue • 212 807 0111

» **www.thebiltmoreroom.com** Open dinner daily

An entrance through thick velvet curtains adds an air of exclusivity to the Biltmore Room. Beyond the threshold lies a swanky bar and stylish dining room. The bar has its own scene, and people often come just to sip signature cocktails such as the Gin Blossom (infused with basil and combined with elderflower syrup). In the dining area – a mixture of gentlemen's-club tradition and something far more chic – chandeliers hang from the high ceiling and mirrors amplify the grandeur. Subtle lighting and funky music create a warm mood, and orchids add color.

The attentive staff serve dishes with Asian and Middle Eastern influences, including Algerian spiced lamb, miso-marinated Alaskan cod, and giant prawns wrapped in crispy noodles with avocado and tomato salad and mango salsa. The warm chocolate tart is not to be missed. **Expensive**

Bolo *more than paella* `6 E5`

23 East 22nd Street • 212 228 2200

» **www.bolorestaurant.com** Open lunch Mon–Fri, dinner daily

Bolo creates modern interpretations of some of the best traditional Spanish dishes. The menu features inventive tapas, such as a 12-layer potato dish with caramelized onions, black squid ink risotto, and egg tortilla with goat cheese. There's a bar, and the atmosphere is upbeat. Good lunch deals. **Expensive**

Tabla *Indian fusion* `6 E5`

11 Madison Avenue • 212 889 0667

Open lunch Mon–Fri, dinner daily

Fusing New American and Indian cuisine, Tabla presents dishes such as Goan spiced crab cake and tandoori breads using inventive flavors. A striking staircase divides the colorful formal upstairs dining room from the downstairs Bread Bar, which offers a less formal, slightly cheaper dining option. **Expensive**

Tamarind *epicurean spices* `6 F5`

41–3 East 22nd Street • 212 674 7400

>> **www.tamarinde22.com** Open lunch & dinner daily

Large glass windows, an unfussy modern interior, and cut flowers on each table set the tone. Tamarind has earned several prestigious culinary accolades, and its two proud owners are often seen milling about with diners, basking in positive feedback, no doubt. Such openness also extends to the kitchens, which are surrounded by glass, so you can watch the food being prepared without getting a noseful of every dish.

House specialties include a signature dish of tandoori scallops presented in a fried potato lattice cup, *bhagerey baignan* (eggplant with coconut, sesame, and peanut sauce), Tamarind's chutneys, and a home-made cheese. Lamb and lobster feature prominently on the menu too.

The Tearoom offers sandwiches, a vast array of teas, and desserts in a more casual, intimate environment. **Moderate**

Dos Caminos *trendy Mexican* `6 F5`

373 Park Avenue South • 212 294 1000

>> **www.brguestrestaurants.com**

Open lunch & dinner Mon–Fri, brunch & dinner Sat & Sun

Hugely popular with a regular crowd of young professionals, this large restaurant and bar is a vibrant place in which to indulge in margaritas and great Mexican fare. The famed guacamole is prepared at your table, so you can dictate the spice factor. **Moderate**

Blue Smoke *upscale American barbecue* `6 F4`

116 East 27th Street • 212 447 7733

>> **www.bluesmoke.com** Open lunch & dinner daily

Chef Ken Callaghan smokes spareribs, beef brisket, organic chicken, and sausages over hickory and apple woods, keeping meats flavorful without sacrificing succulence. The handsome, modern dining room fills with boisterous Manhattanites every night. Excellent beer selection, and live jazz downstairs. **Moderate**

i Trulli *wine & pasta in a warm atmosphere* `6 F4`

122 East 27th Street • 212 481 7372

>> www.itrulli.com Open lunch & dinner Mon–Fri, dinner Sat
i Trulli's delectable cuisine is true to its roots, which
lie in the Italian region of Puglia. Specialties here
include the *panelle* (chickpea fritters with goat
cheese) and home-made pastas. Try a "flight of wine"
(a selection of three to taste from a vast list), and
sample cheeses, olives, and cured meats. **Expensive**

Mandoo Bar *Top-notch Korean cooking* `6 E4`

2 West 32nd Street • 212 279 3075

>> www.mandoobar.com Open all day daily
Uniformed cooks bustle about near the window
preparing plump little *mandoo* – delicate dumplings
stuffed with vegetables, fish, or meat. The salads and
seafood dishes are also superb. Avoid weekday
lunchtimes, though, when this informal restaurant is
packed with local business people. **Cheap**

Artisanal *cheese, please* `6 F4`

2 Park Avenue (entrance on 32nd Street)
• 212 725 8585

Open all day daily (brunch served 11am–3pm Sat & Sun)
The revived tradition of fondue-sharing creates a social
buzz in the high-ceilinged dining room of this bistro
and fromagerie. Various fondues are available, prepared with different cheeses, herbs and oil infusions.
Some are traditional recipes, others experimental.
Cheese is also the focus of salads, and appetizers
such as a three-cheese onion soup. A tarte tatin in a
cheddar crust continues the theme into dessert. There
are non-cheese selections – *cassoulet* (bean stew), or
chicken roasted "under the brick" – but choose at
least one course devoted to the star ingredient.

A requisite cheese plate takes on new meaning as
the *fromagier* guides you through 200-plus selections.
For a five-cheese platter, choose from goat, cow,
sheep, blue, and cheddar varieties. You can also order
a "cheese and wine flight" at the bar (three choices
of each), and buy cheese from the shop. **Moderate**

Cho Dang Gol *Korean creations* `6 E3`
55 West 35th Street • 212 695 8222
Open all day daily

Located in the heart of "Koreatown," this establishment is unusual in catering equally to meat-eaters, vegans, and vegetarians. The authentic yet accessible dishes form a perfect introduction to Korean cuisine.

Gop dol bim bap is a good one to try. With this, a heated stone bowl is filled with rice, vegetables (or meat), broth, spicy red paste, and an egg. You mix the ingredients and let some of the rice crisp at the bottom. You can also expect to receive the *ban chan* – little plates of appetizers that come with any meal and include *kim chi* (spicy pickled cabbage).

Cho Dang Gol is also known for its superb leek pancakes and melt-in-your-mouth tofu (bean curd), which is made on the premises, as is an alcoholic drink called Makkuli. The dishes vary in spiciness – ask the waitstaff for guidance if necessary. The lunchtime specials are great deals. **Cheap**

Sandwich Planet *sliced bread sensation* `5 C2`
534 9th Avenue • 212 273 9768
≫ www.sandwichplanet.com Open 10:30am–8:30pm daily
Despite its closet-like dimensions, this pitstop offers a seemingly limitless choice of custom-made sandwiches. Should one of the five tables be available, linger over a signature creation like the Armani: thin prosciutto, fresh mozzarella, artichoke hearts, and rocket pressed between toasted foccacia. **Cheap**

Mi Nidito *surprisingly good Mexican* `5 C1`
852 8th Avenue • 212 265 0022
Open all day daily

With its gaudy signage hawking dozens of margarita varieties, this unassuming Hell's Kitchen eatery is not the most obvious place to find some of the city's best Mexican food. But the roasted chicken is irresistible – crisp, succulent, and studded with garlic – and the mango margaritas justify all the hoopla. **Moderate**

Churrascaria Plataforma *Brazilian BBQ* `5 C1`
316 West 49th Street • 212 245 0505
➤➤ www.churrascariaplataforma.com Open all day daily
Catering mainly to a post-theater crowd, this Brazilian *churrascaria* is a novel and lively fixed-price barbecue. Guests are led to tables in the capacious, elegant dining room and each given a round disk – one face red, the other green. After trips to the salad bar, the crowd settles in for the impending meat extravaganza.

When the disk's green side is displayed, gracious uniformed servers approach, wielding skewers of top-quality roasted meats – sirloin steaks, sausages, prime rib, chicken, and baby lamb chops – and fish such as salmon. When your plate is sufficiently full, flip the disk to red. When you've emptied it, flip again to green, and repeat the performance until your belly attains the desired level of distension.

Plataforma's perfect *caipirinha* is a refreshing, albeit potent, palette cleanser of cachaça rum, sugar, and mint over cracked ice. **Expensive**

Genki Sushi *sushi on the roll* `6 E1`
9 East 46th Street • 212 983 5018
Open 11:30am–8:30pm Mon–Fri, noon–5pm Sat
A metal conveyor belt stocked with midtown's freshest fish revolves through the colorful dining area. Take your pick from plates (color-coded according to price) of whimsically assembled rolls and succulent sashimi. Lunchtimes are busy, so come in the early evening if you can. **Cheap**

Ess-a-Bagel *classic snacks* `6 F1`
831 3rd Avenue • 212 980 1010
➤➤ www.ess-a-bagel.com Open 6:30am–9pm daily (to 5 Sun)
This spacious midtown bagel shop bakes arguably the city's best example of the dense, rotund breakfast bread. Feel free to linger over any of 14 bagel varieties, coupled with award-winning whitefish salad, Nova Scotia smoked salmon, eggplant salad, or a classic spread of cream cheese. **Cheap**

Acqua Pazza *fresh pasta, seafood & fish* `8 E5`

36 West 52nd Street • 212 582 6900

>> www.acquapazzanyc.com

Open lunch & dinner Mon–Fri, dinner only Sat

Acqua Pazza – "crazy water" – belies its name with serious Italian food. Octopus, crab, and whole baked fish are typical items on the menu. Pasta infused with espresso is an unusual dish, harking back to the days when coffee was used as a preservative. **Expensive**

Aquavit *Swedish sensation* `8 E5`

13 West 54th Street • 212 307 7311

>> www.aquavit.org Open lunch & dinner Mon–Fri, brunch Sun

Swedish chef Marcus Samuelsson, who won a prestigious "Best Chef in New York City" award in 2003, has taken the Scandinavian cuisine at this restaurant to new levels of gastronomic genius. A visit's not cheap, but worth the price, especially if you sit in the main dining room, which is in an atrium that features an indoor waterfall.

The eponymous aquavit is a potent Scandinavian spirit, double distilled, with flavors added in the second distillation. This and glasses of Carlsberg beer are served alongside house specialties such as herrings. Other favorites include seafood stew in a delicious dill sauce, brioche-wrapped salmon, and Kobe beef ravioli. The restaurant also prepares a beguiling gravlax and tandoori smoked salmon.

Three tasting menus, including a vegetarian option, offer seven-course "Aquavit Bite" meals. Another way to sample many of these flavors at a little less expense is to eat upstairs in the Aquavit Café. The café's kitchen is separate from the restaurant's, but both are overseen by the executive chef, so there's a decent amount of overlap. However, Swedish meatballs are available only in the café.

To uphold the restaurant's name, several house-made and unusual aquavits are available; flavors may include black pepper and vanilla, and pear and cloudberry. **Expensive**

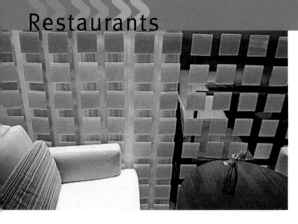

Town *sophistication & pizzazz* `8 E5`
Chambers Hotel, 15 West 56th Street
- 212 582 4445 »
  www.townnyc.com

Open breakfast, lunch & dinner daily, brunch Sun

A fashionable restaurant, where a fanciful interior is matched by creative Euro-American cuisine. The menu changes seasonally, but signature dishes include, in spring, white asparagus with a blood-orange reduction, and, in summer, soft-shell crab. **Expensive**

Norma's *a perfect start to the day* `7 D5`
At Le Parker Meridien Hotel, 118 W. 57th St.
- 212 708 7460 »
  www.parkermeridien.com/normas

Open breakfast & lunch daily

Norma's is a swish place, offering one of the most luxurious breakfasts in town. Between sips of freshly squeezed juice, dig into mango and papaya with cinnamon crêpes, mammoth omelets, and decadent French brioche toast. **Moderate**

Geisha *stylish Japanese-American joint* `8 E4`
33 East 61st Street • 212 813 1112

Open lunch & dinner Mon–Sat

Don your best black outfit and blend in with the crowd sipping cocktails while waiting for tables. The menu focuses on seafood with Japanese flavors, such as lobster served with asparagus and mushroom *udon* noodles. Downstairs is hip and fun; upstairs is a bit more subdued. There's a sushi bar too. **Expensive**

Diner Etiquette

Diners – known as "coffee shops" within New York City limits – are part of the quintessential NY experience. They are social levelers, where a poor poet and a business mogul can rub elbows at the counter over omelets. Diner food is comfort food – all-day breakfast fare, including eggs any style, as well as burgers, French fries, and grilled cheese sandwiches.

Prices don't dictate the quality of a diner; location, longevity, menu, and staff do. Your server should be courteous, but don't get offended if he/she rushes you during a busy period when tables need to be turned over. Coffee is rarely strong but should always be limitless. Kitchen lingo is part of the tradition: eggs are "sunny-side up" or "(easy) over"; rye toast is placed "whiskey down."

Serendipity 3 *American staples* `8 F4`

225 East 60th Street • 212 838 3531
>> www.serendipity3.com Open lunch & dinner daily

A favourite with Upper East Side families, Serendipity 3 is loved for its mammoth portions of American comfort food. The chicken pot pies, juicy burgers, thick soups, and bright salads are, however, mere preambles to dessert: the frozen hot chocolate surely ranks among New York's finest creations. **Cheap**

March *quiet elegance, gourmet food* `8 H4`

405 East 58th Street • 212 754 6272
>> www.marchrestaurant.com Open dinner daily

Superbly presented food in a romantic renovated townhouse. The gourmet food takes in a wide range of influences, but there is a discernible Asian accent in the use of raw fish, soy, sesame, and dishes such as shrimp and wild mushroom tempura. You can dine outdoors from May to October. **Expensive**

Mezzaluna *heart-melting tiramisu* `8 F2`

1295 3rd Avenue • 212 535 9600
Open lunch & dinner daily (cash or Amex only)

A lively and intimate spot for northern Italian cuisine, Mezzaluna excels in freshly made pastas, fish dishes, and brick-oven-baked pizzas. The creamy, light tiramisu is one of the best you'll find in New York. Artistic depictions of half-moons *(mezzaluna)* adorn the walls. Staff are very friendly. **Moderate**

Annie's *hearty brunches* `8 F1`

1381 3rd Avenue • 212 327 4853
Open 8am–11:30pm daily (to midnight Fri & Sat)

An excellent Sunday brunch (served until 4pm) packs young families into this warm, classic New York bistro. Wicked Bloody Marys and generous portions are *de rigueur*; omelets could accommodate two appetites. Annie's is also a pancake lover's dream: wholewheat, apple, banana, mixed berry … take your pick. **Cheap**

Atlantic Grill *fresh fish, fresh atmosphere* **8 F1**

1341 3rd Avenue • 212 988 9200
>> www.brguestrestaurants.com
Open lunch & dinner Mon–Sat, brunch & dinner Sun

To please the finicky Upper East Side inhabitants, food, service, and atmosphere have to be of a high order in any establishment here. So the long-standing popularity of the Atlantic Grill attests to its culinary credentials. The restaurant excels at well-prepared, very fresh fish, accompanied by a good wine list, and waitstaff who are both competent and efficient.

A sense of refined informality pervades the spacious dining area, spread throughout two rooms. Additional sidewalk seating is available when weather permits. Specialties include oysters, crabcakes, lightly fried sesame-crusted lobster roll, and barbecued *mahi mahi* (a particularly succulent, slightly sweet fish). There are also daily specials, and you can order small plates from a sushi bar. Book ahead to reserve a table or be prepared to wait – it's worth it. **Moderate**

Candle 79 *fine meat-free dining* **8 F1**

154 East 79th Street • 212 537 7179
>> www.candlecafe.com Open lunch & dinner daily

An upscale restaurant offering wonderful vegetarian and vegan masterpieces, Candle 79 pushes the limit of what you might expect from a meatless menu. Many a dedicated carnivore is won over by the flavors and textures experienced here. Inventive dishes include squash and wild mushroom risotto, and porcini-crusted *seitan* (a meaty wheat protein concoction) with garlicky greens and a wild mushroom red wine sauce.

In addition to organic wine, sake, and beer, the list of non-alcoholic juices and tonics is enough to make one giddy. Options such as an elderberry extract with apple and lemon, and an orange juice, coconut cream, and banana smoothie are divine. The less formal, sister establishment, Candle Café (1307 3rd Avenue; 212 472 0970), also offers creative green food, focusing on tasty salads, wraps, and soups, and has a juice bar at the front. **Moderate**

Sushi of Gari *inspiring sushi* `8 G1`
402 East 78th Street • 212 517 5340
Open dinner Tue–Sun

The tasting menu here allows innovative sushi chef Masatoshi Gari Sugio and his staff to demonstrate their mastery over fish and seafood. An à-la-carte menu is available, but the principal reason for dining at this small, simply decorated treasure is to allow the chefs to surprise and delight. **Expensive**

Ouest *first-rate New American fare* `9 B5`
2315 Broadway • 212 580 8700
>> www.ouestny.com Open dinner daily, brunch Sun

Ouest is about panache in just about every detail. The bar area is the first thing you'll notice, with its wood-paneled walls, shades of deep red, and old-fashioned fans hanging from the ceiling. Beyond this is a corridor that passes a glazed wine cellar and leads to the main dining area. Stylish round, red-leather booths take up most of the room, with square tables along the periphery. There's balcony seating too, though this is a bit cramped and best avoided. The bright kitchen is open for all to see, and the music adds to the atmosphere, tending toward 20s–40s jazz.

Owner/chef Tom Valenti has been much lauded for pleasing the palate and delighting the eye, here and at other top New York restaurants. Highly sophisticated dishes emerge from his kitchen, such as the intriguingly named "truffled omelet soufflé" with mousseline sauce, or lobster ravioli with a herb salad. Well-sourced game and other roast meats are typical offerings. Specials include braised lamb shanks on Mondays and Tuesdays, and the legendary meat loaf on a Sunday. Allow time to peruse the globe-trotting wine list, which has won awards, or ask for advice if the selection proves overwhelming. By contrast, the dessert selection is short and sweet, and includes a panna cotta that can't be beaten.

Ouest's superior brunch menu also wins plaudits by offering refined breakfast food such as scrambled egg with house-smoked sturgeon. **Expensive**

Picholine *traditional excellence* `7 C3`

35 West 64th Street • 212 724 8585
Open lunch Sat, dinner daily

The eponymous picholine (green olive) theme adorns the plates and is evident in some dishes, such as caramelized ribs with an olive sauce. But Picholine is equally renowned for its formidable cheese cart. Jackets are required in the main dining room, but less formal seating is available at the front bar. **Expensive**

Pasha *high-class Turkish* `7 C2`

70 West 71st Street • 212 579 8751
Open dinner daily

A sumptuous eatery fit for Ottoman royalty. The luxurious, deep-red and yellow dining area is hung with vibrant tapestries. Kebabs, stuffed vine leaves, and dozens of other richly seasoned Turkish delights are presented in copper tureens by charming waitstaff. Pasha offers great pre-theater deals. **Moderate**

El Malecón II *Caribbean specialties* `9 B3`

764 Amsterdam Avenue • 212 864 5648
Open breakfast, lunch, and dinner daily

Given New York's sizeable Dominican population, perhaps it is not surprising that some of the best Dominican cooking north of Miami is found here. While the cuisine's staples do not differ greatly from those used in other Caribbean and many Central American kitchens, nuances make all the difference. Few restaurants get the alchemy quite so right as El Malecón II, younger brother of the Washington Heights original.

Diners familiar with the restaurant's namesake – the pulsating seaside boulevard in Santo Domingo – might raise an eyebrow at the modest dining room. But one look at the spice-encrusted, brown skins of chickens turning on rotisseries will quell doubts. A mixed crowd of ex-pat families and students sit down to *mofongo* (sweet plantains mashed with stewed pork), *asopao con longaniza* (rice in broth with spicy Spanish sausage), and seafood paella. **Cheap**

Aix *inspiration from France* `9 B4`
2398 Broadway • 212 874 7400
» www.aixnyc.com Open dinner daily, brunch Sun
The bright oranges and sky blues in this restaurant evoke the colors of Provence. Rather than focusing on traditional Provençal dishes, however, Chef Didier Virot's menu offers a wider range of creative French fare. The star dish is halibut in a garlic cream with oatmeal porcini cake and walnut sauce. **Expensive**

Symposium *genuine Greek* `11 B5`
544 West 113th Street • 212 865 1011
Open all day daily
Symposium has been serving stuffed vine leaves and mousaka for over 20 years to its regulars, who come largely from the Hellenic community. Sit in the cozy taverna or walk through the kitchen to the enclosed back garden. The Symposium Salad provides a little taste of many dishes on the menu. **Moderate**

New Leaf Café *urban renewal enterprise*
Fort Tryon Park • 212 568 5323 • Ⓜ "A" train to 190th Street
» www.nyrp.org/newleaf
Open lunch & dinner Tue–Sat, brunch & dinner Sun
All net proceeds from this café, which is set in a converted stone house in Fort Tryon Park, go to the restoration and maintenance of the park. Organic salad leaves and wild salmon feature on the menu. Try to catch the Thursday evening Jazz Night. **Moderate**

Noodle Pudding *consistently tasty Italian* `13 B3`
38 Henry Street, Brooklyn • 718 625 3737
Open dinner Tue–Sun (cash only)
Don't let the name deceive you: Noodle Pudding refers to a pasta dish, not Asian food here. *Osso buco* (veal knuckle), *penne arrabiata*, real mozzarella, and panna cotta feature among the Italian staples. Locals show their appreciation by packing this casually stylish restaurant nightly. **Moderate**

The River Café *enchanting views & food*   13 A3

1 Water Street • 718 522 5200

>> www.therivercafe.com Open dinner daily, lunch Mon–Sat, brunch Sun (formal dress required in evening)

The River Café began serving sublime food in 1977 and hasn't had time to look back. In a superb setting directly on the waterfront, with a stunning view of the Manhattan skyline and Brooklyn Bridge, this is probably one of the most romantic dining places in the world. Much of the seating allows couples to gaze out at the scene together.

The reputable kitchen tends to gravitate toward unusual meats and seafood. Foie gras, rabbit, suckling pig, and caviar might all feature on the menu, with a token dish for vegetarians. The Maine Lobster is a regular favorite. For novelty value, order the Chocolate Marquise Brooklyn Bridge – a model in fine chocolate.

Lunch is slightly cheaper than dinner. If, however, you just want to savor the atmosphere, go for wine and appetizers in the Terrace Room. **Expensive**

The Grocery *a neighborhood star* 13 B4

288 Smith Street • 718 596 3335

Open dinner Mon–Sat

The petite Grocery offers New American fare and has long been a favorite with locals. It is praised equally for its use of ultra-fresh ingredients and the warmth of its service. Dishes tend to be simple, allowing the flavors of the produce to sing out, as in the juicy and healthily trimmed grilled lamb. **Moderate**

Joya *Thai spice* 13 B4

215 Court Street • 718 222 3484

Open dinner daily

With its industrial-chic interior imparting a level of SoHo sophistication to the quaint Boerum Hill/Carroll Gardens neighborhood, Joya lures discerning Manhattanites across the river. Young professionals flock here for the ambience and the deftly executed Thai dishes that rarely venture above $10. **Cheap**

Park Slope Chip Shop *comfort food* `13 C4`
383 5th Avenue • 718 CHIPSHOP
>> www.chipshopnyc.com Open all day daily
One of Park Slope's most cheerful eateries is inspired by a British phenomenon in dining. Young families and ex-pat students pining for familiar comfort food relish generous platters of chips, fried haddock, crisps, curries, and fishcakes. Dessert? Fried chocolate candy, of course. **Cheap**

Al Di La *Venetian trattoria* `13 C4`
248 5th Avenue • 718 783 4565
>> www.aldilatrattoria.com Open dinner daily except Tue
First-rate food served in a romantic, candlelit setting ensures Al Di La's devoted following. Specials include polenta, gnocchi with fried sage, and grilled sardines. The restaurant doesn't take reservations, so be prepared to have a drink at a neighboring bar while you wait for a table, or go off-peak. **Moderate**

Convivium Osteria *splendid bistro* `13 C4`
68 5th Avenue • 718 857 1833
Open dinner daily
Dim lighting and dark furnishings are a brooding contrast to the bright, bold flavors of the Mediterranean at this little bistro. Pair a reasonably priced wine with braised artichoke hearts, salt cod filets, or roasted rack of lamb. Few people outside the neighborhood know of this gem … yet. **Moderate**

LouLou *a taste of Brittany* `13 C5`
222 DeKalb Avenue • 718 246 0633
Open dinner daily, brunch Sat & Sun
Cozy LouLou is a great stop before or after a visit to the Brooklyn Academy of Music *(see p149)*. Fish, seafood, and scrumptious crêpes are the mainstays of a menu that focuses on the Brittany region of France. Try dining in the lovely back garden; you'll forget that you're in a metropolis. **Moderate**

i-Shebeen Madiba *South African eaterie* `13 C3`
195 DeKalb Avenue, Fort Greene • 718 855 9190
>> www.I-SHEBEEN.com Open all day daily (to 1am Fri & Sat)
Part Zulu trinket shop, part rustic-style bistro, this place holds boundless intrigue. Cosmopolitan neighborhood residents come for authentic *bobotie* (a curried mince bake) and *potjie bredie* (fragrant meat stew served in a cast iron pot). There's outdoor seating and live music, weather permitting. **Moderate**

Butta'Cup Lounge *Southern-style food* `13 C3`
271 Adelphi Street • 718 522 1669
>> www.buttacuplounge.com
Open all day daily (to 2am Fri & Sat)
Sip a signature Applejack cocktail at the bar, then relax in a leopard print-upholstered booth. Notable main dishes include classic fried chicken and a piquant salmon Japonaise. On weekends, the upstairs lounge is good for DJ-spun soul and hip-hop. **Moderate**

DiFara Pizzeria *Neapolitan pizzas*
1424 Avenue J • 718 258 1367 • Ⓜ Subway Q to Avenue J
Open all day daily (cash only)
The thin, round pizza of Naples – arguably New Yorkers' most beloved culinary import – is elevated to an art form at this tiny pizzeria in the predominantly Hasidic Jewish neighborhood of Midwood. Producing these transcendent pies behind a cracked linoleum countertop since 1964 is Domenico DeMarco, a master *pizzaiolo* with an obsessive commitment to fresh ingredients and the precise assembly (one blob of creamy mozzarella at a time) of just about perfect pizzas. Translation: you must wait for your food.

Patience is duly rewarded with the first bite. The robust, basil-laced tomato sauce, crisp crust, light olive oil, and tangy parmigiano reggiano cheese should conspire to put words like "the best" on your lips. They should also distract you from the smoke-stained ceiling, yellowing prints of Naples, and awkwardly arranged tables – just six altogether. **Cheap**

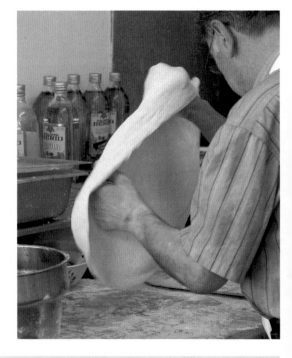

Relish *classic diner* `13 B2`

225 Wythe Avenue • 718 963 4546
Open all day daily (to 1am Fri & Sat)

Archetypal diners like this usually serve greasy, griddle-fried fare. But Josh Cohen's seasonally revised menus feature eclectic American bistro cuisine at diner-friendly prices: think chili-rubbed smoked ribs and tomato soup with chèvre croutons. Locals in the know fill the 1950s-style booths. **Moderate**

Planet Thailand *affordable specialties* `13 B2`

133 North 7th Street • 718 599 5758
Open all day daily to 1am (to 2am Fri & Sat) (cash only)

The dining room here is cavernous, with towering windows and gray, industrial walls hung with sweeping paintings by Williamsburg artists. Within the space, venturesome Manhattanites and stylish Brooklynites nibble Thai papaya salads and Japanese *nigiri* sushi between sips of iced coffee or warm sake. **Cheap**

Peter Luger Steak House *sizzlers* `13 B2`

178 Broadway • 718 387 7400
» www.peterluger.com
Open all day to 9:45pm daily (to 10:45pm Fri & Sat); cash only

Renowned as one of the top meat purveyors in the country, Peter Luger has been in business since 1887, and the generations of experience show. The decor is no-frills, and the menu is simple. Steak – particularly the Porterhouse – rules. **Expensive**

Bamonte's *old-school Italian* `13 C1`

32 Withers Street • 718 384 8831
Open all day except Tue

Home-made pastas and rich red sauces reign supreme at this establishment, which has been in business for more than 100 years. Bamonte's harks back to the past with wonderful photographs on the walls and a waitstaff who look like they've been around almost as long as the restaurant – all part of its charm. **Moderate**

What to Eat in New York

THE VARIETY OF FOOD found in New York is as varied as its cultural and ethnic makeup, and you can find virtually any food you want. For a hearty simple meal, such as marinated vegetables, pasta or salami and cheese, visit one of the Italian restaurants found in every neighborhood. For a more sophisticated meal try a Japanese restaurant for sushi and sashimi – as good in New York as anywhere in Japan. Or try such traditional Jewish foods as pastrami, blintzes and bagels, found in most delis and coffee shops. Spicy curries can be found in the many Indian restaurants around Manhattan. If you are really hungry, visit a steak-house for juicy steaks, fresh seafood and some especially wicked desserts.

Bagel
This chewy Jewish bread roll is most popularly served with lox (smoked salmon) and cream cheese.

Pancakes
Thick, sweet pancakes are usually served with maple syrup as breakfast. Fresh or dried fruit may be mixed into the batter before cooking.

Bacon is often sweet-cured and fried very crisp.

"Home fries" are chunky sautéed potatoes.

Whole-wheat toast

Eggs "over easy" are lightly fried on both sides.

Breakfast or Brunch
Breakfast (or brunch if eaten midmorning) can consist of anything from home fries, eggs, bacon and toast to sweet pancakes or croissants, often with unlimited coffee.

French Toast
A breakfast dish of sliced bread dipped in egg then fried and often served with syrup.

Egg Cream
This drink is made with milk, choco-late syrup and carbon-ated soda water.

Corned Beef on Rye
Cured beef is served on rye bread with mild mustard and a pickle dill gherkin.

Burger and Fries "To Go"
A hamburger and french fries may come with salad and onion rings.

Giant Pretzel
This baked bread twist is sold on many street corners.

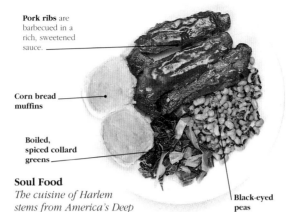

Pork ribs are barbecued in a rich, sweetened sauce.

Corn bread muffins

Boiled, spiced collard greens

Black-eyed peas

Clam Chowder
The Manhattan version of this shellfish soup is made with tomatoes and garnished with crackers.

Soul Food
The cuisine of Harlem stems from America's Deep South. Simple foods are cooked with spices for a unique flavor.

Pizza
The street food of Italian festivals is available all over the city – this uptown version is topped with artichoke hearts.

Sushi
Japanese cuisine, like this ultrafresh raw fish and rice, is a New York favorite.

Dim Sum
Tiny steamed dumplings, stuffed with fish, meat or vegetables, are a specialty of Chinese cuisine.

Waldorf Salad
Created in the 1930s at the Waldorf Hotel, it's made out of apples, nuts and lettuce.

Cappuccino and Cookies
Frothy coffee sprinkled with chocolate is served with cookies in New York cafés.

Apple Pie à la Mode
This traditional American dessert is only "à la mode" when served with ice cream.

New York Cheesecake
This thick, baked Jewish dessert may be served plain or glazed with fruit.

Banana Split
Some New York ice cream concoctions will feed a family. No one will mind if you order extra spoons and share.

shopping

New York is a famously fabulous place to shop. Rich pickings are to be had across the board – in the time-honored department stores of midtown, the designer flagships of Fifth Avenue, and the latest little gem to spring up in buzzing Williamsburg. Follow the lead of New Yorkers and shop where the locals shop – the great delis, bookstores and music outlets downtown, and the funky fashion boutiques in Harlem and Brooklyn.

DEPARTMENT STORES	FOOD	HIGH FASHION

Bergdorf Goodman
754 5th Avenue
A bastion of understated style. Come here for high-end fashions and health treatments in the day spa. *(See p91)*

Dean & DeLuca
560 Broadway
The first stop for foodies. Dean & DeLuca is a delicatessen par excellence, with the largest selection of gourmet foods in NY. *(See p75)*

Miu Miu
100 Prince Street
A label that's adored for girly fashions: sensuous materials, beautifully cut dresses, and sexy underwear. *(See p73)*

>> *www.NYSale.com will give you the lowdown on up-and-coming designer sample sales.*

Dylan's Candy Bar
1011 3rd Avenue
A two-story shop that's choc-a-bloc with sweets and confectionery of all kinds. Cute packaging too. *(See p92)*

Marc by Marc Jacobs
403–405 Bleecker Street
With men's and women's stores next door to each other, this is perfect for couples to get kitted out in Jacobs' effortlessly cool look. *(See p82)*

Barney's New York
660 Madison Avenue
On a more modest scale than New York's really big stores, Barney's is one of the least daunting places for browsing designer clothes. *(See p92)*

Zabar's
2245 Broadway
A family-run New York institution, Zabar's stock includes mouth-watering cheeses, cured meats, and smoked fish. *(See p95)*

INA
21 Prince Street
A treasure-house for girls who want top-end fashions but lack the funds. INA stocks barely worn second-hand designer clothes. *(See p77)*

Century 21
22 Cortlandt Street
A bargain-hunter's dream – despite sometimes surly service – Century 21 is packed with heavily discounted designer clothes. *(See p70)*

Magnolia Bakery
401 Bleecker Street
An irresistible hoard of cakes, muffins, and pastries is prepared daily at this Village bakery. *(See p81)*

Costume National
108 Wooster Street
Typically fine Italian tailoring and a timeless sense of elegance are the hallmarks of the men's and women's clothing at this store. *(See p73)*

Jeffrey
449 West 14th Street
The lion's share of this popular store is given over to shoes – from Prada to Puma. The clothes are top-range and expensive. *(See p84)*

VINTAGE & RETRO	SHOES & ACCESSORIES	COOL STORES

Housing Works Thrift Shop
306 Columbus Avenue
The stock is donated by the most stylish New Yorkers, so you can find cheap design classics here. Profits go to an AIDS charity. *(See p95)*

Felissimo
10 West 56th Street
Felissimo treats household objects as works of art, exhibiting them in a five-floor shop-cum-gallery. *(See p90)*

Mini Minimarket
218 Bedford Avenue
Taking its stylistic lead from 70s and 80s leisurewear, Mini Minimarket is full of funky little numbers for the girl about town. *(See p98)*

Rafe
1 Bleecker Street
Candy-colored sandals with polka-dot insoles, strappy evening shoes, and soft, "ballet shoe" flats – Rafe's collections are fun. *(See p78)*

Takashimaya
693 5th Avenue
Asian influences are strong through-out Takashimaya's seductive store, which sells a mix of vintage furniture and high-tech gadgets. *(See p89)*

ALife Rivington Club
158 Rivington Street
This is *the* place to come for vintage trainers – Nike Air Wovens, old-school Adidas, etc. *(See p79)*

Manolo Blahnik
31 West 54th Street
The doyen of high-end, super sexy footwear, Manolo Blahnik designs shoes that are very desirable, and extremely expensive. *(See p88)*

⟩⟩ *www.lazarshopping.com provides profiles of the city's fashion designers, along with all manner of shopping advice and information, including a list of sales happening each month.*

Christian Louboutin
941 Madison Avenue
A beautiful, Parisian-style shop, with a selection of elegant shoes for wealthy Upper East Siders. *(See p93)*

Flight 001
96 Greenwich Avenue
Be the coolest person on the plane with your own in-flight travel kit and maybe a mobile spice rack to liven up the airline food. *(See p82)*

Blades Board & Skate
120 West 72nd Street
If you want to get around Central Park with more speed and style, get your inline skates here. *(See p94)*

Isa
88 North 6th Street, Brooklyn
Street fashions are mixed with funky beats supplied by DJs. This is a place to hang out, chill out, and buy some cool duds. *(See p99)*

Century 21 *discount designer duds* `1 D3`
22 Cortlandt Street • 212 227 9092
» www.c21stores.com
Open 7:45am–8pm Mon–Fri (to 8:30 Thu), 10–8 Sat, 11–7 Sun
This is a goldmine of a department store, so don't let the aggressive crowds scare you away. The discounted designer men's and women's clothes, shoes, makeup, and linens on offer will make the occasional elbow in the ribs well worth the hassle.

The women's shoe department tends to be the busiest and most chaotic, due to weekly shipments from the likes of Costume National, Dolce & Gabbana, and Marc Jacobs. The top floor is the jewel in the crown, though: it stocks the collections of designers such as Armani, Missoni, and Ralph Lauren, but at a fraction of the price you'd pay at the Madison Avenue flagship stores. The only downside to this heavenly situation is the service (often brusque), long lines, and communal dressing rooms – be prepared to undress in front of 25 other shoppers.

Kate Spade Travel *stylish accessories* `3 C5`
59 Thompson Street • 212 965 8654
» www.katespade.com Open 11am–7pm Tue–Sat, 12–6 Sun
Luxury coupled with whimsy are the key ingredients of Kate Spade Travel. Nylon and leather weekend bags, personalized stationery, and vintage travel books from the 1960s make browsing a delight. (How the beautifully crafted luggage will cope with an airport check-in is another matter.)

Hotel Venus by Patricia Field *Cirque du Soleil meets S&M clothing* `3 D5`
382 West Broadway • 212 966 4066
» www.patriciafield.com Open 11am–8pm daily (to 9pm Sat)
Patricia Field – costume designer for the HBO sitcom *Sex and the City* – has designed this SoHo store to give free rein to her eccentric fantasies. Hip girls, transvestites, and circus performers will all find something here to make them smile.

Keiko *bikinis & maillots* `3 D5`

62 Greene Street • 212 226 6051
>> www.keikonewyork.com
Open 11am–6pm Mon–Fri, noon–6pm Sat, 1–6pm Sun

Take some of the anxiety away from swimsuit shopping with Keiko's wide choice of colors and styles, which ranges from boy-shorts to string bikinis. The assistants will help you find the perfect fit and ensure you'll be a head-turner at the beach.

Pearl River Mart *Far Eastern treasures* `3 D5`

477 Broadway • 212 431 4770
>> www.pearlriver.com Open 10am–7:30pm daily

It has never been easier or more fun to get lost in a store. This three-story shrine to everything Asian feels like a cross between a flea market (yes, the prices are that good) and an exotic department store. The elegant Chinese robes, traditional Mandarin dresses, slippers, embroidered bags, and purses would be triple the price in a more conventional store. The simple ceramic bowls and delicate Japanese tea sets are also the same as those found in pricey boutiques.

The kitchen department offers everything you need to prepare an authentic Asian meal: teas, spices, and sauces are available in bewildering quantities. Among the bathroom products are herbal remedies and beauty treats galore. Many of the exquisite Chinese wedding items make stunning accessories or gifts. There's also a selection of cute and colorful kids' clothes, shoes, and toys.

Gifts and novelty items range from funky alarm clocks and butterfly-shaped kites to windchimes, and there's a selection of fascinating traditional musical instruments. This is not to mention the lanterns, the stationery, the bedding, the homewares, and thousands of other items that will make you suddenly feel as if you've developed adult attention deficit disorder. A word to the wise: if time is of the essence, get here early before the crowds, and keep an eye on the clock – one could easily while away an entire day at the Pearl River Mart and barely notice.

Helmut Lang *luxurious minimalist clothes* `3 D5`
80 Greene Street • 212 925 7214
≫ www.helmutlang.com Open 11–7 Mon–Sat, 12–6 Sun
Splashing out on an outfit from Helmut Lang will reward you for years to come, as the clothes are perennially stylish. This designer epitomizes the world's image of New York chic: basic blacks, whites, and neutrals, in designs that work equally well for a SoHo art opening or a downtown club.

Le Corset by Selima *luxe lingerie* `3 C5`
80 Thompson Street • 212 334 4936
Open 11am–7pm Mon–Fri, 11am–8pm Sat, noon–7pm Sun
The great and the good, from Yoko Ono to Sir Ben Kingsley, have been spotted inside this closet-sized lingerie store. Underwear by Roberto Cavalli and kimonos (new and vintage) will tempt the temptress in you. The hand-dyed corsets are so beautiful that many buyers use them as outerwear.

Barney's CO-OP *hipster clothing* `3 D4`
116 Wooster Street • 212 965 9964
Open 11am–7pm Mon–Sat, noon–6pm Sun
If no-brainer shopping is what you're after, then look no further than this wild-child of Barney's New York *(see p92)*, the city's bastion of good style and taste. The CO-OP's eclectic mix of trendy clothes for young-ish shoppers takes the Barney's brand in a hipper direction. A vast stockpile of jeans (from Seven to Levi's) for men and women guarantees that you'll find the perfect fit. Other lines – such as Theory, Marc by Marc Jacobs, and Prada Sport – mingle with upscale labels and 1970s-inspired athletic gear from the likes of Puma and Adidas. The handmade hats, funky watches, jewelry, and shoes are quirky enough to warrant more than a second glance – in fact, it's almost impossible to make a bad purchase here. What's more, wearing clothes from Barney's CO-OP is sure to increase your likelihood of getting through the velvet ropes at New York's hot night spots.

Clio *whimsical home accessories* `3 C4`
92 Thompson Street • 212 966 8991
>> www.clio-home.com Open 11am–7pm Mon–Sat, noon–6 Sun
Not one to focus on mass brands, Clio concentrates on up-and-coming homeware designers from around the world. Unique pieces, such as a walnut cheese board with turquoise inlay, can be found alongside hand-blown glassware. Look for the stunning Rehabilitated Dinnerware line of revamped vintage serving platters.

Costume National *sleek clothes* `3 D4`
108 Wooster Street • 212 431 1530
>> www.costumenational.com Open 11–7 Mon–Sat, noon–6 Sun
Ennio Capasa's collection of streamlined clothes for men and women includes pieces you'll want in your closet forever because of their enduring style. The Italian designer's perfectly tailored jackets and skirts appear edgy yet elegant, and each season's shoe collection offers sexy heels and urban-style flats.

Kirna Zabate *wearable avant-garde* `3 D4`
96 Greene Street • 212 941 9656
>> www.kirnazabete.com Open 11–7 Mon–Sat, noon–6 Sun
Every item here seems to be letting you in on a fashion secret, hinting at what is absolutely "of-the-moment." The two-story boutique is a hot spot for industry insiders, who love the drama of finding Jean Paul Gaultier next to unknown indie labels. Accessories for babies and dogs make the store even more delightful.

Miu Miu *off-beat elegance* `3 D4`
100 Prince Street • 212 334 5156
>> www.miumiu.com Open 11–7 Mon-Fri, noon–6 Sat & Sun
This flagship store has major browse appeal due to its energetic and flirty designs. While the craftsmanship of parent company Prada can be seen in the details, a let-your-hair-down attitude gives the clothes verve. Miu Miu's fashions may not be cheap, but wearing a shirt that makes you feel happy is priceless.

Moss *museum-worthy designs* `3 D4`
146 Greene Street • 212 204 7100
» www.mossonline.com Open 11–7 Mon–Sat, noon–6 Sun
This store pleases die-hard design fans as well as those who just love pretty things. Step into a world of modern furniture, retro lighting, and Moser crystal. While many of the items are ludicrously expensive, others, like the range of Lomo cameras and stuffed cartoon animals, are both fun and reasonably priced.

Marc Jacobs *fashion's golden boy* `3 D4`
163 Mercer Street • 212 343 1490
» www.marcjacobs.com Open 11–7 Mon–Sat, noon–6 Sun
Given that writer/film director Sophia Coppola is Jacobs' muse, it's not surprising that every item in his store has an air of effortless, super-cool style. From this designer's much-coveted leather bags to his retro-style dresses, jackets, and shoes, there is little that won't please the eye.

Prada *vast flagship store* `3 D4`
575 Broadway • 212 334 8888
» www.prada.com Open 11am–7pm, noon–6pm Sun
Prada's 24,000-sq-ft flagship in the heart of SoHo may have become as overexposed as a pop princess's midriff, but that doesn't mean we won't keep looking. The elegantly futuristic store, designed by Dutch architect Rem Koolhaas, retains the flavor of an art space (the building used to be the downtown arm of the Guggenheim Museum), and will entice travelers to visit just to witness architectural history in the making. Koolhaas included so many technologically advanced gadgets that even science and technology magazines covered the store opening.

As for the clothes, they remain beautiful examples of elegance reinterpreted. For women, the designs do not slavishly follow fashions, but assuredly set their own trends. The men's shoes – with the signature red stripe on the sole of the Prada Sport line – are staples that never lose their popularity.

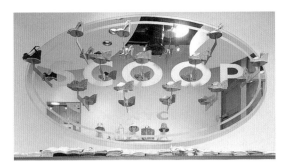

Scoop *high fashion* `3 D4`
532 Broadway • 212 925 2886
≫ www.scoopnyc.com Open 11am–8pm Mon–Sat, noon–7 Sun

The price tags may elicit a tiny (involuntary) gasp, but one piece will go a long way in building a great wardrobe. While the store caters mainly to sample-size fashionistas who don't balk at maxing out their credit cards for a poncho, it's a great place to come for the most sought-after pieces from each season.

Dean & DeLuca *a gourmet's mecca* `3 D4`
560 Broadway • 212 226 6800
≫ www.deandeluca.com Open 9am–8pm Mon–Sat, 10–7 Sun

Should there be a perfect way to stack mangoes, display passion fruit, and organize juice bottles according to the laws of color theory, then Dean & DeLuca will find it. This Aladdin's cave of a gourmet store carries top-quality produce, be it fresh, cured, made locally, or flown in from distant shores. All the produce looks wonderfully wholesome and good. Spices are clearly chosen with care, and the bottles of olive oil from Italy are almost too beautiful to open. And one of the best things about shopping here is that there are always free tasters to sample.

Each department carries delicacies from around the world. The cheese section stocks an ample selection of Goudas and Bries, as well as more exotic delights, such as Brillo de Treviso (a sweet cheese from Italy that is dipped in wine). There are also fine American cheeses, such as the creamy goat's cheese Humbolt Fog. The seafood department carries sushi-grade tuna, and the bakery produces tasty numbers such as Portuguese corn bread – it's good enough to make you throw out the low-carb lifestyle for good.

Head to the back of the store for every type of kichen appliance you never knew you needed, from sushi trays and crème brûlée dishes to mixers, suede oven mitts, and cedar grilling planks (they keep food moist, apparently). And, lest you become overwhelmed by the choice of food on offer, there is an entire library of cookbooks to help sort things out.

Kate's Paperie *stationery with panache* `3 D4`

561 Broadway • 212 941 9816

>> www.katespaperie.com Open 10–8 Mon–Sat, 11–7 Sun

Luddites who prefer the tactile pleasures of pen and paper to the ease of electronic mail should check out Kate's for all their stationery needs. Quirky thank-you cards, giant leather-bound photo albums, fountain pens, stamps, and tactile handmade paper sold by the sheet are here in abundance.

The Apartment *dream apartment loot* `3 D4`

101 Crosby Street • 212 219 3661

>> www.theapt.com Open Mon–Fri by appt only

Once you enter this experimental design studio set up to look like a real apartment, you may have difficulty returning to your own abode. Every aspect of The Apartment has been put together with an eye for what is both minimalist and sensuous. From the multicolored broom in the kitchen to the Philippe Starck fixtures in the bathroom to the Edith Mezard linens on the bed – everything exudes exemplary design. And, of course, everything you see is for sale: the clothes hanging in the closet, the toothpaste in the bathroom, even the food in the fridge.

The point of it all? To emphasize that by putting objects in a real, living, breathing space, design becomes more accessible. More than just a store, The Apartment hosts happenings and events, works with major corporations on brand development, and can be hired to re-style private and commercial spaces.

Rescue Nail Spa *velvet-rope nail spa* `4 E5`

21 Cleveland Place • 212 431 3805

Open 11am–8pm Mon–Fri, 10am–6pm Sat

Ji Baek – the super-stylish, Gucci-clad owner of Rescue – has put together NY's most hip beauty salon. As well as pedicures and manicures, Rescue offers many other treatments and all the lotions and potions associated with top-notch aromatherapy, massage, waxing, and brow-shaping.

SCO *customized skincare*   4 E4
230 Mulberry Street • 866 966 7268
>> **www.scocare.com** Open 11am–7pm Mon–Sat

Giant test tubes of pure infusions stand sentinel at the entrance to this tiny, bright, and crisply decorated skincare shop. SCO stands for Skin Care Options, and the products – which include facial cleansers, tonics and creams, a lip balm, body scrubs and polishes – are universal to all skin types. The infusions are used to customize them to each person's needs.

The consultant will ask you a series of health-related questions, then mix up a product appropriate to your requirements, choosing from more than 20 natural ingredients: caffeine for toning and tightening skin; vitamins A, C, and E for helping skin renewal; willow bark for its antiseptic properites; and mushroom for evening out skin tone. Products are packaged in elegant bottles and labelled with your name. Your prescription is filed for repeat orders, and any changes in skin condition can be accommodated.

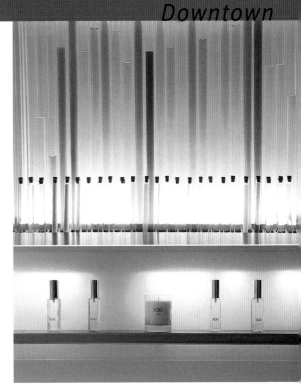

INA *runway cast-offs*   4 E4
21 Prince Street • 212 334 9048
Open noon–7pm daily (to 8pm Fri & Sat)

Ever longed for Prada heels but just couldn't afford them? Now you can find designer goods at a fraction of the original price at this store for girls with high-end tastes but low budgets. Many of the clothes are brand new, and legend has it that models occasionally bring in their just-off-the-catwalk items.

Calypso *hip hippy beachwear*   4 E4
280 Mott Street • 212 965 0990
Open 11am–7pm Mon–Sat, noon–7 Sun

This famously chic store carries clothes for the girl who spends half the year in Spain's Ibiza and the other half in the Caribbean's St. Barth's. Every item here oozes bohemian beach luxury. Flowing peasant skirts, colorful silk tops, and sandals can lend summer in the city a gloriously tropical appeal.

Hable Construction *beautiful interiors* `4 E4`
230 Elizabeth Street • 212 343 8555
» www.hableconstruction.com Open 11–7 Mon–Sat, noon–5 Sun

The Hable sisters named their company after their grandfather's construction business. But rather than building houses, they design pretty, practical things for the home. The adorable canvas pillows, printed boxes, beach towels, and garden accessories will add color and a dash of fun to any home.

Mayle *dressing up for real life* `4 E4`
242 Elizabeth Street • 212 625 0406
Open noon–7pm Mon–Sat, noon–6pm Sun

Jane Mayle's vintage-style, super-sexy clothes are on every young Hollywood starlet's must-have list. Actress Kirsten Dunst (of *Spiderman* fame) is among the many fans of Mayle's slip dresses, girly blouses, and slouchy pants. The designer has recently extended her collection to include shoes, which have won rave reviews.

Rafe *eye-catching modern handbags* `4 E4`
1 Bleecker Street • 877–7 RAFENY
» www.rafe.com
Open noon–7pm Mon–Thu, Sat, noon–8 Fri

Designer Ramon Felix creates glamorous bags and shoes that transport the imagination. His straw-and-leather Corsica bag looks like something Audrey Hepburn could have held, and the St. Germain clutch is pure Parisian chic. There are bags for men too.

Bond 07 by Selima *neo-bohemian looks* `3 D3`
7 Bond Street • 212 677 8487
» www.selimaoptique.com Open 11–7 Mon–Sat, noon–7 Sun

Selima Salaun, known for her eye-catching optical wear, is behind this NoHo boutique, which caters to women who favor unusual styles. An eclectic selection of shoes, bags, hats, lingerie, highly stylized dresses, and, of course, glasses is displayed for discerning customers.

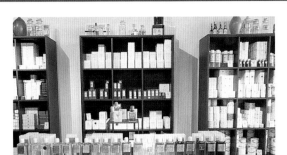

LAFCO *highly coveted beauty products* `4 E4`
285 Lafayette Street • 212 925 0001
>> www.lafcony.com Open 11am–7pm Mon–Sat (to 8pm Thu), noon–6pm Sun (closed on Sun in summer)
LAFCO sells a variety of exclusive beauty products, including the creams and tonics of Lorenzo Villoresi. This is also the NY base for Santa Maria Novella, a coveted Italian skincare line. (LA and Florence are the only other places where you'll find the entire range.)

TG-170 *clothes that epitomize downtown cool* `4 F4`
170 Ludlow Street • 212 995 8660
>> www.tg170.com Open noon–8pm daily
If you've ever wondered what the cutting-edge kids wear to hip Lower East Side parties, TG-170 will let you in on the secret. The shop stocks small quantities of choice clothes and accessories that never seem to miss the fashion bull's-eye. Owner Terri Gillis is often in the shop to personally sort out shoppers' style dilemmas.

ALife Rivington Club *sneaker joint* `4 G4`
158 Rivington Street • 212 375 8128
>> http://rivingtonclub.com Open noon–7pm Tue–Sat
If an exquisite pair of retro trainers is what you're after, you need to be willing to put up with a few headaches. To begin with, ALife pretends not to want to be found – there is no sign out front, and you must ring a doorbell to enter. Such discretion may give you the impression that you've intruded on a members-only club – in fact, their business cards say "members only." But this is all retail theater, and once you're inside the wood-paneled shop any misgivings you have will soon be forgotten.

The knockout shoes are individually displayed, each allotted its own back-lit mahogany shelf space, like a row of rare finds in a local museum. This is fitting, as the items stocked here would be hard to track down elsewhere. Vintage Air Jordans, Nike Air Wovens, and old-school Adidas are just some of the lines available that will grant you instant street credibility.

Shop *fun, feminine finds* `4 F4`
105 Stanton Street • 212 375 0304
Open noon–7pm daily

A rack of sexy dresses, lacy cover-ups for the beach, and cashmere sweaters makes Shop feel a little like an intimate dressing room for college sorority girls. The salespeople are extremely friendly too, treating you just like one of the girls. For more standard fare, there's an entire wall devoted to jeans.

Teany *Moby's tea shop* `4 F4`
90 Rivington Street • 212 475 9190
⟫ www.teany.com Open 9am–midnight daily

Electronica music maven Moby has created his own vision of what a teahouse should be (and very teeny it is indeed). The cozy interior is minimalist white, and the sound system reverberates with low-key club music, giving the shop a futuristic Zen-like ambience.

There are over 93 different teas to sample and buy, ranging from the exotic to the highly exotic. Try the Silver Needle (a white tea with a superior level of antioxidants), the Golden Nepal (just because the name is so cool), and the Earl Grey Creme (the unequivocal best-seller). Alongside metal canisters of leaf tea, the tiny retail section sells every accessory needed for the perfect brew, from the actual teapot – with the Teany logo – to cups, glasses, tea caddies, and milk jugs. Don't leave Teany without sampling the vegan and vegetarian menu, which features organic muffins, delicate sandwiches, and tofu scramble.

Chain Stores

New York has no shortage of chain stores offering reasonably priced fashion. There is a **Gap** on practically every corner – always good for basic T-shirts, jeans, khakis, and bookbags. Equally prevalent is Gap's more upscale sister store, **Banana Republic**. Popular with Wall Street yuppies, Banana offers clean-cut fashion. Prices can be a bit high for fashion with such little soul, but there is always a sale rack with bargains. The all-American, casual-preppy look of **J. Crew** is popular with all age groups, and can even make it into a fashionista's closet. For pseudo-punk flair, try **Urban Outfitters**, where you'll find the latest trends, such as Puma zip-ups, and funky household items like shower curtains and kitchenware. For individual contact details, *see p275–76.*

Subterranean Records *60s–70s vinyl* `3 C3`
5 Cornelia Street • 212 463 8900
≫ www.recordsnyc.com Open noon–8pm daily

In the heart of the West Village, Subterranean Records is the kind of music store any die-hard rocker would be hard pressed to fault. Specializing in 70s-era NYC punk and 60s-era rock, the shop is crammed with 7-inch singles and LPs. There's soul, jazz, and blues, too, and plenty of CDs alongside the old-school vinyl.

Fat Beats *hip-hop & def sounds* `3 C2`
406 6th Avenue • 212 673 3883
≫ www.fatbeats.com Open noon–9pm Mon–Sat, noon–6 Sun

Fat Beats caters to DJs and collectors of hip-hop vinyl. If you are a true connoisseur of underground hip-hop, you'll probably have the shop at the top of your NY itinerary. If, on the other hand, you're merely a dabbler in the music, at least go for the experience – especially the too-cool-for-school staff.

Fresh *decadent bath & body tonics* `3 B3`
388 Bleecker Street • 917 408 1850
≫ www.fresh.com Open noon–8 Mon–Fri, 11–8 Sat, noon–6 Sun

The lotions and potions found here sound more like culinary ingredients than bathroom products. Sugar scrubs, sake bath gel, milk soaps, rice face washes, and soy hand cream are a few of the more exotic creations. All Fresh products are beautifully packaged, making them ideal gifts to take back home.

Magnolia Bakery *classic cupcakes* `3 B3`
401 Bleecker Street • 212 462 2572
Open noon–11:30pm Mon–Thu; 9am–12:30am Fri, 10am–12:30am Sat, 10am–11:30pm Sun

Instantly recognizable by the line of happy customers at the door, Magnolia is a Village institution, famed for its beautifully decorated and superb-tasting cupcakes. Don't be shy about guzzling one as soon as you've paid – everyone does.

Marc by Marc Jacobs *downtown cool* `3 D4`
403–405 Bleecker Street • 212 343 1490
≫ **www.marcjacobs.com** Open 11–7 Mon–Sat, noon–7 Sun
Ever wondered how models obtain that effortlessly chic, just-rolled-out-of-bed appearance? Step inside Marc's store, and you too can achieve that devil-may-care look, with a pair of 70s-inspired corduroys and a bomber jacket – the designer's perennial favorites. The men's and women's stores are next to each other.

Flight 001 *quirky accessories for jet-setters* `3 B2`
96 Greenwich Avenue • 212 691 1001
≫ **www.flight001.com** Open 11am–8pm Mon–Sat, noon–6 Sun
Ever thought you could do with a petal pink passport cover? You will be convinced you need more cool accessories and gadgets than 007 after visiting this West Village gem. A mobile spice rack to liven up airplane food, a cigarette lighter that will work in storm-force gales, and adorable laundry bags are among the essentials. For the transcontinental sophisticate, there are *New York Times* trivia games, airplane yoga books, travel candles, and Dr. Hauschka beauty products. This is also your chance to stock up on travel books locating the planet's hippest hotels. Walking-tour CDs of Brooklyn, Manhattan and the Bronx can be burnt on to your iPod, to ensure that you never get lost on the street. Still got money to burn? Then indulge in the silver, hardcase luggage, because nothing looks more dashing in an airport than a traveler who knows how to get there in style.

Bonsignour *coffee & beautiful people* `3 B2`
35 Jane Street • 212 229 9700
Open 7am–8pm Mon–Sun
The reason why so many shoppers pack into this Lilliputian space is because it offers good coffee, even better baked goods, and has the friendliest vibe of any café/bakery in the West Village. The bench outside is arguably the best place in the neighborhood to sit and watch the world go by.

MXYPLYZYK *eclectic urban homeware* `3 B2`
125 Greenwich Avenue • 212 989 4300
>> www.mxyplyzyk.com Open 11am–7pm Mon–Sat, noon–5 Sun

Keep your hands in your pockets at this unique store, as you're bound to want to touch, stroke, or squeeze *everything*. From puggy banks (pug-dog piggy banks – get it?) to purses resembling Bocce bowling balls, whimsy is the *raison d'être* of almost every item at MXYPLYZYK. (It's pronounced "mixyplitsick," by the way.) Vinyl bowls look like warped LPs, a shiny chrome toaster is suggestive of a prop in a 1950s sci-fi movie, and a nutcracker comes in the guise of a squirrel. Utilitarian products, such as cups and saucers, make the occasional appearance alongside a wealth of semi-useful stuff like salt and pepper dogs, psychedelic plates, wonky glasses, and rubber-bladed desk fans.

There are items for every corner of your home: modern measuring bowls and Japanese dishes for the kitchen, Korres skin care products and giant rubber ducks for the bathroom, a coffee table book of *Turkish Wrestling*, and sleek Martini shakers for your evening cocktails. The most sophisticated pieces (not outrageously priced considering the exclusive West-Village location) include office lamps and metal "industrial-style" jewelry. The point of this store is to bring a little humor and frivolity into the overly studious atmosphere that frequently surrounds contemporary design. Linking all the varied products in this fun store is the perennial question of what is functional design and what is art.

Stella McCartney *high chic/rocker chick* `3 A2`
429 West 14th Street • 212 255 1556
>> www.stellamccartney.com Open 12–7 Mon–Sat, 12:30–6 Sun

Set in the newly fashionable Meatpacking District, Stella McCartney's store is a lesson in cool. Green stilettos with plastic cherries dangling off the straps epitomize her vision of elegance mixed with a little *joie de vivre*. The inlaid wood and mother-of-pearl dressing rooms are exquisite.

La Cafetiere *French-style homewares* `3 A1`
160 9th Avenue • 646 486 0667
Open 10am–7:30pm Tue–Sat, noon–7pm Sun–Mon

Francophiles and those who think a smattering of Provençal style might look good in their homes should head to this shop. While some of the rural-style tableware is pleasant but commonplace, the furniture – such as a weather-beaten armoire by Campagne Premiere – is exceptional.

Jeffrey *boutique department store* `3 A2`
449 West 14th Street • 212 206 1272
Open 10am–8pm Mon–Sat (to 9pm Thu, 7pm Sat), 12:30–6 Sun

A trailblazing store at the edge of the luxuriously gritty Meatpacking District *(see p183)*, Jeffrey is where beautiful people and celebrities shop (you'll often see tinted-glass limousines parked out front). While the store is not large, the stock is a discerning selection, and avant-garde labels such as Dries Van Noten and Balenciaga are much in evidence. This means that you won't have to spend hours digging around for the choicest outfits, but it also means that you won't find bargains either.

The women's shoe department – which takes up the entire center of the store – is quite possibly the best collection of footwear in New York. You'll find flirty sandals made in Capri, Prada flats, Yves Saint Laurent stilettos, Puma trainers, and a selection of other equally stylish brands. Adding to the enjoyment of shopping at Jeffrey are old-school touches, such as formal greeters at the doorway and an abundance of cheery salespeople at your beck and call.

Carapan Urban Spa & Store *city oasis*

`3 C1`

5 West 16th Street • 212 633 6220
>> www.carapan.com
Spa open 10am–9:45pm daily; store open 10am–8pm daily

Carapan's all-natural restorative products are made from plants, flowers, and minerals. Buy them here, or indulge fully at the on-site holistic spa, which offers some of the best massage and treatments in the city.

ABC Carpet and Home *beautiful, budget-breaking furniture*

`3 D1`

888 Broadway • 212 473 3000
>> www.abchome.com
Open 10am–8pm Mon–Fri, 10am–7pm Sat, 11am–6:30pm Sun

The six massive floors of ABC will be like the skies of heaven to many shoppers – there's a vision of unparalleled beauty wherever you look.

The first floor is an assortment of treasures, such as hand-blown Venetian glass chandeliers, vintage nursery furniture from France, and cast-iron Buddha heads. This level may look like a Parisian flea market, but don't expect flea market prices.

Walk upstairs to find modern furniture and retro 1960s-style chairs and light fixtures. The third floor stocks some of the world's finest linens, Frette and Pratesi among them. Head to floors five and six for Belle Époque French antiques. Many pieces – whether rustic cooking pots or formal chairs – would look at home in a museum.

Many native New Yorkers don't even know about the top-notch, top-floor restaurants at this extraordinary store. Le Pain Quotidien is a French-Belgian Bakery serving breads, pastries, gourmet sandwiches, and coffee. It's a popular place for brunch. There is also Pipa, a tapas restaurant, which has a lively atmosphere for larger parties. Lucy is a Mexican barbecue.

Without leaving the store, you can visit the Mudhoney Salon. This is a full-service luxury hair salon with a beguiling element of punk set amid the beauty of East Asian furniture.

Paragon Sporting

3 D1

Goods *clothes and equipment for the sporty*
867 Broadway • 800 961 3030
>> www.paragonsports.com
Open 10am–8pm Mon–Sat, 11:30am–7pm Sun

A three-floor megastore for your inner athlete, Paragon offers everything needed for just about any sport you care to mention. The basement is filled to the brim with trainers, including New Balance (the serious jogger's choice), Nike, and Puma. All manner of running paraphernalia is stocked: heart monitors, lap timers, even breathable underwear.

The first floor caters to the more genteel country club set, with tennis rackets, Lacoste shirts, and adorable tennis skirts. There's a wide selection of golf equipment too. Don't miss the large back room for swimwear (from delicate bikini sets made for lounging to serious one-piece Speedos for racing).

The top floor is the preserve of adventure sports: kayaking equipment, diving watches, and a full assortment of camping gear.

Department Stores

Manhattan's department stores are legendary, and visitors rarely feel a visit to New York is complete without venturing to at least one of the city's great shopping behemoths.

Macy's *(see p275)* is usually high on the list; this century-old icon spans a full city block and carries mostly moderately priced goods from homewares to fashion. You'll need to exercise patience, though, as Macy's is always crowded and easy to get lost in. But, if you have time to spare, you will uncover generous sale racks, with all-American brands such as DKNY, Tommy Hilfiger, and Polo.

If you're looking for a more upscale, less crowded variation, **Bloomingdale's** and **Saks Fifth Avenue** *(see p275 for both)* offer not only hundreds of everyday brands but also boutique labels and high-end designer showrooms. Chanel, Stella McCartney, and Yves Saint-Laurent are among the fashion houses represented at these department stores. During the amazing end-of-season sales, luxury items are reduced by as much as 50 per cent.

Henri Bendel *(see p275)* is much loved by New Yorkers and visitors alike because it feels deceptively more like a boutique than a large department store. This is due, in part, to its clever layout of split levels and winding staircases. Yet the selection here is vast, from hip make-up lines such as MAC and Laura Mercier to private label sweaters. There is a mini boutique of Diane Von Furstenburg wrap dresses and an impressive selection of evening frocks. Unlike the other department stores though, Bendels (as it's affectionately called by New Yorkers) does not sell everything from mixers to mattresses, but limits itself to cutting-edge designers and beauty products. *(See also **Bergdorf Goodman**, p91.)*

Kiehl's *world-famous for beauty products* `4 E2`

109 3rd Avenue • 800 543 4572

>> www.kiehls.com Open 10am–7pm Mon–Sat, noon–6 Sun

Conveniently located just steps away from the Third Avenue stop on the L train, this flagship store for Kiehl's has an awesome product line of plant-based beauty creams, tonics, powders, and soaps. In keeping with the simplicity of the products, the packaging is kept equally minimal.

Grab a basket upon entering and start walking down the rows of cucumber body washes, rose toners, coconut hair conditioners, and more. Friendly and well-informed staff are on hand to answer questions and offer suggestions. A few suggestions for your shopping list: Kiehl's Silk Groom (which does wonders for conditioning and styling hair); the excellent Lip Balm; and Kiehl's Original Musk Oil (which has been known to stop people in their tracks, so intoxicating is its aroma). Kiehl's is also very good at offering free samples of any item you are curious about.

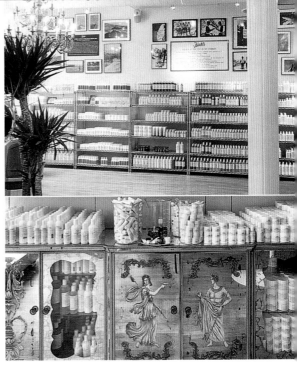

The Strand *the first and last word in books* `3 D1`

828 Broadway • 212 473 1452

Open 9:30am–10:30pm Mon–Sat, 11am–10:30pm Sun

The Strand is a downtown institution, and all visitors to the city should pay a visit here to participate in a New York rite of passage. This is not a bookstore with neatly arranged shelves and space to sit on sofas and sip lattes. And that is precisely why The Strand is so precious to bibliophiles. Books are its sole *raison d'être*; they seem to spill from every direction, and book-hunters duly crowd the store to scour the shelves for out-of-print books, first editions, and obscure tomes at greatly discounted prices.

A large collection of photography, architecture, and design books sits alongside shelf upon shelf of fiction, from pulp to literary classics. A treasure trove of children's books can be found downstairs. Outside, there are always hundreds of books stacked up, on sale for a dollar each. Whatever you're looking for, there are always astonishing discoveries to be made.

St. Mark's Sounds *new & used CDs* `4 E3`
16 St. Mark's Place • 212 677 2727
Open noon–8pm Mon–Sun

This is no place in which to worry about surly service, dust collecting on the CD covers, or the absence of listening booths. However, it is the place to go wild about an amazing selection of used and new CDs of rock, jazz, new wave, soul, and more at prices that rarely go above double digits.

Jazz Record Center *hidden store of jazz jewels* `5 C5`
236 West 26th Street (8th floor) • 212 675 4480
» www.jazzrecordcenter.com
Open 10am–6pm Mon–Sat

A music store for those who know that jazz isn't just about Miles Davis, John Coltrane, and Dizzy Gillespie. The Jazz Record Center specializes in rare vinyl for true jazz fanatics. Auctions are held via the store's website, through which you can purchase books, magazines, jazz ephemera, and LPs, including coveted first pressings.

Jimmy Choo *shoes that pinch the wallet* `8 E5`
645 5th Avenue • 212 593 0800
» www.jimmychoo.com Open 10am–6pm Mon–Sat

If the shoe fits (or even if it hurts a bit), don't deny yourself the luxury of owning a pair of status-making Jimmy Choos. There is a style to match any aspect of your life (except maybe hiking): flat sandals for holidays, strappy stilettos for the evening, sporty pumps, and even a bridal collection.

Manolo Blahnik *shoe shrine* `8 E5`
31 West 54th Street • 212 582 3007
Open 10:30am–6pm Mon–Fri, 10:30am–5:30pm Sat

If shoes can be considered works of art, then Manolo Blahniks are masterpieces. Every pair is meticulously hand-crafted, and any woman who wears them gains instant sex appeal (that is, if she can master walking in such dainty heels). Plan on paying a hefty price though: such stylistic wizardry does not come cheap.

Takashimaya *hand-picked exotica* `8 E5`
693 5th Avenue • 800 753 2038
Open 10am–7pm Mon–Sat, noon–5pm Sun

If you find yourself on the crowded streets of Fifth Avenue, duck into Takashimaya for some peace and tranquillity. A hushed quality fills this six-level store, and the objects therein form a refined selection of goods from around the world (many of them with an Asian influence). Comfort and luxury come in many forms: vintage furniture, state-of-the-art gadgetry, pamperingly soft bathrobes, lacquered bowls, handmade sweaters, and exotic flower arrangements.

The top floor carries deluxe beauty items, such as outrageously decadent silk Japanese slippers that release a perfume as you walk in them. This department also stocks the most coveted and hard-to-find beauty products and fragrances. You'll find ranges by Czech & Speake, Different Company perfumes, and Takashimaya's own T fragrance line.

The slick "lifestyle" floor sells everything from modern dishes to ancient-looking tables and wardrobes. If a one-of-a kind gift is what you're after, there is an endless selection of pretty little things, such as delicate Japanese writing paper and old-fashioned photo albums. Everything is displayed in a sparse Zen-like fashion, and every item is specially selected for its uniqueness and high quality.

The Tea Box Café on the bottom floor is the best place to rest tired feet and reinvigorate the tired shopper. It serves authentic Japanese green teas and bento boxes filled with healthy East-West fusion morsels to munch on.

Felissimo *half-gallery, half-boutique* `8 E5`
10 West 56th Street • 212 247 5656
» www.felissimo.com
Open 11am–6pm Mon–Thu & Sat, 11am–8pm Fri

The five-story design house of Felissimo is unlike any other store you'll find in New York – or anywhere else, for that matter. It is a hybrid gallery/design boutique, filled with one-of-a kind products to contemplate and to buy. The owners of Felissimo (which means "beyond happy" in Italian) collaborate with designers from around the world to produce temporary exhibitions. The beautiful and often highly original objects on display may be prototypes for goods not yet mass-produced. Each exhibition has a theme, and aims to make the audience/customers question the effect of design on society. During 2004, for example, one of the exhibitions was called "White Out." All five floors were filled with white furniture, clothes, and objects for the duration of the show, which explored the perception of white.

If this all seems a little pretentious, take comfort in the fact that proceeds from the sale of many of the designs go to good causes. For example, a portion of the price of the Tribute Plates – ceramic plates individually designed by famous actors, designers, and artists – goes to the charity of the designer's choice, as well as UNESCO.

In the gift shop downstairs, you can view and buy more down-to-earth objects, such as modern steel tea pots, metal earrings, funky wrapping paper, T-shirts, and other eclectic but well-designed items.

Niketown *a Nike for everyone* `8 E5`
6 East 57th Street • 212 891 6453
» www.niketown.com Open 10am–8pm Mon–Sat, 11–7 Sun

Much as the name implies, this is, if not quite a town, then certainly a decent-sized village of Nike products. The newest trainers are on display alongside men's and women's workout clothes – cool enough for street wear. If you're less concerned about the latest craze, seek out the Clearance Department for great bargains.

Bergdorf Goodman *old-school charm*   8 E4

754 5th Avenue • 800 558 1855

≫ www.bergdorfgoodman.com

Open 10am–7pm Mon–Sat (to 8pm Thu), noon–6pm Sun

Bergdorf's, as New Yorkers affectionately call this landmark department store, is almost as definitive a symbol of the city as the Statue of Liberty. Located near the Trump Tower and across the street from the Plaza Hotel *(see p205)*, this is where the well-heeled ladies who lunch choose to shop.

The basement level has been converted into the beauty floor. This bright and cheerful space showcases skincare brands, such as La Prairie, and make-up lines including Shu Umera. The Buff Spa is a manicure/pedicure stand (no appointment necessary). More beauty needs can be fulfilled upstairs at the Susan Ciminelli Day Spa (which is known for its use of soothing, seaweed-based products) and the John Barett Salon.

As for fashion and accessories, everything you could ever need (and didn't even know you needed) is all under the same roof. There's a stunningly fine jewelry selection on the first floor, while a large collection of Marc Jacobs, Gucci, Prada, and Chanel jostles for space on the second floor. The very sophisticated clothes are all displayed as mini-boutiques, showcasing renowned design labels such as Moschino and Dolce & Gabbana.

Dylan's Candy Bar *sugar-lover's dream* 8 F4
1011 3rd Avenue • 646 735 0078
»» www.dylanscandybar.com Open 11am–9pm Mon–Thu,
11am–11pm Fri & Sat, 11am–7pm Sun
Dylan Lauren, daughter of American designer Ralph
Lauren, offers a fantasy for both kids and adults: a
two-story candy store. Not one to do anything run-of-
the mill, she stocks hard-to-find candy in tins that
you'll cherish long after the contents are eaten.

Barney's New York *hip versus classic* 8 E4
660 Madison Avenue • 888 822 7639
»» www.barneys.com
Open 10am–8pm Mon–Fri, 10am–7pm Sat, 11am–6pm Sun
Too original to be called a department store and too
large to be a boutique, Barney's is unique. Off-beat
clothes by little-known designers are carried right
next to heavy hitters, such as Marc Jacobs and Prada.
The top-floor restaurant lures New York's power elite.

La Perla *luxurious lingerie* 8 E3
803 Madison Avenue • 212 570 0050
»» www.laperla.com
Open 10am–6pm Mon–Sat
Bikinis and lingerie couldn't be sexier. Glamorous
and risqué tulle-knit bathing suits play peek-a-boo
with the body, while the lingerie selection goes from
nice to naughty in no time at all. The sporty Studio
and saucy La Perla Black collections are included.

Bra Smyth *tailored bras & underwear* 8 E2
905 Madison Avenue • 212 772 9400
»» www.brasmyth.com Open 10am–6pm Mon–Sat, noon–5 Sun
Just as no two snowflakes are identical, neither are
two breasts – a fact not lost on Bra Smyth. With more
than 3,000 bras to choose from, and full-time seam-
stresses on board to customize each bra to fit
perfectly, falling straps and poking underwire should
never be an issue again.

Liliblue *feast of accessories for Europhiles* `8 E2`
955 Madison Avenue • 212 249 5356
Open 10am–6pm Mon–Sat, noon–6pm Sun

This French-owned boutique imports hats, scarves, purses, and other accessories from Italy and France. The reasonably priced jewelry comes mostly from two Parisian brands: Satellite and Poggi. Both are known for their bright, characterful costume jewelry and silver rings, set with semiprecious stones.

Clyde's *boutique pharmacy* `8 E2`
926 Madison Avenue • 800 RXCLYDES
>> www.clydesonmadison.com
Open 9am–7.30pm Mon–Sat (to 8pm Thu), 10am–6pm Sun

Yes, Clyde's is a pharmacy in the sense that you can buy vitamins and cough syrup, but this popular neighborhood institution offers so much more. The store is stocked with high-end beauty and skincare products, candles, and imported bathroom goods.

Christian Louboutin *scarlet soles* `8 E2`
941 Madison Avenue • 212 396 1884
Open 10am–6pm Mon–Sat

The quirky designs and scarlet soles that mark every Louboutin shoe signify that you've arrived in the style-conscious world of Madison Avenue. Well-heeled fans include New York socialites and Hollywood A-listers. Even if you're not buying, drop by to admire the glorious, Parisian-style interior.

Diane B *clothes & shoes for uptown girls* `8 F1`
1414 3rd Avenue • 212 570 5360
Open 11–7:30 Mon–Fri, 10–6:30 Sat; closed Sun in summer

Situated in the lonely shopping territory of the far eastern Upper East Side, Diane B is a good stop for French and Italian women's clothing if you don't feel like venturing downtown. Finding a hot number isn't hard with brands such as Stephan Kelian and Vera Wang, but don't expect to find Prada and Gucci.

ABH Designs *creature comforts* `8 H1`
401 East 76th Street • 212 249 2276
Open 11–6:30 Mon–Sat
Owner Aude Bronson-Howard's career as a
Hollywood costume designer is evident in her eye for
detail when choosing items for her store. Linen
napkins with silk trim, Italian plates, down shawls,
and faux-mink slippers are some of the items that
will bring a touch of luxury to any home.

Searle *coats and cashmere tops* `10 E5`
1124 Madison Avenue • 212 988 7318
» www.searlenyc.com
Open 10–7 Mon–Fri, 10–6 Sat, noon–6 Sun
What began as a store focusing on stylish shearling
coats has expanded to include the full gamut of delectable women's clothing. From TSE cashmere sweaters
to casual lines such as Blue Dot, Trina Turk, and
classic Lacoste, Searle provides a great mix of styles.

Intermix *must-have clothing* `7 C3`
210 Columbus Avenue • 212 769 9116
Open 11–7 Mon–Wed, 11–7:30 Thu–Sat, noon–6 Sun
Intermix is a beacon of style in the relative fashion
desert of the Upper West Side, where pickings can be
slim for trend-conscious shoppers. The staff can be
less than helpful and the prices are high enough to
leave you temporarily broke, but Intermix provides an
irresistible selection of cool, slinky outfits.

Blades Board
& Skate *gear for movers and skaters* `7 B2`
120 West 72nd Street • 888 552 5233
» www.blades.com Open 10–9 Mon–Sat, 11–7 Sun
The name says it all. Kneepads, goggles, and
helmets are among the essential equipment sold
here for skateboarders, snowboarders, and inline
skaters. Make your choice from an impressive array
of skates then head across the street to Central Park.

Housing Works
Thrift Shop *treasures at bargain prices*

`7 C2`

306 Columbus Avenue • 212 579 7566
>> www.housingworks.org
Open 11–7 Mon–Fri, 10–6 Sat, noon–5 Sun

This is not just a thrift shop, but a store with heart. It was conceived in 1990 by Keith Cylar and other activists as a not-for-profit shop to help homeless New Yorkers living with AIDS. Housing Works has now become the largest community-based AIDS activist group in the U.S. Cylar passed away in April 2004 after a long AIDS-related illness, but the shop continues his work.

The soul and integrity of the project encourages New York's most stylish residents to donate anything from couches to lamps to coveted clothes. It's not uncommon to find rare and sought-after furniture, designer clothes, antiques, and even collectable art. Despite all this, prices remain rock bottom, in contrast to those found in other trendy thrift stores.

Super Runners *joggers paradise*

`7 B1`

360 Amsterdam Avenue • 212 787 7665
>> www.superrunnersshop.com Open 10–7 Mon–Fri
(to 9pm Thu), 10–6 Sat, 11–5 Sun

Even if you're not training for the New York marathon, this shop has a running shoe for every terrain, from the gym treadmill to Central Park nature trails. Stock is not restricted to trainers; you can also buy a watch for keeping a check on lap times.

Zabar's *top-notch deli*

2245 Broadway • 212 787 2000
>> www.zabars.com
Open 8–7:30 Mon–Fri, 8–8 Sat, 9–6 Sun

Were Zabar's to close, the city could well descend into chaos. Since the 1920s, New Yorkers have relied on this family-run business for all their gourmet kitchen needs, from fine cheeses to the best smoked fish. Don't leave without buying a famous Zabar's coffee.

Xukuma *cool lifestyle store* `11 D4`

183 Lenox Avenue • 212 222 0490

>> www.xukuma.com

Open noon–7 Wed–Sat, 10–6 Sun

Xukuma, pronounced "zoo-koo-ma," is a lifestyle store for hip city-dwellers. The shop-owners define Xukuma (a word they dreamed up) as "life the way you want it to be." Their vision encompasses homewares – groovy lamps, frames, clocks, etc. – and clothing lines that bank heavily on 1960s/70s-influenced "sista-soul" appeal.

You'll see the lanky, sexy silhouette of a black woman with an Afro (dubbed "X Girl") on everything from T-shirts to posters and cards. Her best cameo is on the tank top and panty sets emblazoned with phrases such as "obey me" and "please me." There's a range of men's underwear with "hustler," "dirty devil," and "bad boy" emblems. Xukuma also stocks gourmet food, teas, and Sia candles, as well as chandeliers and gift baskets.

Demolition Depot *historic artifacts* `12 G3`

216 East 125th Street • 212 860 1138

>> www.demolitiondepot.com

Open 10–6 Mon–Fri, 11–5 Sat

Many a New Yorker can thank Demolition Depot for helping to spruce up a bland apartment with objects from a bygone era. At the four-story warehouse in Harlem, you'll uncover treasures such as 19th-century light fixtures, mirrors that once hung in American farmhouses, fireplace mantles, and oil paintings.

Owner and antiques dealer Evan Blum salvages most of his stock from homes and buildings that are about to be destroyed. Because of this, he can buy cheap and sell a beguiling range of architectural pieces – from plumbing fixtures and door furniture to stone sculptures, stained-glass windows, gates and railings – at far more reasonable prices than you'd expect to pay at an auction. Demolition Depot's smaller items include decorative tiles, clocks, old shop signs, and NYC subway signage.

Butter *current trends for women* `13 B4`
389 Atlantic Avenue • 718 260 9033
Open noon–7 Mon–Sat, noon–6 Sun

Though not completely original by NYC standards, Butter has been a ground-breaking store for Brooklyn, being the first in the neighborhood to offer top-end women's clothing. With lines such as Dries Van Noten, Rick Owens, and Rogan jeans available here, Brooklyn girls no longer have to trek across the bridge.

Bark *one-of-a-kind gifts* `13 B4`
495 Atlantic Avenue • 718 625 8997
» www.breukelenny.com
Open noon–7 Wed–Sat, noon–6 Sun

"Lifestyle stores" are becoming something of a phenomenon in New York, and Bark is hailed as the first example of this genre in Brooklyn. In old-fashioned parlance, however, Bark is an interior design store, predominantly stocking contemporary pieces, such as Japanese glass, South African wooden bowls, and jewelry by local artists.

Because the selection offered at Bark is so unusual and distinctive, even Manhattanites are prepared to leave the island once in a while to visit it. Expensive kitchen supplies, such as coffee-makers, handmade ceramic dishes, and stainless steel mixers offer endless appeal. The wonderfully elegant, aromatic Diptyque candles are the store's most affordable and best-selling items, but this is not really the place for bargain-hunting.

Loom *groovy knick-knacks* `13 C4`
115 7th Avenue, Brooklyn • 718 789 0061
Open 11–7 Mon–Sat, 11–6 Sun

Loom is a design store catering to the well-heeled, stroller-pushing crowd of Park Slope. Italian stationery, mod jewelry, and cute little *objets* make wonderful gifts for the friend who has everything. Come and agonize over the discerning selection of glass vases and hand-embroidered bed linen.

Nest *clutch of delectable home furnishings* `13 C5`

396a 7th Avenue, Brooklyn • 718 965 3491
Open noon–7 Mon, 11–7 Tue–Sat, noon–6 Sun

When graphic designer Jihan Kim and his wife decided to settle down together and have a baby, they decided to open a store that would combine this cozy time in their lives and their artistic backgrounds. Thus Nest was born (and their baby girl) to fill the niche in Park Slope for off-beat *objets* and furniture for starting a home.

Their range of products for a groovy home include sleek, handmade ceramic vases – made by Kim's aunt – and Japanese mugs with bold graphic prints. Nest also stocks hand-embroidered pillows and stylish window shades, tiny wooden children's chairs in bold colors (really adorable), and space-age Blue Dot desks, made of white Lucite. The perfect buy if space is tight in your suitcase are Nest's giant, adhesive dots, which come in bright colors and are designed to decorate walls, ceilings, and floors.

Mini Minimarket *ironic girly lifestyle store* `13 B2`

218 Bedford Avenue • 718 302 9337
>> www.miniminimarket.com Open noon–8 daily

A hodgepodge of all things cool, this store has everything for the hipster Williamsburg girl: playful jewelry, fashions from Tokyo, sexy underwear, Gola trainers, and 1980s-inspired tops. The minimarket stocks only small quantities of each item, so it's unlikely you'll find anyone else wearing the same thing.

Spoonbill & Sugartown Booksellers *rare tomes* `13 B2`

218 Bedford Avenue • 718 387 7322 Open 11–9 daily

Books on painting, photography, architecture, and graphic design cater to Brooklyn's bohemians. At the back of the store, you'll find used books on everything from religion to geography. What you won't find at Spoonbill & Sugartown is anything off the current *New York Times* best-seller list.

Spacial *high-end crafts* `13 B2`
199 Bedford Avenue • 718 599 7962
≫**www.spacialetc.com** 11–9 Mon–Sat, noon–8 Sun

Spacial (sic) feels simultaneously folksy and urban.
In the window are handmade ponchos, clogs, and
precious children's clothes. Step inside to find highly
stylized lamps, jewelry, and bowls, as well as
imported design journals and soaps. The only factor
that unites all these items is their evident coolness.

Isa *trend-setting clothes* `13 B2`
88 North 6th Street • 718 387 3363
Open 1–9 Mon–Fri, noon–10 Sat, noon–8 Sun

Walking into Isa is like stumbling upon the closet of
pop prince Justin Timberlake. An array of vintage-
looking (but new) T-shirts adorn the wall, each
bearing a dramatic or provocative slogan, such as
"Hold On To Young Ideas," and "Dine At The Y."
Another popular design is Jean-Michel Basquiat's
image of Cassius Clay. The hip urban gear includes
limited-edition Nikes, high-end Levi's, and a
selection of expensive sweaters.

Beautiful people work the counter, and DJs spin
the sounds to remind you what a very cool shop this
is. But Isa is not just a great boutique selling of-the-
moment clothes; it also functions as a gallery and
"happening" space in the heart of Brooklyn's fast
up-and-coming Williamsburg district. The owner, Isa,
often moves the clothing racks to one side and turns
the place into an all-night DJ dance party.

Beacon's Closet *vintage clothes trader* `13 B1`
88 North 11th Street • 718 486 0816
≫**www.beaconscloset.com**
Open 12–9 Mon–Fri, 11–8 Sat & Sun

Sick of all your old clothes? Then take your suitcase
to Beacon's Closet and either sell your garments for
cash or trade them for in-store credit. In the shop,
you'll find lots of second-hand clothing and
accessories for men and women. There are also
brand-new CDs.

Earwax *sounds to clean out your ears* `13 B2`

218 Bedford Avenue • 718 486 3771
Open noon–8pm Mon–Fri, 11am–9pm Sat & Sun

Earwax is the antithesis of record store chains: there is no adjoining coffee shop/bookstore and you can't pre-listen to CDs. But what you do get is a hand-picked selection of music that won't let you down. New CDs are biased towards indie rock, while the formidable second-hand section runs the full gamut of tastes.

Fortuna *boutique clothes store* `13 C2`

370 Metropolitan Avenue • 718 486 2682
Open 2–9pm Thu & Fri, 1–9pm Sat & Sun

It is very hard to visit this old-school style salon and leave empty handed. All the beautifully displayed vintage men's and women's clothes are carefully selected by the owner, who scours the country in her search. There are slips from the 1930s, wedge shoes from the 1970s, and even the occasional top hat.

MiniMall *alternative retail space* `13 B2`

218 Bedford Avenue
Stores at MiniMall have differing opening times, but most are open between 10am and 7pm daily

Located on Williamsburg's hippest boulevard *(see p187)*, the MiniMall is one of the best places for shopping and lounging in Brooklyn. This retail space-cum-club house takes up the entire ground floor of a loft building, and houses myriad stores.

Once inside the cavernous entryway (where computers and tables are set up for Internet perusal), you can venture into shops such as **The Girdle Factory**, in which vintage treasures can be found (a $30 Gucci wallet!). **Otte**, on the other hand, sells only what the uptown girl wants: Seven jeans and flirty dresses. **Go Yoga** offers some of the best yoga classes in the city, and the **Tibet Boutique** will help you look the part. One of the most popular stores is the **UVA Wine Shop**. There, you'll find young connoisseurs deliberating over their purchases.

Astroturf *vintage homewares* `13 B4`
290 Smith Street • 718 522 6182
Open 11am–7pm Tue–Fri, 11am–5pm Sat & Sun

There is something comforting about setting foot into this Cobble Hill homewares and furniture store. It's almost as if you've just stepped into a really groovy grandmother's attic. Astroturf sells everything that was left carelessly behind from the 1950s and 60s: orange plastic bowl sets, curvy lamps, now-prized vintage lunchboxes, turquoise coffee thermoses, and Formica tables. Everything in this store yells – no, screams – kitsch!

If all the fun and funky appeal is too much for the pottery-barn aesthetic you have studiously cultivated in your home, take a sleekly sculpted ashtray or vase to add a dash of *Austin Powers* grooviness to your decor. There are shelves and shelves of knick-knacks, so the choices are practically endless. Best of all, prices are still pretty retro here, so you can afford to have fun with the cheap-and-chic look.

Two Jakes *period furniture* `13 B2`
320 Wythe Avenue • 718 782 7780
>> www.twojakes.com
Open 11am–7pm Tue–Sun

Head to this industrial-chic area of Williamsburg for used metal office furniture that would be triple the price if it were sold in SoHo. Two Jakes' massive warehouse space offers classic 20th-century office furniture in remarkably good condition.

Moon River Chattel *farmhouse furniture* `13 B2`
62 Grand Street • 718 388 1121
Open noon–7pm Tue–Sat, noon–5pm Sun

In the urban jungle of Brooklyn sits a store that offers items more befitting a country cottage than a city pad. Light fixtures look as if they were taken from an early 20th-century soda shop, old clocks tick ponderously, wooden tables carry the burden of age, and appliances seem more artistic than purposeful.

art & architecture

New York is the pre-eminent city for Modernist art and architecture, famously evident in its towering skyscrapers and in the unsurpassed collections of the Guggenheim and the Whitney. Along with great cultural icons, such as The Met and Brooklyn Museum of Art, New York also has a thriving contemporary art scene, split between Manhattan's galleries and a dynamic community of artists in Brooklyn.

U.S. Custom House *Beaux Arts affair* `1 D5`

1 Bowling Green

Open 10am–5pm daily (to 8pm Thu)

New York's grandest example of Beaux Arts architecture has figures representing the four continents incorporated into its facade. They were sculpted by Daniel Chester French, most famous for his work at the Lincoln Memorial in Washington. The National Museum of the American Indian is housed here.

St. Paul's Chapel *New York's oldest* `1 D3`

209 Broadway, between Fulton & Vesey streets

» www.saintpaulschapel.org

It has served the residents of Lower Manhattan for well over 200 years, but St. Paul's Chapel gained wider public attention in the wake of the 9/11 attack on the World Trade Center, when it acted as a steadfast beacon for New Yorkers.

Modelled on St-Martin-in-the-Fields in London, the church was completed in 1766, making it New York's oldest building in continuous use. George Washington worshipped here during the two-year period (1789–91) when New York served as the nation's capital. His pew is singled out, and above it hangs what is believed to be the first oil painting of the Great Seal of the United States – the image of the bald eagle, with a red-and-white striped shield, thirteen arrows, and an olive branch.

The chapel bore witness to another kind of history on September 11, 2001, as debris from the collapsing North Tower of the World Trade Center rained down, cloaking the building in pale ash. Within hours of the catastrophe, St. Paul's converted into a base for recovery squads. Firefighters, police officers, and medical personnel ate, slept, and grieved here, while volunteers ministered, the city's top chefs cooked, and students from the Julliard School of Music performed impromptu concerts.

The chapel has an exhibition of memorabilia and testimonies from 9/11 survivors called *Out of the Dust: A Year of Ministry at Ground Zero*.

Ground Zero *poignant reconstruction site* `1 C3`

In 2002, the Lower Manhattan Development Corporation – in collaboration with families of victims, local business owners, and politicians – selected a master plan for Ground Zero: site of the former World Trade Center. The design was by Daniel Libeskind, an architect renowned for his ground-breaking Holocaust Museum in Germany. His scheme intended to retain the twin towers' footprints at 30 ft (9 m) below sidewalk level, creating a contemplative space for a memorial. But the most dramatic part of his design was an astonishing 1,776-ft (540-m) skyscraper, the Freedom Tower, its height echoing the date of the signing of the Declaration of Independence – 1776.

Libeskind's designs have undergone significant alterations, however, due to the commercial imperative to maximize office space. Until it is completed, visitors can view the site from a pedestrian platform at Vesey and West streets. The memorial is scheduled to open in 2006, with a museum to follow.

Skyscraper Museum *homage to height* `1 D5`
39 Battery Place • 212 968 1961
>> www.skyscraper.org
Open noon–6pm Wed–Sun

After seven years bouncing from one office lobby to the next, the Skyscraper Museum finally found a home in 2004. One of the city's most ingeniously designed museums, it honors its soaring subjects through illusion and intriguing details. Freestanding white columns are vertically reflected between stainless steel floors and mirrored ceilings, creating the appearance of infinite height. Throughout this echoing space, architectural fragments from Manhattan's most notable skyscrapers are displayed. The museum contextualizes New York's 100 year-old obsession with building tall in terms of economic cycles, an interesting counterpoint to the apparent brashness of the form. The museum also mounts temporary exhibitions, and future shows are set to redress the current NY bias with more international subjects. **Adm**

Art & Architecture

Woolworth Building *pinnacled tower* `1 D2`

Gothic in style and topped off by a green turret, the Woolworth Building is utterly distinct from its clean-edged, Lower Manhattan neighbors. Erected in 1913 for the houseware-catalogue magnate Frank Woolworth, it was, at 55 stories, the tallest structure in New York until the 1930s, when the Chrysler Building was constructed. The nave-like lobby contains a statue depicting the thrifty Mr. Woolworth counting his dimes.

Broken Kilometer *relative distance* `3 D5`

393 West Broadway • 212 989 5566 (Dia offices)
» www.brokenkilometer.org Check website for opening times

In five parallel rows, 500 gleaming brass rods lie on a SoHo hardwood floor in Walter De Maria's 1979 installation. Lain end to end, the rods would measure exactly one kilometer. The seemingly straightforward arrangement plays subtly with perspective in a work loved by mathematicians, despised by real estate agents.

Earth Room *deep, dark soil* `3 D4`

141 Wooster Street • 212 989 5566 (Dia offices)
» www.earthroom.org Check website for opening times

Commissioned by the trailblazing Dia Art Foundation, Walter De Maria's *Earth Room* (1977) is a white-walled exhibition space, filled to a depth of about 2 ft (55 cm) with moist, dark soil. Viewers stand at the threshold to the space and quietly stare in. The third of De Maria's earth sculptures, it is the only one still in existence.

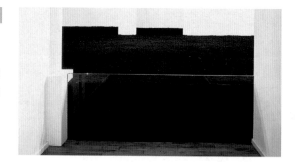

Contemporary Art Galleries

Some of the hottest galleries in the contemporary art world are grouped in Manhattan. The SoHo nexus, comprising Wooster, Grand, Greene, and Spring streets, boasts the highest concentration of galleries. **Deitch Projects** mounts some of the area's most highly anticipated shows, from paintings inspired by skateboard design to performances. Chelsea has welcomed defecting SoHo dealers for years. **Pace Wildenstein** and **Mary Boone** have Chelsea outposts as well as midtown locations, and **Larry Gagosian's** little empire, extending from Beverly Hills to London, mounts prestigious exhibitions at his large Chelsea space. Elsewhere, Chinatown's **Leo Koenig Gallery** deals in lively work from emerging artists. For individual contact details, *see p278*.

Lower East Side Tenement

4 F5

Museum *home of NY's early immigrants*
90 & 97 Orchard Street • 212 431 0233
>> www.tenement.org
Open for guided tours only: Sep–Jun Tue–Sun, Jul & Aug Mon

In the heart of the old garment district in the Lower East Side, the Tenement Museum offers an enlightening overview of how pioneering immigrants lived and worked in the late 19th and early 20th centuries. Guided tours explore an 1863 tenement, which was home to some 7,000 immigrants from 20 countries during its 72 years as a residential building.

Engaging tour guides lead visitors through the humble, virtually unchanged units, peppering biographical accounts of former tenants' lives with fascinating facts about the neighborhood's social organizations, businesses, sights, sounds, and smells. It is advisable to book a few days ahead. The museum also arranges historical walking tours of the Lower East Side. **Adm**

Merchant's House

4 E3

Museum *19th-century opulence*
29 East 4th Street • 212 777 1089
>> www.merchantshouse.com Open afternoons Thu–Mon

Between the Bowery's punk-rock bars and Broadway's name-brand shops rises a magnificent Federal-style house of around 1832. It is one of the last vestiges of a prosperous merchant-class suburbia that once thrived in downtown Manhattan. The hardware-importing Tredwell family lived here until 1933, resisting the late-19th century trend among Manhattan's elite to construct estates bordering Central Park.

Opened as a museum in 1936, the Merchant's House provides an unparalleled glimpse into how the high life was lived in mid-19th-century Manhattan. Tours (weekdays only) take visitors through a Greek Revival interior of Ionic columns, ornate plasterwork, and beautiful black-and-gold marble mantelpieces. The backyard garden is a delightful mix of arbors, perennials, and 19th-century iron furniture. **Adm**

Art & Architecture

Jefferson Market Courthouse *architectural treasure* `3 C2`

A building loved by West Villagers, the fairytale Venetian-Gothic courthouse was saved from the wrecking ball when local residents campaigned to have it converted into a public library. The former civic court is now the library's main reading room and the children's reading room occupies the police court; the reference section in the basement used to be the holding cell.

Forbes Magazine Gallery *toys/games* `3 D2`
60 5th Avenue at West 12th Street • 212 206 5548
Open 10–4 Tue, Wed, Fri & Sat

The private art estate of publishing magnate Malcolm Forbes is displayed here. Although his unrivaled Fabergé egg collection recently sold for $100 million, visitors can still glimpse a frivolous side to the notoriously pragmatic Mr. Forbes in his vintage toy collection and staggering array of boardgames.

Block Beautiful *decorous abodes* `4 E1`

Among Manhattan's most picturesque residential blocks is this fanciful melange of Tudor, late-Federal, and brownstone houses. Attractive paint schemes, varied door arch designs, and intricate wrought-iron gates distinguish each home from the next. In fair weather, the block enchants with window-mounted planter boxes brimful of color, and slender trees sprouting acid-green leaves.

Museum at the Fashion Institute of Technology *past and future trends* `5 D4`
7th Avenue at 27th Street • 212 217 5970
» **www.fitnyc.suny.edu** Open noon–8 Tue–Fri, 10–5 Sat

Do Andy Warhol's early footwear sketches bear hints of future greatness? Contemplate this question and scores of other fashion designs at F.I.T.'s free museum. Special exhibitions draw on the school's textile, illustration, and photography collections.

Midtown Deco *classic buildings*   6 F1–6 G2

Evoking an age of tuxedoed jazz orchestras, jet-black limousines, high hems, and cocked fedoras, midtown's Art Deco skyscrapers are, for many, quintessential emblems of New York. Beyond the well-known destinations (most obviously the **Empire State Building,** *see p18*) rise equally impressive yet less-visited landmarks. The following buildings are not open to the public, but you can admire the exterior forms and nearly always venture into the foyers, which often contain the buildings' most elaborate designs. The **General Electric Building** (570 Lexington Ave.), for example, has a rare, nickel-silver embellished lobby. Over on 42nd Street, look for the **Chanin Building's** intricately carved facade and doorway with elaborate, gold-plated convector grilles (122 E. 42nd St. at Lexington Ave.). Also on 42nd Street, you'll find a huge revolving globe and antiquated weather instrumentation in the lobby of the **New York Daily News Building** (220 E. 42nd St.). Though not exactly a hidden gem, the shimmering **Chrysler Building** (405 Lexington Ave.) is a revelation if you've never seen the lobby; mosaics, multicolored African marble, and whimsical automotive motifs make it a must-see.

111

International Center of Photography `5 D2`
massive photo archive

1133 Avenue of the Americas • 212 860 0000
>> www.icp.org Open 10–5 Tue–Thu, 10–8 Fri, 10–6 Sat & Sun
Combining a school, an archive, and frequent exhibitions, the ICP is one of the world's biggest centers of photography. The subject of a show here might be historical – a 1920s French avant-gardist, perhaps – or contemporary, such as reportage from Iraq. **Adm**

Whitney Museum of American Art at Altria `6 F2`

120 Park Avenue at 42nd Street • 917 663 2453
>> www.whitney.org
Open 11am–6pm Mon–Fri; sculpture garden daily
The airy, bright lobby of Altria Group, Inc. serves as an exhibition space for cutting-edge contemporary art. There are two spaces, in fact – an intimate gallery and a glass-walled indoor sculpture court. The focus of the exhibition program is emerging contemporary artists. Recent shows put the spotlight on Mark Bradford, Louis Gispert, and Dario Robleto.

Rose Museum at Carnegie Hall `7 D5`
musical memorabilia

154 West 57th Street, 2nd Floor • 212 903 9600
>> www.carnegiehall.org Open 11am–4:30pm daily
The Rose Museum gives an insight into the status of the prestigious Carnegie Hall *(see p145)* and is a treasure trove of intriguing memorabilia, from concert programs to vintage costumes. For tours of the concert hall (11:30am, 2pm, and 3pm, Sep–Jun) call 212 903 9765.

Icons

Ever since King Kong scaled the **Empire State Building** *(see pp124–5)* in his 1933 film debut, the 86th-floor observatory has been a compulsory visitor destination. Eleven blocks south, the **Flatiron Building** was New York's first skyscraper (1902). In midtown, **Grand Central Terminal** (Map 6 F2) is a Beaux Arts sculpture brought to frenetic life each morning. You can shop for souvenirs, buy fresh goods at the market, and count stars twinkling on the concourse ceiling. Nearby **Times Square** is site of dizzying neon lights and the world's most famous New Year's Eve celebration. Stately **Brooklyn Bridge** was one of the world's first steel-cable suspension bridges – walk across it for majestic views of Manhattan and glimpses of the **Statue of Liberty** *(see p18)*.

Museum of Modern Art *home at last* 8 E5
11 West 53rd Street • 212 708 9400

>> www.moma.org Open 10–5 Mon & Thu–Sun (to 7:45pm Fri)

After leading itinerant lives in cities around the world and in a temporary space in Queens, MoMA's most highly prized holdings have returned to their dramatically revamped six-story gallery back in Manhattan. Reopened in late 2004 after the most ambitious building project of the museum's 75-year history, MoMA has reaffirmed its status as the world's foremost modern art institution.

Yoshio Taniguchi's renovation has doubled the museum's exhibition capacity and restored one of its most beloved attributes, the Abby Aldrich Rockefeller Sculpture Garden. The redesign also incorporates a smart new restaurant. Set off by the refreshed gallery spaces, the collection continues to impress, with such delights as Vincent Van Gogh's *Starry Night*, Picasso's formidable *Les Demoiselles d'Avignon*, and Dalí's seminal *The Persistence of Memory*. **Adm**

Whitney Museum 8 E2
of American Art *America's finest*
945 Madison Avenue • 800 WHITNEY

>> www.whitney.org Open 11–6 Wed, Thu, Sat & Sun, 1–9 Fri

As with Frank Lloyd Wright's Guggenheim building *(see p116)*, Marcel Breuer's cantilevered Whitney is more than just a home for an art collection, it is a statement of radical intent. Built in the mid-1960s, it is distinctive, powerful and Modernist, reflecting the strongest elements of the exclusively American art it holds. The permanent collection boasts works by Warhol, Pollock, and Jasper Johns, and by abstract sculptors David Smith and Alexander Calder. It also has an extensive collection of paintings by Georgia O'Keeffe and Edward Hopper.

The Whitney's program of temporary exhibitions is excellent, including one-person retrospectives (Philip Guston, for example) and themed shows, such as on film and video (shorts by John Baldessari and Ed Ruscha were shown in 2004). **Adm**

Frick Collection *art in a glorious setting* 8 E2

1 East 70th Street (at 5th Avenue) • 212 288 0700

>> **www.frick.org** Open 10am–6pm Tue–Sat, 1–6 Sun

The family of steel tycoon Henry Clay Frick bequeathed their Fifth Avenue mansion to the city shortly after Henry's death in 1919. Included in the gift was one of the country's most spectacular collections of fine and decorative arts, spanning more than five centuries, from the Renaissance to the late 19th century.

Henry took incredible care over situating his most prized pieces in specific rooms and halls, a habit not forgotten by the collection's present directors, who may arrange entire floorpans in order to showcase one single piece. The Whistler portraits in the Oval Room, for example, are a mere backdrop to the room's main focal point, Houdon's life-size sculpture *Diana the Huntress*. The capacious West Gallery is more egalitarian with its hanging arrangements, granting Old Masters Rembrandt, Velásquez, Van Dyck, and Goya equal wallspace. On the rich, oak-paneled walls of the intimate Living Hall, at the heart of the residence, are major works by Titian, El Greco, and Bellini. Elsewhere are Jan van Eyck's *Virgin and Child with Saints and Donor*, El Greco's fearsome *The Purification of the Temple*, and Holbein's luminous portrait of *Sir Thomas More*.

However, it's the house itself that makes a visit so unforgettable. Furnishings range from Louis XVI opulence to 19th-century English restraint. Plant-filled atriums and a charming outdoor garden, with graceful magnolia trees and views of Central Park, also add extra dimensions to the Frick experience. **Adm**

Metropolitan Museum of Art *cultural behemoth*

8 E1

1000 5th Ave • 212 535 7710
>> **www.metmuseum.org** 9:30–5:30 Tue–Sun (to 9pm Fri & Sat)

The Met's two million objects form one of the world's largest museum collections. Among the myriad galleries of the hulking Beaux Arts structure are estimable collections of Egyptian artifacts, Islamic art, and European paintings. Among the paintings are works by Renaissance giants Botticelli and Leonardo, and canvases by Rembrandt, Cézanne, and Monet.

If the prospect of such a vast museum seems daunting, consider attending an informal gallery talk. More in-depth than the museum highlight tours, they are led by art historians and offer the opportunity to learn more about specific works. Check the Met's website for the talks calendar. Also note the Met's highly varied program of temporary exhibitions, which range from ancient Chinese art to the photographs of Diane Arbus and a Max Ernst retrospective in 2005. **Adm**

Museum of Television and Radio *classic footage & recordings*

8 E5

25 West 52nd Street • 212 621 6800
>> **www.mtr.org** Open noon–6pm Tue–Sun (to 8pm Thu)

Yearning to revisit a classic *Muppets* episode? The Museum of Television and Radio exists for just such desires, with its constant streams of vintage newsreel, landmark radio broadcasts, and classic comedy shows. There's a huge searchable archive too. **Adm**

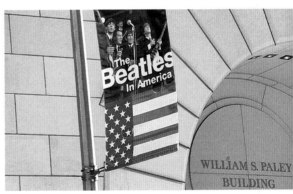

Asia Society *Asian arts*

8 F2

725 Park Avenue at 70th Street • 212 288 6400
>> **www.asiasociety.org** Open 11am–6pm Tue–Sun (to 9pm Fri)

The superb Asian art collection of American philanthropist John D. Rockefeller III is housed in this bright, modern building. Japanese screens and bronze Buddhist deities are among the exhibits spread throughout a series of galleries. Shows by contemporary Asian and Asian-American artists are often staged, and the building acts as a venue for performances of Asian music and dance. **Adm**

Guggenheim Museum

10 E4

1071 5th Avenue (at 89th Street) • 212 423 3500
>> www.guggenheim.org

Open 10am–5:45pm Sat–Wed, 10am–8pm Fri

With museums now bearing the name in Las Vegas, Venice, Berlin, New York, and Bilbao in Spain, "Guggenheim" has penetrated the world's cultural vocabulary. But before becoming the art-world jugger-naut that it is today, Guggenheim was simply the surname of Solomon, a private collector who wanted to publicly exhibit his collection of abstract art.

In the minds of Guggenheim and his advisor, the painter and curator Hilla Rebay, the collection required a new kind of gallery space – one that complemented the pioneering, iconoclastic form of the paintings in his collection. What resulted was one of the world's most instantly recognizable buildings. Designed by American Modernist architect Frank Lloyd Wright, the building shattered notions of rectilinear exhibition space. Rather than walk through traditional galleries and wings, only to turn around and experience the same art while returning to the entrance hall, visitors were encouraged to ride elevators to the top of a spiral-shaped tower, the Great Rotunda, and descend via a gently sloping ramp along the spiral's perimeter. Adorning the tower's walls were works by Wassily Kandinsky, Piet Mondrian, and Joan Miró.

This specific vision for the building is no longer upheld, however. Some six years after the building's completion in 1959, the strictly abstract collection was augmented with figurative works by Impressionists Cézanne, Degas, and Renoir, and with paintings by Van Gogh and Picasso. The building was extended, and today the Great Rotunda is used only for temporary exhibitions, while the permanent collection is housed in the adjoining Tower. The Small Rotunda is used to display the "greatest hits" of the Impressionist and Post-Impressionist collection. The museum's temporary shows tend to relate to the Modern Movement, some very obviously, such as the conceptual abstraction of Daniel Buren, others more obliquely, such as art from the Aztec Empire, which influenced some early 20th-century avant-garde painters. **Adm**

Museum of the City of New York `10 E2`
focus on New York
1250 5th Avenue (at E. 103rd St.) • 212 534 1672
>> www.mcny.org
Open 10–5 Tue–Sun
Dedicated to New York's development from its past to its present and future, this museum is housed in a handsome Georgian Colonial building, noted for period rooms from actual homes. Donations appreciated.

The Jewish Museum *all things Jewish* `10 E4`
1109 5th Avenue (at 92nd Street) • 212 423 3200
>> www.thejewishmuseum.org
Open 11am–5:45pm Sun–Wed, 11am–9pm Thu, 11am–5pm Fri
The Jewish Museum presents an unparalleled overview of Jewish art and culture. A stunning French Gothic house holds four floors of ceremonial art, photographs, paintings, textiles, sculptures, and video screenings. Each piece in the permanent collection – whether it be a self-portrait by Viennese artist Max Beckmann, a 3,000-year-old ceramic vase, or a vibrant 19th-century quilt from a Jerusalem workshop – encourages the viewer to explore how the object informs, or is informed by, Jewish identity.

Popular temporary exhibitions take place on the ground floor, such as *Kafka's Prague* and *Entertaining America: Jews, Media, and Broadcasting*, as well as retrospectives of individual Jewish artists, such as Marc Chagall and Chaim Soutine. A kosher café in the basement is on hand for refreshments.

Cooper-Hewitt National Design Museum *design classics* `10 E4`
2 East 91st Street • 212 849 8400
>> www.ndm.si.edu Open 10am–5pm Tue–Sat, 10am–9pm Fri, 10am–6pm Sat, noon–6pm Sun
Housed in the imposing Andrew Carnegie mansion, the Cooper-Hewitt is a shrine to design in all its forms. Exhibits range from a sketch of candelabra by Michelangelo to highly coveted Eames chairs. **Adm**

The Cloisters *portal to the Middle Ages*

Fort Tryon Park • 212 923 3700 • M4 bus or A train to 190th St.
» www.metmuseum.org

Open 9:30am–5:15pm Tue–Sun (to 4:45pm Nov–Feb)

One of New York's most cherished assets seems, paradoxically, about as native to the Manhattan landscape as a Boston Red Sox fan at the Yankee Stadium. The Metropolitan Museum of Art's Cloisters is a neo-medieval composite of stained glass, painstakingly landscaped gardens, cavernous halls, and solemn chapels grafted onto the craggy northern fringes of Manhattan island.

It was the philanthropic might of John D. Rockefeller Jr. that facilitated the building's construction in 1938. The project was undertaken to provide a harmonious context for displaying the Met's superb collection of medieval European art and architecture. It provides a splendid setting for such masterpieces as Robert

Campin's *Annunciation* triptych of 1425. It also integrates relics of medieval buildings, such as a 900-year-old apse from a Spanish church, seamlessly woven into a limestone wall. Elsewhere, a unicorn hunt is vibrantly portrayed through a series of 16th-century Dutch tapestries, and scores of ecclesiastical objects from the length and breadth of Europe are scattered throughout the complex. So complete is the illusion of medieval Europe that the Cloisters creates, the visitor experiences a sensation of distance, both temporal and geographical. Glimpsing New Jersey's rugged cliffs across the Hudson through a 12th-century portico is positively disorientating.

Turning to more earthly needs, during warm months visitors can stave off hunger at the on-site café in Bonnefort Cloister. But savvy diners take lunch at the nearby New Leaf Café *(see p59)* for moderately priced bistro fare, such as juicy sirloin burgers. **Adm**

El Museo del Barrio *Latin art* `10 E2`
1230 5th Avenue at 104th Street • 212 831 7272
» www.elmuseo.org Open 11am–5pm Wed–Sun (to 8pm Thu)

Founded in 1969 by artists and activists from Spanish Harlem, El Museo del Barrio was a response to the lack of exhibition space for specifically Puerto Rican art. Since then, the museum has broadened its scope to the whole of the Caribbean and Latin America.

The permanent collection spans two millennia of art production, from Pre-Columbian artifacts to prints, paintings, installations, and film and video works by the latest generation of Latin American artists. Among more than 8,000 objects are wooden *santos* (colorful, often comical, depictions of Catholic saints that incorporate Afro-Caribbean motifs); fascinating documents of the early years of immigration in New York; and films of life in Spanish Harlem from the 1970s to the present day. The adjoining Teatro Heckscher is an enchanting venue for live Caribbean music, film screenings, and book readings. **Adm**

Studio Museum in Harlem `11 D3`
144 West 125th Street • 212 864 4500
» www.studiomuseum.org
Open noon–6pm Wed–Sun (from 10am Sat)

The SMH is a contemporary art gallery and resource specializing in African-American culture. As well as holding a large permanent collection, the gallery puts on temporary exhibitions, such as its recent showcase for young Harlem photographers.

Prospect Park West *beautiful setting* `13 C5`
Between Union and 15th streets
» www.prospectpark.org

This genteel stretch of 19th-century brownstone, brick, and limestone residences borders Prospect Park. Beginning at Grand Army Plaza's majestic Memorial Arch, a southward stroll takes you past the imposing bronze statue of the Marquis de LaFayette at 9th Street, the park's Concert Shell, and beautiful playgrounds.

Brooklyn Museum of Art
world-class repository

`13 D4`

200 Eastern Parkway • 718 638 5000
>> www.brooklynmuseum.org
Open 10–5 Wed–Fri, 11–6 Sat & Sun (to 11pm first Sat of month)

The Beaux Arts BMA dates from 1893 and has as diverse and staggering a collection as its larger cross-river contemporary, the Metropolitan Museum of Art. This is no idle boast – spread over the five floors of the BMA is a collection that embraces Egyptian sarcophagi and mummy cases; statues, masks, and jewelry from Central Africa; Hiroshige's woodblock prints of *One Hundred Famous Views of Edo*; and a vast selection of paintings and sculpture from Europe and America, including works by Rodin, Degas, Pissaro, Matisse, Louise Bourgeois, and Mark Rothko. There is also a strong photography collection, with significant prints by Edward Weston and Paul Strand. On the Fifth floor, *American Identities* explores the American dream through exhibits that range from Native American totems to Georgia O'Keefe's 1948 meditation *Brooklyn Bridge*.

The BMA's First Saturday events (first Saturday of every month) make for one of the city's best nights out: free admission after 5pm, free concerts and dance performances, and a bar (cash only). **Adm**

Williamsburg Galleries

Priced out of Manhattan's lofts and studios during the late 1980s, frustrated but intrepid artists boarded the L Train and disembarked in Williamsburg, until then a predominantly Polish and Hasidic Jewish working-class neighborhood. There they found vacant industrial warehouses, which were easily converted into studios. Since then, Williamsburg artists have influenced tastes and styles worldwide, from fashion to painting to music. Supporting the neighborhood's visual arts scene from a spectacular c.1867 building is the **Williamsburg Art & Historical Center** (135 Broadway at Bedford Avenue), which mounts eclectic shows and performances by local artists. **Pierogi 2000** (177 North 9th Street) artists exhibit around the world, but visitors will always see at least one local artist featured at any time. Since 1992, not-for-profit **Momenta Art** (72 Berry Street) has given two artists per exhibition cycle a forum for what is often their first non-group show. The touring **Eyewash** gallery is quintessential Williamsburg: artists exhibit in multiple spaces around the neighborhood. Check **www.freewilliamsburg.com** for the latest exhibition information. For contact details of all the galleries mentioned here, *see p278*.

Brooklyn Historical Society   `2 H5`
local culture, historical setting

128 Pierrepont Street • 718 222 4111
>> www.brooklynhistory.org
Open 10am–5pm Wed–Sat, noon–5pm Sun

Thousands of Brooklyn-related objects, from slave deeds to Brooklyn Dodgers baseball memorabilia, are housed in a stunning 1880s mansion. The BHS also arranges walking tours and outdoor concerts. **Adm**

Williamsburg Savings Bank Building   `13 C4`
opulent interior

1 Hanson Place, corner of Flatbush & Atlantic avenues

At night, Brooklyn's tallest building is distinguished by the neon red clock face of its 512-ft (156-m) tower. But the greatest highlight of this building (currently a branch of the HSBC bank) is its Neo-Romanesque interior: imposing iron chandeliers, mosaic-covered ceilings, intricately tiled floors, and graceful arches.

P.S.1   *cutting-edge contemporary art*
22–5 Jackson Ave. • 718 784 2084 • Ⓜ E or V to 23 St./Ely Ave.
>> www.ps1.org   Open noon–6pm Thu–Mon

Modern art aficionados with adventurous tastes and an urge to break from the SoHo and Chelsea scenes need only venture as far as Long Island City to experience one of the world's foremost contemporary art institutions. Housed inside a late-19th-century high school building, P.S.1 consistently presents groundbreaking multimedia, painting, photography, and sculpture exhibitions that challenge conventions and blaze new aesthetic trails.

Featured artists have included the 1980s art star Keith Haring, actor/director/painter Dennis Hopper, and the late Spanish sculptor Juan Muñoz. A 1997 redesign by Frederick Fisher introduced a courtyard. Every summer, artists are selected to create thematic installations in this space for P.S.1's Saturday afternoon party series, Warm Up. The event draws a savvy crowd to hear top local DJs. **Adm**

Ellis Island Museum

NO OTHER PLACE EXPLAINS so well the "melting pot" that formed the character of the United States of America as Ellis Island in New York Harbor. Over one-third of Americans can trace their point of arrival here, the country's immigration depot from 1890 until 1954.

Nearly 17 million people passed through its gates and were dispersed across the country in the greatest wave of migration ever known. Outside, the American Immigrant Wall of Honor is the largest wall of names in the world. Abandoned for over 35 years, the restored site now centres on the Great Hall or Registry Room, and houses a three-storey museum with permanent exhibits and an electronic database for Americans to trace their ancestors.

Immigrants being transferred to Ellis Island for processing

TRAVEL IN STEERAGE

By the end of the 19th century, steam-powered ocean liners had cut the Atlantic passage time to two weeks. The poorest passengers travelled in "steerage", the lowest decks that also housed the ship's steering mechanism. Here, narrow compartments were divided into separate dormitories for single men, single women and families. The air was rank with the odours of communal living and many were seasick. The food was poor, consisting, at best, of potatoes, soup, eggs and unrefrigerated food brought from home. Arrival in New York did not bring better conditions, as immigrants sometimes had to wait on board for days before being ferried to Ellis Island.

THE ADMISSION PROCESS

Immigrants landing on Ellis Island joined a queue for the ▷ Great Hall, a wait that could last five hours. During this time, doctors checked them for a variety of diseases including cholera and tuberculosis, as well as insanity and trachoma, a contagious eye infection that could cause blindness and death. Immigrants who did not pass were sent either to the island's hospital to recover or, if incurable, back to their country of origin. In the Registry Room, the immigrants' socio-economic background was established to ensure that they would not become a burden on society. Unescorted women were detained until their safety could be assured, through the arrival of a telegram or letter.

Main building

The train station office sold tickets onward to the final destination.

Rail Ticket
A special fare for immigrants led many on to California.

★ **Dormitory**
There were separate sleeping quarters for male and female detainees.

The ferry office sold tickets to New Jersey.

THE RESTORATION

In 1990 a $189 million project, by a company called the Statue of Liberty-Ellis Island Foundation, rebuilt the ruined buildings, replaced the copper domes and restored the interior with surviving original fixtures.

★ **Baggage Room** *The immigrants' meagre possessions were checked here on arrival.*

★ **Great Hall**
Immigrants were made to wait for "processing" in the Registry Room. The old metal railings were replaced with wooden benches in 1911.

The metal and glass awning is a re-creation of the original.

BEFORE ELLIS ISLAND

Immigration into the US was formerly regulated by individual states and from 1855 to 1890, more than 5 million immigrants passed through Castle Garden at the foot of Manhattan. When the federal government took over immigration in 1890, it undertook to build a new reception centre on Ellis Island to handle the huge influx.

VISITORS' CHECKLIST

Ellis Island. **Map** 1 A5. **Tel** (212) 363-3200. **Subway** 4, 5 to Bowling Green; 1, 9, R to Whitehall/South Ferry. **Ferry** Circle Line/Statue of Liberty Ferry from the Battery every 30–45 mins, 8:30am–3:30pm summer (winter hours vary). **Open** 8:30am–5:15pm daily. **Adm** Ferry fare includes entry to Ellis and Liberty Islands. **www**.nps.gov/elis

Arrival
Steerage passengers crowd the deck as the ship approaches Ellis Island.

Main entrance

Immigrant Family
An Italian mother and her children arrive in 1905.

STAR FEATURES

★ **Dormitory**

★ **Baggage Room**

★ **Great Hall**

Medical Examining Rooms
Immigrants with contagious diseases could be refused entry and sent back home.

KEY DATES

1890 Construction of a reception centre begins.

1897 Original pine structure burns to the ground.

1900 New masonry structure opens.

1954 Ellis Island ceases to function as an immigration station.

MUSEUM

The three-storey Ellis Island Immigration Museum has permanent exhibits that include audiovisual displays detailing the history of the immigration processing station between 1892 and 1954. Artifacts include baggage, immigrant articles of clothing and costumes, passports, steamer and train tickets, and ship passenger manifests. Sound is a crucial part of three of the museum's major exhibits called "Through America's Gate", "Peak Immigration Years" and the "Baggage and Registry Rooms". There is a collection of over 200 hours of oral history including original interviews with immigrants and their descendants. These sources tell the immigrants' stories as no other exhibit can. Like the immigrants, visitors arrive by ferry and proceed through the ▷ *Baggage Room*, where they can pick up audio devices that will accompany them along the same route taken by the immigrants to the ▷ *Great Hall* and beyond.

Statue of Liberty

BUILDING THE LADY

In his Parisian workshop, the sculptor Bartholdi began by creating four scale models, the largest at one-fourth the actual size. This was divided into 300 plaster sections, and each section was then enlarged to full size. A mould of laminated wood was made from each of these sections, and sheets of copper were pounded into the moulds to a thickness of only 2.5 mm (0.1 in). In all, 350 sheets were connected with 50 mm- (2 in-) wide iron straps. The straps acted like springs, which allowed the surface to flex in high winds or extremes of temperature. The statue arrived in New York packed in over 200 crates and was attached to the frame using some 300,000 copper rivets.

Statue construction workshop in France, c.1882

FUND-RAISING

Although the French contributed to the cost of the statue, early on in the plan it was decided that funds for the pedestal would come from the US. As fund-raising was going slowly, media baron Joseph Pulitzer used the editorial clout of his newspaper *The World* to criticize the wealthy for withholding their financial support and the middle class for relying on the wealthy. He pointed out that the statue was a gift to the entire US and attacked those who were not supporting it on the grounds that it was a New York project. Soon the whole nation was involved. When the crated statue arrived on 19 June 1885, fund-raising rose to fever pitch. It reached its target in just two months.

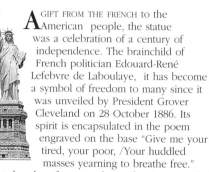

A GIFT FROM THE FRENCH to the American people, the statue was a celebration of a century of independence. The brainchild of French politician Edouard-René Lefebvre de Laboulaye, it has become a symbol of freedom to many since it was unveiled by President Grover Cleveland on 28 October 1886. Its spirit is encapsulated in the poem engraved on the base "Give me your tired, your poor, /Your huddled masses yearning to breathe free." After decades of wear and tear, the statue needed restoration work and was given an expensive facelift in time for its 100th anniversary in 1986.

From Her Toes to Her Torch
Three hundred moulded copper sheets riveted together make up Lady Liberty.

★ **Statue of Liberty Museum**
Posters featuring the statue are among the items on display.

The original torch now stands in the main lobby.

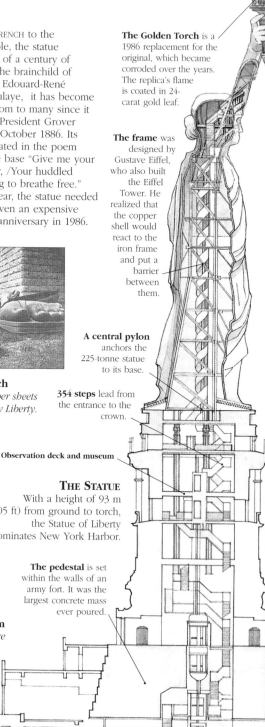

The Golden Torch is a 1986 replacement for the original, which became corroded over the years. The replica's flame is coated in 24-carat gold leaf.

The frame was designed by Gustave Eiffel, who also built the Eiffel Tower. He realized that the copper shell would react to the iron frame and put a barrier between them.

A central pylon anchors the 225-tonne statue to its base.

354 steps lead from the entrance to the crown.

Observation deck and museum

THE STATUE
With a height of 93 m (305 ft) from ground to torch, the Statue of Liberty dominates New York Harbor.

The pedestal is set within the walls of an army fort. It was the largest concrete mass ever poured.

★ Ferries to Liberty Island
Ferries cross New York Harbor to Liberty Island, which was originally known as Bedloe's Island.

STRUCTURAL GENIUS

The French engineer Gustave Eiffel was commissioned to solve the problems of building such a large hollow statue that could withstand the forces of wind and weather. His solution was an internal diagonally braced ▷ *frame* of 1,350 ribs and verticals. This, and his use of steel posts, were seen as structural innovations.

VISITORS' CHECKLIST

Liberty Island. **Map** 1 A5. *Tel (212) 363-3200.* **Subway** 1, 9, R to Whitehall/South Ferry; 4, 5 to Bowling Green. **Ferry** Circle Line/Statue of Liberty Ferry from the Battery every 30–45 mins, 8:30am–3:30pm summer (winter hours vary). **Open** Jul–Aug: 9am–6pm daily; Sep–Jun: 9:30am–5pm daily. **Adm** Ferry fare includes entry to Ellis and Liberty Islands.
www.nps.gov/stli

Face of Liberty
The sculptor's mother was the model for Liberty's face. The seven rays of her crown represent the seven seas and seven continents.

Making the Hand
To make the copper shell, the hand was made first in plaster, then in wood. The scale of the project can be seen by the figures around it.

KEY DATES

1865 Bartholdi has the idea of building a tribute to Liberty in America.

1876 Bartholdi is given the commission to create the Statue of Liberty.

1886 The Statue of Liberty is unveiled.

1986 The Statue of Liberty is reopened after extensive restoration.

THE MUSEUM

The ▷ *Statue of Liberty Museum* is located in the base of the structure. The Torch Exhibit in the lobby holds the much-altered flame and the ▷ *original 1886 torch.* Overlooking the lobby is a display covering the history of the torch and flame. The Statue of Liberty Exhibit, on the pedestal's second level, is a biography of Lady Liberty and an examination of the ideals for which she stands. Through artifacts, prints, photographs, videos and oral histories, seven sections with topics such as "From Image to Ideal" and "Stretching Technology" focus on her history. Another area has five sections on her symbolism, exploring ideas such as "Mother of Exiles," and "The Statue in Popular Culture." There is also a display of full-scale models of Liberty's face and left foot (▷ *A Model Figure*). A plaque dedicated to Emma Lazarus's famous sonnet *The New Colossus* was added to the pedestal in the early 1900s.

FRÉDÉRIC-AUGUSTE BARTHOLDI (1834–1904)

Initially called "Liberty Enlightening the World", the Statue of Liberty was intended by its designer the French sculptor Bartholdi as a monument to the freedom he thought was lacking in his own country. He said "I will try to glorify the Republic and Liberty over there, in the hope that some day I will find it again here." He devoted 21 years of his life to the project, travelling to the US in 1871 to persuade President Ulysses S Grant and others to help to fund the pedestal.

A Model Figure
A series of graduated scale models enabled Bartholdi to build the largest metal statue ever constructed.

Restoration Celebration
On 4 July 1986, after a $100 million clean-up, the statue was revealed. The $2 million fireworks display was the largest ever seen in America.

STAR FEATURES

★ **Statue of Liberty Museum**

★ **Ferries to Liberty Island**

Empire State Building

THE SKYSCRAPER RACE

With the construction of the Eiffel Tower in 1889, American architects were challenged to build ever higher, so at the beginning of the 20th century the skyscraper race began. By 1929, New York's Bank of Manhattan Building, at 283 m (972 ft), was the tallest skyscraper but Walter Chrysler, the famous car manufacturer, was planning to top that height. John Jakob Raskob, of rival General Motors, decided to join the race and, with Pierre S Du Pont, was a major investor in the Empire State project. Since Chrysler was keeping the height of his building a secret, Raskob had to be flexible in his planning. He first aimed at building 85 floors but, unsure of Chrysler's goal, he kept going until the building reached 102 floors, and by adding a spire beat Chrysler by 62 m (204 ft).

WHO DESIGNED IT?

The Shreve, Lamb & Harmon company has designed some of the most notable skyscrapers in Manhattan. By the time work on the Empire State Building began, they had designed seven buildings, including 40 Wall Street (now the Trump Building), at 70 floors, which was completed in only 11 months. With a team of top engineers and contractors, using up to 3,000 workers, the Empire State Building, too, was completed under budget and in record time.

Al Smith, former governor of NY State, with a model of the ESB

Empire State Building

ONE OF THE WORLD'S most famous buildings, the Empire State broke all height records when it was finished. Construction began in March 1930, not long after the Wall Street Crash but by the time it opened in 1931, it was so hard to find anyone to fill it that it was nicknamed "the Empty State Building". Only the popularity of its observatories saved it from bankruptcy. However, the building was soon seen as a symbol of New York throughout the world.

Art Deco Medallions
Displayed throughout the lobby, these depict symbols of the modern age.

CONSTRUCTION
The building was designed to be erected easily and speedily with everything possible prefabricated and slotted into place at a rate of about four storeys per week.

The framework is made from 60,000 tons of steel and was built in 23 weeks.

Aluminium panels were used instead of stone around the 6,500 windows. The steel trim masks rough edges on the facing.

Ten million bricks were used to line the whole building.

Sandwich space between the floors houses the wiring, pipes and cables.

Over 200 steel and concrete piles support the 365,000-ton building.

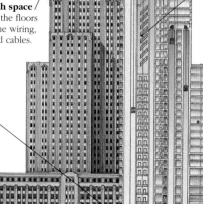

The Empire State has 102 floors, but only 85 have office space. A 46 m (150 ft) mooring mast for Zeppelins was added. Now 62 m (204 ft), the mast transmits TV and radio to the city and four states.

Coloured floodlighting of the top 30 floors marks special and seasonal events.

High-speed lifts travel at up to 366 m (1,200 ft) a minute.

Ten minutes is all it takes for fit runners to race up the 1,576 steps from the lobby to the 86th floor, in the annual Empire State Run-Up.

STAR FEATURES

★ **Views from the Observatories**

★ **Fifth Avenue Entrance Lobby**

ART DECO DESIGN

The Empire State Building is considered New York City's last Art Deco masterpiece. The movement flourished from the 1920s to the 1940s and was noted for its use of crisp, graphic lines, geometric shapes, and vertical setbacks evocative of Aztec ziggurats.

VISITORS' CHECKLIST

350 5th Ave. **Map** 6 E3. **Tel** (212) 736-3100. **Subway** B, D, F, N, Q, R, 1, 2, 3, 9 to 34th St; 6 to 33rd St. **Observatory open** 9:30am–midnight (last adm: 11:15pm) daily. **Adm.** www.esbnyc.com

★ Views from the Observatories

The 86th floor has outdoor observation decks for bird's-eye views of Manhattan. On a clear day, visitors can see more than 80 miles (125 km) in all directions. The observatory on the 102nd floor closed in 1994.

KEY DATES

1930 Building work begins.

1931 Empire State Building is tallest building in the world.

1977 The first annual Empire State Run-Up takes place.

2002 Donald Trump sells the Empire State Building to a real estate consortium.

BUILDING SKYSCRAPERS

The modern skyscraper would not have been possible without several building developments. Lifts had been in use for some time, but it was not until Elisha Otis's 1854 demonstration of his safety brake that the public began to trust them. The second necessary innovation was the use of the structural steel skeleton, seen in the world's first skyscraper in 1885. With this kind of construction, the walls became merely a sheathing, not a load-bearing element, and enormously tall, heavy buildings could now rise ever higher. Building in the heart of Manhattan presented a further problem; large amounts of essential construction materials could not be kept in the street. To solve this, the aluminium elements were prefabricated and only three days' worth of structural steel was kept on site, creating an extremely complicated organization job. Although no longer the world's tallest, the Empire State Building is arguably still the most famous.

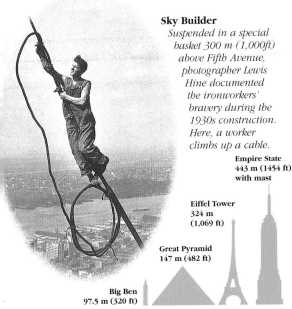

Sky Builder

Suspended in a special basket 300 m (1,000ft) above Fifth Avenue, photographer Lewis Hine documented the ironworkers' bravery during the 1930s construction. Here, a worker climbs up a cable.

Empire State
443 m (1454 ft)
with mast

Eiffel Tower
324 m
(1,069 ft)

Great Pyramid
147 m (482 ft)

Big Ben
97.5 m (320 ft)

Lightning Strikes

A natural lightning conductor, the building is struck up to 100 times a year. The observation decks are closed during inclement weather.

★ Fifth Avenue Entrance Lobby

A relief image of the skyscraper is superimposed on a map of New York State in the marble-lined lobby.

Pecking Order

New Yorkers are justly proud of their city's symbol, which towers above the icons of other countries.

STARRING ROLE

The Empire State Building has been seen in many films. However, the finale from the 1933 classic *King Kong* is easily its most famous guest appearance, as the giant ape straddles the spire to do battle with army aircraft. In 1945 a real bomber flew too low over Manhattan in fog and struck the building just above the 78th floor. The luckiest escape was that of a young lift operator whose cabin plunged 79 floors. The emergency brakes saved her life.

performance

Broadway shows may be the big sellers, but the city's creative heart beats in a host of other artistic venues devoted to music, theater, dance, cinema, poetry, comedy, and literature. The official Music Under New York program promotes talents year-round on the subway and at street level, while the summer months bring superb outdoor entertainments, such as plays and opera in the parks.

CLASSICAL VENUES	DANCE & PERFORMANCE	CUTTING-EDGE

Barge Music
Fulton Ferry Landing, Brooklyn
With the Manhattan skyline in front of you and water lapping beneath, this is a magical setting for chamber music. *(See p150)*

>> *www.entertainment-link.com is a handy site which gives the percentage of seats already sold for a given performance.*

Carnegie Hall
881 7th Avenue
The three concert halls of this hallowed venue have hosted the world's best classical performers for more than a century. *(See p145)*

Brooklyn Academy of Music
30 Lafayette Avenue, Brooklyn
World-class dance and theater productions often preview here, especially during Brooklyn's international Next Wave festival. *(See p149)*

The Kitchen
512 West 19th Street
Experimental performances and more straightforward literary readings are combined at this Chelsea hub of creativity. *(See p140)*

New Jersey Performing Arts Center
One Center Street, Newark
International artists and the NJ Symphony Orchestra perform at this state-of-the-art complex. *(See p151)*

The Joyce Theater
175 8th Avenue
Dance is the main attraction at this former movie house. Mid-sized U.S. and international companies are showcased year-round. *(See p140)*

Bowery Poetry Club
308 Bowery
Rarely delivering anything mainstream, the Bowery plays host to literary performers who challenge the audience's minds. *(See p138)*

Alice Tully Hall, Lincoln Center
Broadway & Amsterdam, 62nd–66th Sts
This hall is known for spectacular performances and an energetic program of choir, quintet, and full orchestra concerts. *(See p146)*

The Public Theater
425 Lafayette Street
Five on-site theaters and the Shakespeare in the Park festival entrance drama fans. *(See p139)*

P.S.122
150 1st Avenue
East Village's innovative, not-for-profit arts center has two theaters offering some of the city's most daring productions. *(See p140)*

GIG VENUES	JAZZ & BLUES	COMEDY

Tonic
107 Norfolk Street
The thing that sets this cool space apart from other gig venues is the highly diverse and experimental music it programs. *(See p137)*

Village Vanguard
178 7th Avenue
A jazz institution not to be missed for its good acoustics and line-up of great musicians. *(See p136)*

The Comic Strip
1568 2nd Avenue
A stalwart of the stand-up tradition, this is a place to see both budding and established comedians. *(See p145)*

>> *For a basic listing of every kind of popular music, from bluegrass to hip-hop, go to www.citidex.com. It also gives info about comedy venues.*

Mercury Lounge
217 East Houston Street
There's a good bar scene in the front room here, while at the back, behind a deep red curtain, is a secretive room for live music. *(See p136)*

Cornelia Street Café
29 Cornelia Street
This intimate space hosts a wealth of musical styles, including jazz, a cappella singing, and the lilting rhythms of samba. *(See p135)*

Lenox Lounge
288 Lenox Avenue
This famous Harlem venue has a local vibe. It attracts regulars from the neighborhood and jazz junkies from much farther afield. *(See p149)*

Upright Citizen's Brigade
307 West 26th Street
An informal space that buzzes with off-the-cuff jokes and well-executed skits. *(See p141)*

Knitting Factory
74 Leonard Street
It's less cutting edge these days, but Knitting Factory still has a great music line-up. The air guitar competition always sells out. *(See p134)*

55 Bar
55 Christopher Street
Get close up and personal with jazz and blues maestros as you sip a drink and gaze at the photos of historic greats. *(See p136)*

>> *The website www.nytheatre.com gives comprehensive listings.*

Smoke
2751 Broadway
The Monday night jam session in this intimate room lures an audience of accomplished musicians and jazz devotees. *(See p147)*

Knitting Factory *experimental mecca* `1 D1`
74 Leonard Street • 212 219 3132
>> www.knittingfactory.com Open 6pm–4am nightly

Arriving here is like entering a funfair attraction; you're not sure which door to go through first. There are three main performance spaces – Main Space, Tap Bar, and Old Office – as well as a free bar area, where late-night jazz jams are often hosted. The media company that runs this venue, and also the Knitting Factory Record label, styles itself "a genre-bending presenter of established avant-garde." The types of music you're most likely to hear are experimental rock, klezmer, and jazz, though recent performances have also included an Eastern European women's choir. The Old Office is the most intimate space of the three and sometimes hosts poetry evenings and alternative screenings, as well as regular music slots. This has also been one of the venues used for the June JVC Jazz Festival. Tickets for all events can be ordered from the Knitting Factory website.

Film Forum *independent & vintage films* `3 C4`
209 West Houston Street • 212 727 8110
>> www.filmforum.com Box office 12:30pm–midnight daily

Cineastes can delight in this three-theater venue, where each screen has Dolby Digital Sound. The selection of films shown is widely varied, from old classics such as an Orson Welles season, to the latest underground hit. Director talks, fresh food concessions, and film-related merchandise are also offered.

S.O.B.'s *Latin beats* `3 C4`
204 Varick Street • 212 243 4940
>> www.sobs.com Open 6:30pm–4am Mon–Sat

Shake your body and celebrate the Sounds of Brazil (S.O.B.) – the very best in Latin, French Caribbean, salsa, hip-hop, reggae, and African beats. Live music is performed every night, with musicians coming from around the globe. For a free dance lesson, get here on a Monday or Friday night between 6pm and 8pm.

Blue Note *gold-standard jazz* `3 C3`
131 West 3rd Street • 212 475 8592
>> www.bluenotejazz.com
Open from 7pm nightly; to 4am Fri & Sat

Now a franchised chain, with venues in Japan, Korea, and Europe, Blue Note first took root in Greenwich Village. The premise is simple: sophisticated surroundings for seriously good music (not just jazz), with the option of dinner service, and a classy interior to match the top-notch performers who come to play. Dizzy Gillespie, Ray Charles, and Sarah Vaughan have ripped the roof off the place in the past, and the club has also witnessed the talents of Oscar Peterson, George Benson, and Tony Bennett.

If it all sounds a little too highfalutin' for the gutsy world of live improvised music, join New York's poorer musicians, who turn up for the late-night Friday and Saturday jam sessions – it's a mere $5 cover. Blue Note is also known for the reasonable Sunday Jazz brunch and its Saturday afternoon master classes.

The Comedy Cellar *gritty stand-up* `3 C3`
117 MacDougal Street • 212 254 3480
>> www.comedycellar.com Evening shows nightly

This basement space has had comics, famous and infamous, performing nightly for over 20 years. The cramped seating, brick wall backdrop and spotlit stage set the tone. The cover charge is normally $10–15, depending on the night, but you can get free passes via the website. Rude heckling isn't tolerated.

Cornelia Street Cafe *eclectic acts* `3 C3`
29 Cornelia Street • 212 989 9319
>> www.corneliastreetcafe.com Evening shows nightly

Performed on a tiny stage in a narrow room beneath a restaurant, acts here have ranged from Inuit poetry to Suzanne Vega. In any given week you might encounter poetry and prose readings, one-act plays, comedy, singing, and live Latin, jazz, or samba music. Art on the walls changes regularly and is often for sale.

Performance

Duplex *kitsch & cabaret* `3 B3`
61 Christopher Street • 212 255 5438
Open 4pm–4am nightly
Anything goes in this dual-level space, which features a piano bar, complete with disco ball, on the first level, and an intimate-sized cabaret room, with pool table, upstairs. The monthly schedule is always packed, and usually includes comedy, cabaret, comedians, and open mic for singers of varying abilities.

55 Bar *NYC-style jazz/funk/blues* `3 C3`
55 Christopher Street • 212 929 9883
» www.55bar.com Open 1pm–4am nightly
Walk down a few steps and soak up an atmosphere that's been brewing in this West Village stalwart since 1919. The music packs a punch in a space small enough for the vibes to resonate against the walls, which are hung with black-and-white photos of Miles Davis and John Coltrane.

Village Vanguard *amazing acoustics* `3 B2`
178 7th Avenue • 212 255 4037
» www.villagevanguard.com Open from 8pm nightly
One of the world's most famous jazz venues, the Village Vanguard has hosted singers and musicians of phenomenal talent since 1935. It continues to take music very seriously, and socializing during sets is discouraged. Genres include mainstream jazz (for popular standards), bebop, fusion, Latin, and funk.

Mercury Lounge *musical excellence* `4 F4`
217 East Houston Street • 212 260 4700
» www.mercuryloungenyc.com Open 6pm–4am nightly
The Mercury Lounge hosts a mix of new and established musical talent. You enter a long, narrow room dominated by a wooden, candle-lit bar. A heavy, deep-red curtain separates this from the performance space (with superb sound system), where Lou Reed, Jeff Buckley, and Tony Bennett have played.

Bowery Ballroom *music in style* `4 F5`

6 Delancey Street • 212 533 2111 • Box office 866 468 7619
>> www.boweryballroom.com

This Beaux Arts ballroom, dating from 1929, makes a
wonderful setting in which to hear a band and have a
drink. Although the venue has been fully updated to
accommodate state-of-the-art acoustics and facilities,
many of the building's architectural details have been
retained. The mezzanine bar is wisely positioned in
front of a gorgeous set of arched windows, providing
a view of the city lights. The stage can be seen from
the wooden ballroom area or the mezzanine. If you'd
like a break from the music, you can drink more
peacefully in the lower-level cocktail lounge. David
Byrne, Beth Orton, Patti Smith, the John Spencer
Blues Explosion, and DJ Shadow are among those
who have played here. Tickets for shows often sell
out, so buy early either by phone or at the box office,
located at the Mercury Lounge *(see opposite)*,
between noon and 7pm from Monday to Saturday.

Tonic *adventurous music* `4 G4`

107 Norfolk Street • 212 358 7501
>> www.tonic107.com Open from 7:30pm nightly

From jazz funk to the sounds of "industrial waste per-
cussion" to the whirs of an electronic theremin to the
bleeps of a palm pilot – the range of music and instruments at Tonic often surprises and inspires. The main
space is hip, with its no-frills decor and basic seating;
downstairs is Subtonic, where DJs spin eclectic beats.

Arlene's Grocery *multi-band options* `4 F4`

95 Stanton Street • 212 358 1633
>> www.arlene-grocery.com Open from 6pm nightly

It was, indeed, once a grocery store – hence the
colorful frontage and welcoming atmosphere – and it
gets a little crazy when more than four bands are
billed in one evening. The music is invariably grunge,
indie, pop, and metal. Come on Monday for a
raucous and rocking Punk Rock Karaoke Night.

Bowery Poetry Club *literary café* `4 E4`
308 Bowery • 212 614 0505
>> www.bowerypoetry.com Open 11am–midnight daily

First-time visitors with any anti-intellectual angst will soon feel at ease in this welcoming, unpretentious venue. Even imaginative readings for children are included on the bill.

The main glass doors open to a café with uneven wooden floorboards and mismatched tables, in which you can order organic goodies, espresso, juices, and alcoholic drinks. The back of the room widens out considerably to a high-ceilinged performance area with its own tables and chairs, which can pack in 200 word-lovers; there's also a smaller room for intimate readings. An alluring, slightly bohemian atmosphere is accentuated by local artists exhibiting their works on one wall, and flyers and notes about events and goods for sale pinned up on another. Readings include works by new writers and those of established poets and authors. Sunday brunch is a good time to come.

CBGB *echoes of rock history* `4 E4`
315 Bowery • 212 982 4052
>> www.cbgb.com Open 6:30pm–3am nightly

Come here to pay respects to the world of punk and progressive rock. The Ramones, Blondie, The Police, and Talking Heads are among those who owe something to this venue. The bar's a bit cleaner, the music's changed to metal and new punk, but the basic gritty stage and loud amps are the same.

Landmark's Sunshine *film theater* `4 F4`
143 East Houston Street • 212 330 8182
>> www.landmarktheatres.com

Formerly home to a Yiddish Vaudeville Theater, this beautifully renovated film house has five screens, all with Dolby Digital Sound and comfortable seats. Mostly foreign and independent films are shown. A good concession stand serves espresso and freshly baked snacks. For info about late-night screenings, *see p25*.

The Public Theater *integrity on stage* `4 E3`
425 Lafayette Street • 212 539 8500;
212 539 8750 for Shakespeare in the Park tickets (free)
» www.publictheater.org
Box office 1–7:30pm (to 6pm Sun & Mon)

With five theaters, a private rehearsal space, and the recent addition of neighboring performance space/bar Joe's Pub, The Public Theater is a long-established venue for groundbreaking drama. It is where the musical *Hair* had its world premiere in 1967. The main building – formerly the Astor Library – has a grand entrance hall with the theaters leading off, and a small wine and coffee bar in the far corner. Joe's Pub focuses on experimental theater and solo performances of drama and music.

The company is also responsible for the summer Shakespeare in the Park season, performed from June to August at Central Park's Delacorte Theater. You can buy tickets from The Public Theater box office or at the park on the day of performance.

Nuyorican Poets Cafe *beats & poetry* `4 G3`
236 East 3rd Street • 212 505 8183
» www.nuyorican.org Events nightly, except Mon

This once "underground" café has become a cutting-edge venue for people of all ethnicities to read, slam, rhyme, perform, or play an instrument. The dimly lit, cozy café is a place for contemplative, poetic thought by day and original spoken-word performances by night. *(See also p23.)*

C-Note *musical dive bar* `4 G2`
157 Avenue C • 212 677 8142
» www.thecnote.com Open 7pm–4am (from 4pm weekends)

Live music – from jazz and blues to funk, rock, and country – is played nightly. C-Note also hosts superb jam sessions – jazz on Saturdays (4–7pm), blues on Sundays (10pm–3am) – and an open mic for singers and songwriters on Sundays (5–9pm). Have a go on the 1980s table version of the video game *Galaxian*.

Performance

P.S.122 *innovative performances*   4 F2

150 1st Avenue • 212 477 5829 • Box office 212 477 5288
>> www.ps122.org
Open daily; box office 2–6pm Tue–Sun

This performance space in East Village was once a public school, a shadow of which is seen in the original stairwell, complete with wooden banisters and wrought-iron safety gates. In 1979 a small group of innovative performers began transforming the rooms into spaces for performance workshops, movement classes, and community meetings. The old school gym was converted into a theater in 1986, used by small avant-garde groups and cutting-edge productions. Now a major hub of creative energy, the not-for-profit arts center boasts two theaters and galleries, with a constantly changing program of theatrical, video, musical, and film presentations. Experimental in all that it does, and contributing much vibrancy to New York's arts community, P.S.122 has been nicely described as the "Petri dish of downtown culture."

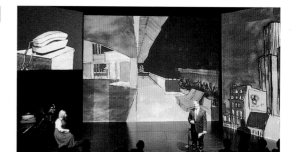

The Kitchen *multimedia creations*   3 A1

512 West 19th Street • 212 255 5793
>> www.thekitchen.org Box office 2–6pm Tue–Sat

For many years, The Kitchen has brought together artists from varied disciplines, taking pride in its innovation. The two black-box theaters serve as backdrops for literary readings, multimedia installations, dance, and music. Family-friendly presentations often feature on Saturday afternoons.

The Joyce Theater *delightful dance*   3 B1

175 8th Avenue • 212 242 0800
>> www.joyce.org Box office noon–around 6pm daily

Presenting small- to medium-sized national and international companies, The Joyce Theater is a center of dance, from contemporary to traditional. The auditorium seats 452 in a functional interior that once housed a movie theater. Joyce's satellite space in SoHo (155 Mercer St.) hosts further performances.

Upright Citizen's Brigade *improv* `5 C5`

307 West 26th Street • 212 366 9176
» www.ucbtheater.com Performances nightly (cash only)
Step into a world of zany and clever comic sketches and improvisation at the UCB Theater. Home-grown Brigade shows and visiting comic troupes are both on the schedule. Ticket prices are very reasonable, and you have the possibility of seeing future stars of the U.S. favorite TV show *Saturday Night Live*.

Kavehaz *gallery & music café* `6 E5`

37 West 26th Street • 212 343 0612
» www.kavehaz.com Open 5pm–midnight or later nightly
The music and artwork on the walls dictate the ambience of the month at this popular Chelsea spot. Sample one of the featured wines or indulge in a hot drink gulped from a bowl as you listen to the music. Monday is reserved for an open mic singers' showcase; Wednesday is for the Ray Vega Latin Jazz band.

Gotham Comedy Club *funny shows* `6 E5`

34 West 22nd Street • 212 367 9000
» www.gothamcomedyclub.com Shows nightly
This comfortable, casual comedy club is given an added air of sophistication by its solid oak bar and shimmering chandelier. The line-up mixes budding comics and surprise guests from the world of TV – comedians who may have appeared on *Conan O'Brien, The Tonight Show*, or on the Comedy Central network.

Hammerstein Ballroom *music venue* `5 C3`

311 West 34th Street • 212 279 7740
» www.mcstudios.com Check website for upcoming events
Ambience and acoustics rate high at this Art Deco space with a capacity of 2,500. Historic fixtures and a beautiful ceiling mural have been kept, while there's enough rigging to support impressive light and sound equipment for shows by bands such as indie-rockers the Pixies or modern jazzers Medeski, Martin & Wood.

Performance

Rodeo Bar *country music crossover* `6 F5`
375 3rd Avenue • 212 683 6500
>> www.rodeobar.com Open noon–4am daily; live music 10pm
Leave NYC and voyage into a world of bluegrass, rockabilly, flavors of country music, an amicable atmosphere, drinks served from a converted horse-trailer, and no cover charge for the entertainment! Refreshment comes in the form of Tex-Mex snacks, free peanuts, and powerful margaritas. Yeeee-haw!

The Soul Cafe *soul food* `5 B2`
444 West 42nd Street • 212 244 7685
>> www.soulcaferestaurant.com Open all day from 5.30pm
Attracting a mixed clientele of regulars and theater district visitors, this is a fun place to party with the almost nightly live entertainment. Have a drink in the bar and let the music take you. Also consider the Sunday gospel brunch (11:30am–3pm), for an uplifting mix of soul food and powerful song.

Roundabout/AA *magical theater space* `5 D2`
227 West 42nd Street • 212 719 1300
>> www.roundabouttheatre.org
This repertory theater company has moved several times and is now based at the beautifully renovated American Airlines Theatre (formerly called the Selwyn), which was built in 1918. Slick productions often feature well-known guest actors; some shows are also performed at Studio 54 (254 West 54th St.).

B.B. King Blues Club *gospel & blues* `5 C2`
237 West 42nd Street • 212 997 4144
>> www.bbkingblues.com Box office 10am–midnight daily
Legends such as James Brown and, of course, B.B. King himself have played in the club's Showcase Room. It has a tourist vibe, but the aim to entertain prevails, and wins over New Yorkers too. Food is served all day and there's nightly music at Lucille's, the more intimate space, named after B.B. King's favorite guitar.

Swing 46 *jazz & swing dance* `5 C1`
349 West 46th Street • 212 262 9554
>> www.swing46.com Open from 5pm nightly

Try your two-step or lindy between courses at this dinner and dance club, or have drinks up by the bar – away from the frenzy on the floor, but close enough to hear the music. There's no dress code, but a bit of sartorial elegance is encouraged. Bring your tap shoes for the Tap Jam on Sundays between 5 and 8pm!

Don't Tell Mama *piano & cabaret* `5 C1`
343 West 46th Street • 212 757 0788
>> www.donttellmama.com Open from 6pm nightly (cash only)

Life is indeed a cabaret, and all believers need to visit this venue at least once, either to listen or to perform. Grab your Liza Minnelli songbook and come on over to the piano bar or one of three intimate theaters, where you can also eat. *The* place to hear the standards, see diva wannabes, and enjoy hilarious musical comedy.

Rainbow Room *vintage sophistication* `6 E1`
30 Rockefeller Plaza, 65th Floor • 212 632 5100
>> www.cipriani.com
Open from 7pm Fri & Sat; Sunday brunch 11am–3pm

A glorious Art Deco institution with awesome views from the 65th floor to help you forget the $150 per person tab for dinner and dancing. Big band orchestras play for the evening as you sway above the shimmering lights of the city. Black tie is preferred.

City Center *music, drama & dance* `7 D5`
131 West 55th Street • 212 581 1212
>> www.citycenter.org

The colorful tiles and pillars of the beautiful Moorish facade welcome you to the City Center. Inside, the main stage is used for concerts and performances by the Alvin Ailey, American Ballet, Paul Taylor, and Martha Graham dance companies. The Manhattan Theater Club performs in the center's smaller spaces.

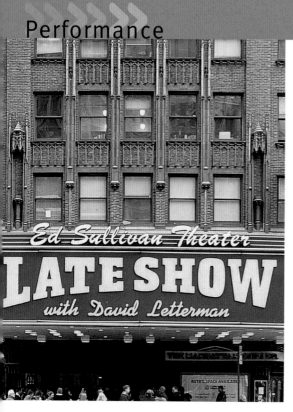

NBC Studios/ Ed Sullivan Theater *three seconds of fame?* | 6 E1

If you'd like to have your head filmed in the studio audience for NBC's news and entertainment *Today Show*, which goes out live on weekday mornings, hang around 49th Street between Fifth and Sixth avenues, between 8:30 and 10am, and join the masses who have the "Hi Mom, Bergen County Loves You" signs. You can also try your luck for last-minute studio audience tickets to see *Saturday Night Live* or *Light Night* with Conan O'Brien by lining up outside NBC's main lobby on the 49th Street entrance at 30 Rockefeller Plaza. Both lines often form before 7am (tickets are given out after 9am); unfortunately there are no guarantees that you'll get in.

It's easier to obtain tickets to see *The Late Show* with wise-cracking David Letterman, which is staged at the Ed Sullivan Theater at 1697 Broadway (Map 7 D5). For standby tickets, call 212 247 6497 at 11am on the day of the show (Monday to Thursday).

Florence Gould Hall *for Francophiles* | 8 F4
55 East 59th Street • 212 355 6160
» www.fiaf.org Box office 11am–7pm Tue–Fri, 11am–3pm Sat
Associated with the French Institute and the location of a series of interesting lectures and weekly French films, this space is also open for productions ranging from light opera and ballet to various concerts. Acoustics are great in the main 400-person auditorium, while next door's Tinker Auditorium is more intimate.

Tickets for Broadway Theaters

The two main agencies selling theater tickets are **Telecharge** (212 239 6200, www.telecharge.com) and **TicketMaster** (212 307 4100, www.ticketmaster.com). These are convenient ways to purchase tickets, but you may be charged up to $9 extra for handling fees. If you want to try your luck at a discount agency on the day of performance, **TKTS** offers great deals on theater tickets – often 25–50% off the full price – but you will have to line up and you can't use a credit card. The main outlet is on the little island called Duffy Square at 47th and Broadway (Mon–Sat 3–8pm, Sun 11am–7:30pm; for matinees Wed & Sat 10am–2pm). The other outlet is at the South Street Seaport on the corner of John Street and Front Street (Mon–Fri 11am–6pm, Sat 11am–7pm).

The Comic Strip *stand-up showcase*   8 G1

1568 2nd Avenue • 212 861 9386

>> www.comicstriplive.com Shows nightly

Jerry Seinfeld started his career with a regular act here. There's a casual atmosphere, cabaret-style seating, and traditional stand-up. Thursday is "new talent night," while Mondays often feature comics from far and wide auditioning for regular spots. Reserve tickets by phone, and check out discounts on the website.

92nd Street Y *emporium of activity*   10 F4

1395 Lexington Avenue • 212 415 5500

>> www.92y.org

Established in the 19th century as a men's Hebrew association, the 92nd Street Y has since become a more diverse cultural institution. With a wide-ranging bill of artists, entrepreneurs, and politicians, the Y's two halls have hosted performances and talks by Yo-Yo Ma, Bill Gates, and Kofi Annan.

Carnegie Hall *supreme concert hall*   7 D5

881 7th Avenue at 57th Street • 212 247 7800

>> www.carnegiehall.org

Tchaikovsky conducted the Carnegie Hall's inaugural concert over a century ago and thus the standard was set. The main hall, the Isaac Stern Auditorium, seats just under 3,000; the Zankel Hall focuses on jazz and contemporary music; the smaller Weill Hall has good acoustics for recitals and chamber music.

Merkin Concert Hall *on-air sound*   7 B3

129 West 67th Street • 212 501 3330

>> www.elainekaufmancenter.org/merkin.htm

The resonance in this mid-sized auditorium is wonderful and it is often used for live radio recordings. Assorted performances cover classical, jazz, funk, and many other genres. Both the balcony and the orchestra seating provide good views, and the art gallery makes a nice diversion during intermissions.

Lincoln Center for the Performing Arts

7 B3

rich pickings for culture vultures

Straddling Broadway and Amsterdam between
62nd Street and 66th Street
Box office 212 721 6500 • Tours 212 875 5350
➤➤www.lincolncenter.org

One of the world leaders in performing arts since the 1960s, Lincoln Center has 12 resident organizations, including a Chamber Music Society, a Film Society, Jazz at Lincoln Center, The New York City Ballet, Metropolitan Opera, New York City Opera, and the New York Philharmonic.

Formerly the slum area of Lincoln Square, the 15-acre site was first envisaged as an arts complex in the 1950s, the scheme being eventually realized with the support of John D. Rockefeller and President Eisenhower, among others. The **Philharmonic Hall** opened in 1962, and was followed a few years later by the **New York State Theater**, the **Vivian Beaumont Theater**, the **Metropolitan Opera House**, and the **Alice** Tully Hall. Altogether there are nearly 20 performance spaces and a host of other facilities, including a library and studios for budding musicians and actors. Tours of the complex run regularly and last an hour, focusing on history, stories, and architecture.

The central outdoor fountain, designed by American Modernist architect Philip Johnson, is a popular meeting point before a show. It is also close to the spot where the Christmas tree, bedecked in musical instrument ornaments, stands during the holiday period. **Damrosch Park** hosts a free outdoor concert series, usually in August. The **Mostly Mozart Festival** is a perennial favorite, while **Midsummer Night Swing** features a wide range of dance music.

Renovations are expected to take place over the next few years to give some of the buildings a facelift and to enhance acoustics. The Vivian Beaumont Theater, beyond the reflecting pool and Henry Moore sculpture, has already been refurbished and hosts wonderful theatrical productions.

Makor *culture with hip twist* `7 C3`
35 West 67th Street • 212 601 1000
≫ www.makor.org

Frequented by a 20- to 30-something crowd, Makor – associated with the 92nd Street Y *(see p145)* – offers film, discussions, theater, and music, including jazz, funk, and a cappella. Allow time to relax in the lobby lounge before a show, or have a drink in the café. There's a healthy singles scene here too.

Stand-Up NY *heard the one about...?* `7 B2`
236 West 78th Street • 212 595 0850
≫ www.standupny.com

Stand-Up is the only comedy club on the Upper West Side, so it's a popular venue for locals. Get to know your table neighbors up close and personal as you sit in on a string of comics delivering their routines. The standard ranges from decent to hilarious, and past circuit performers include Robin Williams.

Symphony Space *reggae & throat-singing* `9 B3`
2537 Broadway • 212 864 5400
≫ www.symphonyspace.org Box office noon–7pm Tue–Sun

This newly renovated complex offers a vast array of theater, film, dance, and music. The main Peter Jay Sharp Theatre – which seats nearly 700 on a gentle slope with plenty of legroom – is often used by guest musicians of the World Music Institute. The Leonard Nimoy Thalia building now includes a café.

Smoke *hot jazz, no tobacco* `9 B2`
2751 Broadway • 212 864 6662
≫ www.smokejazz.com Open 5pm–4am most nights

Red velvet curtains and low-hanging chandeliers set the scene in this cozy jazz bar/lounge. If you can't accessorize with an instrument, then at least bring an attentive pair of ears, because the live music is taken seriously here. There's seating for 70, with overflow accommodated at the bar.

Apollo Theater *where stars are born* `11 D3`

253 West 125th Street • 212 531 5300

>> www.apollotheater.com

Box office 10am–6pm Mon, Tue, Thu, Fri; 10am–8:30pm Wed; noon–6pm Sat

The Apollo – Harlem's top attraction – has made such an important contribution to music history and the cultural life of New York that it was designated a National Landmark in 1983. Originally a burlesque theater, in the 1930s the venue became a showcase for African American musicians, singers, dancers, and comedians, who would perform at the theater's Amateur Night. The careers of many internationally famous musicians and singers were launched here – Ella Fitzgerald and Michael Jackson were among those who were first recognized at the Apollo.

Today, the venue welcomes any talent good enough to withstand the potential boos from the crowd on Wednesday's Amateur Night. Latino music has also been showcased since 2001, and *Showtime at the Apollo* is produced as a syndicated television program.

As well as coming here to see a performance, it is also worth taking a close look around the theater. The lobby Walk of Fame highlights some of the eminent past performers, such as James Brown, Aretha Franklin, and Duke Ellington. The guided backstage tour offers fascinating oral anecdotes and musical history. You'll also get to touch the renowned Tree of Hope – in reality, a wooden stump mounted on an Ionic column. Legendary in the show business world, it is touched by performers before they start their act to bring them good luck.

Lenox Lounge *booze & Billie Holliday* `11 D3`

288 Lenox Avenue (between 124th & 125th streets)
212 427 0253
>> www.lenoxlounge.com Open noon–4am daily

Lenox is a leading music club with a solid repertoire of live jazz, DJs, and an open jam session on Monday nights. The front bar is Art Deco in character, and the lounge has been restored to its original plush design, including built-in banquettes and zebra stripes in the back room. Southern-style food is served all day.

A sense of history permeates the proceedings – jazz heroes such as Miles Davis, Billie Holiday, and John Coltrane have played in this space. And Malcolm X is said to have spent many an hour at the Lenox before being galvanized by the political fight. Nowadays, the live music ranges from mainstream jazz through to more esoteric genres. Use the front room for mingling – the clientele includes regulars, locals, and jazz aficionados – and then head to the back for listening and dining pleasure.

Brooklyn Academy of Music *performing arts center* `13 C4`

30 Lafayette Avenue • 718 636 4100
>> www.bam.org Box office noon–6pm Mon–Sat

Far more than just a music academy, the BAM is a hive of cultural activity, offering live music, opera, dance, film, and theater. The academy's first production was in 1861, and the legendary Ellen Terry was one of the first actors to perform here.

The main building straddles most of the block and has a grand lobby. The Rose Cinema has four screens and very comfortable seating. The Howard Gillman Opera House has a capacity of a little over 2,000, while the smaller Harvey Lichtenstein Theater holds 874. From Thursday to Saturday, you can also catch live performances in the BAM café, which is a great place for a quick drink or light meal before or after a show. The famed Next Wave Festival takes place over three months in the Fall and features modern and experimental works from around the globe.

Warsaw *pierogi & pro sound*   `13 C1`

261 Driggs Avenue • 718 387 0505

➤➤ **www.warsawconcerts.com**

A curious collaborative doubling: hip music venue and main ballroom of the Polish National Home. Some nights feature indie and rock groups; others involve Polish festivals and Polka dance evenings. The bistro offers *kielbasa* (sausage) and *pierogi* (dumplings), and the bar serves strong Polish beer.

Barge Music *classical music on the water*   `13 A3`

Fulton Ferry Landing • 718 624 4061

➤➤ **www.bargemusic.org**

Performances at 7:30pm Thu, Fri & Sat; 4pm Sun

This chamber music concert space is absolutely worth the trip for the quality of the performers, the unique setting, and the superb views of the Manhattan skyline and Brooklyn Bridge.

As suggested by the venue's name, performances do, indeed, take place on the water, in a converted barge that features wood paneling and an open fireplace. Seating arrangements cater to a maximum of just 125, which encourages an intimacy and immediacy for the audience and the musicians.

The barge does move gently during performances but there's little danger of sea-sickness.

Unusually for chamber music, there is no regard for the seasons, and the concert hall is used year-round. Highly polished performances of Mozart, Bach, Schubert, Debussy, and Prokofiev might all feature in a typical month, and guest musicians add zest to the program. A fortnight in December each year is given over to Bach's Brandenburg Concertos.

Before a concert, allow time to wander around the revamped ferry landing and enjoy some ice cream at the Brooklyn Ice Cream Factory. Round off the evening by taking a yellow New York water taxi (212 742 1969, www.nywatertaxi.com) back to Manhattan.

New Jersey Performing Arts Center (NJPAC) *notable in Newark*

One Center Street, Newark • 888 GO-NJPAC (466-5722)
▶▶ www.njpac.org • Train from Penn Station (New York) to Penn Station (Newark), then LOOP shuttle or short walk to NJPAC
Box office noon–6pm Mon–Sat; 10am–3 pm Sun

Newark has never looked so appealing. This stunning, multi-million-dollar arts complex was built in 1997, breathing new life into a downtrodden city and giving Manhattan residents and tourists alike reason enough to cross the water to New Jersey.

The architecture of the main part of the complex – defined by glass and brick, and cubed shapes – was the brainchild of Barton Myers and honors the idea of casual urban living. The two performance spaces, Prudential Hall (2,730 seats) and Victoria Theater (514 seats) are wonderfully appointed and functional, with first-rate sight lines and excellent acoustics for all seats. The Alvin Ailey American Dance Theater and the New Jersey Symphony Orchestra are regular performers. The complex has also hosted touring productions of musicals (*Les Misérables*, *The Mikado*) and such diverse performers as Yo-Yo Ma, the Vienna Boys Choir, Lauryn Hill, and teen band 'N Synch.

Getting to the NJPAC is not too difficult, but does involve either walking five blocks from Newark's Penn Station, or taking the purple-signed LOOP shuttle bus for one dollar. The complex has two restaurants: the Theater Square Grill, which has a lounge bar, and the Calcada restaurant, which offers alfresco dining.

Sports Venues

New York has several capacious sports venues. The **Yankee Stadium** was built for the famous baseball team in 1923, and is fun to visit via the Yankee Clipper ferry. **Shea Stadium** is home to the New York Mets baseball team and lies beneath a flight path to LaGuardia airport. The Beatles famously played here in 1965 and 1966. Part of the Meadowlands complex, **Giants Stadium** is the home of three soccer teams: the New York Giants, New York Jets (both always sold out), and Metrostars. **Madison Square Garden** is home to ice hockey team New York Rangers and basketball teams Knicks and Liberty. The Garden also hosts big-name concerts, monster truck rallies, wrestling, boxing, and top dog and cat shows. For contact details, *see p279.*

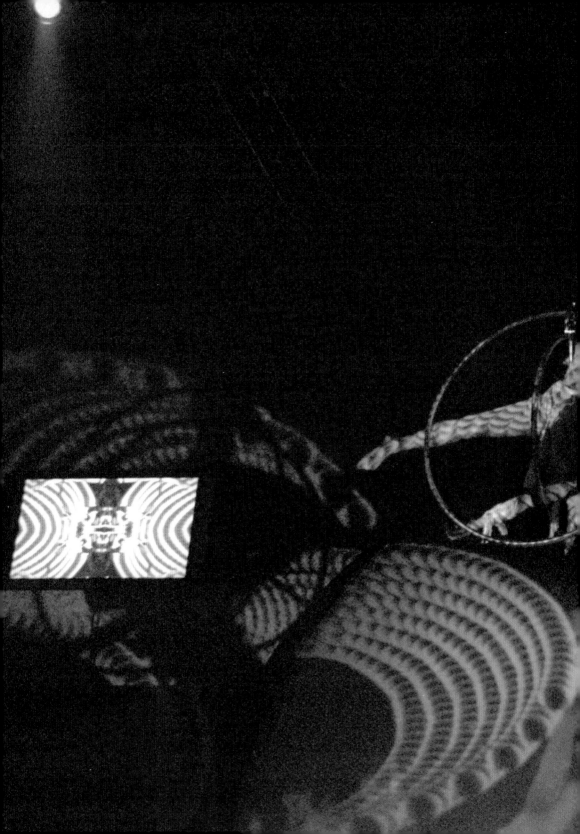

bars & clubs

From super-cool cocktail lounges to dark old ale houses to neighborhood joints with jukeboxes and pool tables, New York has bars to suit everyone. For those in search of an energetic night out, downtown and Chelsea have the most lively DJ bars and clubs, though Brooklyn is catching up fast. More laid-back drinkers may prefer to slip into an easy chair in the swanky cocktail bars of midtown and the Upper East Side.

DJ BARS	GAY BARS & CLUBS	STAR BARS
Beauty Bar 231 East 14th Street Expect plenty of 70s and 80s punk and glam rock at this lively East Village bar, decked out like an old-fashioned beauty salon. *(See p164)*	**Cubbyhole** 281 West 12th Street Cheeky decor, mammoth Martinis, and a relaxed, friendly vibe are enjoyed by a predominantly lesbian clientele here. *(See p168)*	**2A** 25 Avenue A Downtown rockers The Strokes are among the street-credible names associated with this Alphabet City dive bar. *(See p161)*
Sullivan Room 218 Sullivan Street The warm tones and cushy alcoves induce a loungy atmosphere, the mood matched by soulful house played by resident DJs. *(See p166)*		**Hiro** 366 West 17th Street Japanese-themed Hiro is a top spot for the city's youthful models, musicians, and actors to congregate. *(See p170)*
TriBeCa Grand's Studio Room 2 Avenue of the Americas The Studio attracts a knowledgeable crowd, appreciative of the club's top DJ talent, such as Junior Sanchez and LCD Soundsystem. *(See p205)*	**Roxy** 515 West 18th Street Evoking the last days of disco, the cavernous Roxy hosts the city's longest running, most popular gay club night on Saturdays. *(See p169)*	**Serena** Chelsea Hotel, 222 West 23rd Street This subterranean lounge caters to artists and film makers hoping to become a part of the Chelsea Hotel's eventful history. *(See p169)*
Uncle Ming's 225 Avenue B Fashion-conscious Lower East Siders flock to Ming's to hear retro electro beats and bask in the dim light of ancient chandeliers. *(See p166)*	**Stonewall** 53 Christopher Street With regular drag shows, this icon of 60s gay activism is as much about pleasure as politics. *(See p167)*	**Bungalow 8** 515 West 27th Street A tribute to Tinseltown, with palms, mock sunsets, and a strict door policy to help homesick Hollywood babies feel at ease. *(See p170)*
>> *In New York there are strict laws governing where you can dance. Dancing is permitted in clubs, but not in the city's DJ bars unless they are hosting special events.* 		
	Trash 256 Grand Street, Brooklyn Punk-glam vinyl upholstery, beautiful gay boys and girls, and the dirtiest rock 'n' roll weekend parties east of Alphabet City. *(See p176)*	

HISTORIC BARS

Bemelmans Bar
Carlyle Hotel, 35 East 76th Street
This uptown lounge has a whimsical mural by *Madeline* creator, Ludwig Bemelmans. *(See p173)*

McSorley's Old Ale House
15 East 7th Street
The furnishings, robust ales, and good cheer remain largely unchanged since the days when Abraham Lincoln drank at this inn. *(See p162)*

White Horse Tavern
567 Hudson Street
This bar attained fame when, as legend has it, poet Dylan Thomas met his demise after a whiskey-drinking session here. *(See p167)*

Chumley's
86 Bedford Street
A favorite of writers thirsting for liquid inspiration ever since the 1920s Prohibition era. *(See p166)*

ALFRESCO DRINKING

Glass
287 10th Avenue
Beyond the sleek, Cubist bar here lies a patio surrounded by bamboo trees – the destination of choice for local sophisticates. *(See p150)*

Gowanus Yacht Club
323 Smith Street, Brooklyn
Typifying summer in Brooklyn, this convivial, all-outdoor bar lures a young clientele with cheap beer and nightly barbecues. *(See p175)*

Barramundi
147 Ludlow Street
A Lower East Side rarity, Barramundi has a flower-filled garden, complete with fairytale lighting. *(See p160)*

Ava Lounge
Majestic Hotel, 210 West 55th Street
On warm nights Ava's best feature is its patio filled with stylish cocktail-quaffers. Times Square lies within view. *(See p172)*

B-Bar & Grill
40 East 4th Street
At the crossroads of East Village and West Village, B-Bar invites both camps into its large, illuminated back patio. *(See p163)*

DANCE CLUBS

Cielo
18 Little West 12th Street
Seasoned DJs combine with a full-on crowd of clubbers in this small venue for nights of enjoyable mayhem on a sunken dance floor. *(See p168)*

Volume
Wythe Ave. & North 13th St., Brooklyn
Underground hip-hop DJs, electro producers, and other creative music makers get Brooklynites moving at this warehouse. *(See p176)*

>> *The website http://nyc.flavorpill.net gives a roundup of forthcoming club nights and DJs playing in the city's bars.*

Avalon
47 West 20th Street
A church converted into a cavernous dancing and lounging space for Ibiza-scale crowds of clubbers and top international DJs. *(See p169)*

Galapagos
70 North 6th Street, Brooklyn
Brooklyn's home for performance art, films, and irresistible DJ parties. Musical styles include glam rock, techno, and new wave. *(See p177)*

Pussycat Lounge *trash & banter* `1 D4`

96 Greenwich Street • 212 349 4800
>> www.pussycatlounge.com Open Mon–Sat from around 9pm
A quiet block near Ground Zero adopts a delectably sleazy air when the Pussycat Lounge opens up for the night. Skip the first floor's depressing, 60s-style go-go strip club, and head upstairs for trashy burlesque shows, live bands, and ribald weekend dance parties. Try to wear something a little daring. **Adm**

Winnie's *Chinatown's livelist karaoke bar* `2 E1`

104 Bayard Street • 212 732 2384
Open noon–4am daily
Someone is singing, and probably butchering, your favorite song right now at Winnie's. Know before you go: 1. You'll pay $1 per song; 2. Swinging the microphone is not allowed; 3. You should anticipate sharing any well-known chorus (such as in Neil Diamond's *Sweet Caroline*) with the boisterous young crowd.

Antarctica *chilled beer hall* `3 C5`

287 Hudson Street • 212 352 1666
>> www.antarcticabar.com
Open from 4:30pm Mon–Fri, from 7pm Sat
The owners of Antarctica claim that their bar has been in continuous business since the year in which Guinness was invented: 1759. You don't have to believe this, but there is certainly a feeling of age about the weathered wood floor planks, shining brass taps, and the picture of 19th-century, mustachioed drinkers on the wall. The overall effect is not of Earth's last frontier either, though Antarctica's location in the far reaches of SoHo lends it a certain remoteness that's appealing.

The bar has received many plaudits for its down-to-earth appeal in an upscale neighborhood. It has also won the "Best Bar to Shoot Pool" title from *NY Mag*. Booth seating and pitchers of beer ensure a merry crowd. Check the website to see if your first name qualifies you for free drinks on the night.

THOM's Bar *classy hotel bar*   3 C5

60 Thompson Street • 212 431 0400

>> www.60thompson.com Open from 5pm nightly

The boutique hotel bar craze that swept Manhattan in the 1990s shows no signs of fatigue at this bar set in the lobby of the sleek 60 Thompson Hotel.

A sense of occasion starts to build from the moment you approach the chic SoHo address. The glass entrance is grandly set back from the curb and manned by cordial, black-clad doormen. You'll be directed up to THOM's Bar, which instantly gives the impression of classic sophistication with its leather parlor chairs, massive marble fireplace, and lofty ceilings. Modern touches can be seen in the lacquer-black bar, gracefully arching chrome lamps, and strongly geometric purple sofas and banquettes.

A typical weekend night attracts an international, casually fashionable crowd partial to specialty cocktails. The signature THOM is a blend of the very pure Skyy citrus vodka, fresh lime, and mint. Sidecars, lychee Martinis, Tom Collins, and others are deftly mixed by bartenders who look as if they've stepped off the pages of hip lifestyle magazine *Wallpaper**.

On particularly crowded nights, patrons have no compunction about taking their drinks to the adjacent lobby, where the acid jazz music plays at lower decibels than in the bar, and where seating does not come at such a premium.

ñ *atmospheric Spanish bar* 3 D5
33 Crosby Street • 212 219 8856
Open from 5pm nightly (to 4am Fri & Sat; cash only)

The labyrinthine lanes of Madrid's old quarter lie a considerable distance from SoHo, but past midnight – especially on Wednesdays – this somewhat desolate stretch of Crosby Street adopts a distinctly *madrileño* mood. As you open the door to ñ (pronounced "enyay"), the insistent, passionate rhythms of flamenco immediately grab you.

An intimate and authentic Spanish tapas bar, ñ is just wide enough to accommodate a few musicians and dancers for its Wednesday flamenco showcase. It compensates for its diminutive size, however, with a genial, Iberian atmosphere. An international mix of artists and professionals gathers at the long, gleaming copper bar to choose from a selection of 20 sherries and affordable Spanish wines by the glass. Among the popular tapas plates are savory toasted almonds, addictive, briny olives, and luscious *tetilla con membrillo*: mild, creamy cheese served with a sweet quince paste.

At weekends patrons pack four-deep at the bar, which can result in brusque drink service, but weeknights – Wednesdays excepted – are comparatively quiet and easygoing. A homely bar, ñ concedes few points to its style-driven downtown environs. Except, that is, for the one-way glass on the bathroom doors. Fear not, however: you can be assured that the only visibility afforded is experienced from inside the stall looking out.

Temple Bar *for lounging lovers* 4 E4
332 Lafayette Street • 212 925 4242
Open from 5pm Mon–Sat, from 7pm Sun

Exuding luxury and romance from every dimmed Deco wall lamp, Temple Bar is a favorite destination among amorous NoHo couples. Discreet servers bring deftly mixed Martinis to the table, while the sultry crooning of one female jazz legend or another drifting from the speakers raises the seduction ante.

Pravda *Russian speakeasy* `4 E4`

281 Lafayette Street • 212 226 4944

>> www.pravdany.com Open from 5pm Mon–Sat, from 6 Sun

Keen eyes are indispensable for locating this subterranean SoHo destination, indicated by a lone red lamp atop an iron banister. At the entrance, crimson velvet curtains part to reveal a sprawling lounge painted terra cotta and furnished with burgundy parlor chairs, candlelit cocktail tables, and leaded glass wall lamps. Combined with the Cyrillic characters and Roman numerals stenciled on low ceiling arches, the scene evokes the gritty romance of a Moscow train station, circa 1929. Statuesque, black-clad servers weave between throngs of chic patrons, balancing cocktail trays laden with generous vodka shots, single-malt Scotches and house specialties such as the Nolita: chilled mango-infused vodka, apricot liqueur, and lime juice. In true vodka-room style, Pravda also offers an appealing menu of European finger foods, from garlicky mussels and fries to smoked-fish plates and caviar.

Upstairs, a diminutive lounge, with no more than one couch and a tiny bar, is a prime spot for amorous couples – providing, that is, they can blissfully ignore the constant parade of drinkers traipsing up to use Pravda's bathrooms.

Lansky Lounge *discreet cocktail bar* `4 G4`

104 Norfolk Street • 212 677 9489

>> www.lanskylounge.com Open from 6pm nightly

A spacious, modern bar, named after one of the neighborhood's most notorious sons, Jewish gangster Meyer Lansky. The uptown, attractive crowd enters through the "speakeasy" entrance, distinguished by the neon letter "L." Excellent classic cocktails, plus DJs spinning hip-hop on Wednesdays and weekends.

Welcome to the Johnson's *the real dive bar*

`4 F4`

123 Rivington Street • 212 420 9911
Open 11am–5pm, 6pm–4am daily (cash only)

While some New York bars may classify themselves as "dives," a close inspection often reveals that the shabby decor has been painstakingly cultivated, the jukebox song catalogue caters only to esoteric tastes, the place is full of elitist poseurs, and the beer is $7 a glass. Whereas the genuine requirements of an American dive bar are cheap beer, anthemic rock music, decrepit furniture, and graffitied bathrooms – nothing else will do.

Fortunately, there is a Lower East Side bar that delivers the requisite attributes with just the right touch of self-assured, devil-may-care attitude: Welcome to the Johnson's – or, as it's known to the regulars, The Johnson's.

Though it opens mid-afternoon, the fun really begins from around 5pm, as the neighborhood's young musicians, professionals, and students make themselves comfortable on thrift-shop sofas. The favorite beer, Pabst Blue Ribbon, is absurdly cheap. Diversions involve playing pool on a warped billiard table, waging intergalactic warfare on the vintage video game machine, and feeding dollar bills into the hard-rocking juke.

A word of caution: The Johnson's gets very crowded after 10pm. Also, the bathroom stalls are not for the squeamish. Consider yourself informed.

Barramundi *backpackers' hangout*

`4 F4`

147 Ludlow Street • 212 529 6900
Open 6pm–4am daily

Young travelers feel at home at this funky, Australian-owned Lower East Side bar. An international crowd sips reasonably priced beverages on the back room's couches while gesturing at the otherworldly wall sculptures. During summer, Barramundi's garden (which closes at 10pm) is a beautiful setting.

Slipper Room *lively entertainment* `4 F4`
167 Orchard Street • 212 253 7246
>> www.slipperroom.com Open from 8pm nightly

Five dollars is usually all that's required to experience anything from burlesque and classic vaudeville theater to cash-prize trivia nights at this inviting Lower East Side lounge. The crowd changes according to the event schedule, but patrons infallibly arrive equipped with sharp wits and playful attitudes.

Parkside Lounge *easygoing joint* `4 G4`
317 East Houston Street • 212 673 6270
>> www.parksidelounge.com Open from 1pm daily

Cheap beers, generous cocktails, and zero attitude draw neighborhood residents young and old to the Parkside. In the afternoon, the affable crowd's banter mixes with the jukebox's classic country. Nighttime arrivals head straight to the back room, where bluegrass bands and burlesque troupes perform.

Chez es Saada *North African vibe* `4 F4`
42 East 1st Street • 212 777 5617
>> www.chezessaada.com Open from 6pm nightly

Follow the trail of fresh rose petals from the undistinguished street-level lounge down into a sumptuous Moroccan-style grotto. Here, fashionable lovebirds steal kisses across candlelit alcove tables, singles flirt at the bar over signature plum Martinis, and North African rhythms evoke a world far away.

2A *rocking bar & upstairs lounge* `4 F3`
25 Avenue A • 212 505 2466
Open from 4pm–4am daily

For better or worse, 2A has become an easy place to spot a hip celebrity. New Wave and punk music from the 70s set the tone at the street-level bar. The couch-filled upstairs lounge is cozier, with a more flirtatious atmosphere. Though most of the clientele drinks beer, 2A's red wine selection should not be overlooked.

KGB *vodka & old Russia* `4 E3`
85 East 4th Street • 212 505 3360
›› www.kgbbar.com Open from 6pm nightly

Detached from the frenetic barhopping of nearby 2nd Avenue is this Bolshevik-red, dimly lit den of Soviet nostalgia. Staff keep glasses full of vodka or Central European imported pilsners, while bookish patrons turn up for occasional readings by guest novelists. Vintage Leninist posters adorn the walls.

Swift Hibernian Lounge *Celtic vibe* `4 E3`
34 East 4th Street • 212 260 3600
Open noon–4am daily

A mural depicting Irish satirist Jonathan Swift raising a pint of Guinness welcomes Irish expats, NYU students, and everyone else besides to this spacious public house. Come for Swift's extensive draft beer selection, hearty pub food, sharp-witted bartenders, weekly live Irish music, and infectious cheer.

McSorley's *historic ale house* `4 E3`
15 East 7th Street • 212 473 9148
Open from 11am Mon–Sat, from 1pm Sun

Reputedly New York's oldest bar, McSorley's hasn't changed much since Civil War president Abraham Lincoln hoisted his tankard here. You'll still find sawdust littering the wooden floor, drinkers from around the globe crowding the rustic booths, and robust dark and pale ales on draft. *(See also p23.)*

Angel's Share *cocktails with a Tokyo flavor* `4 E2`
8 Stuyvesant Street • 212 777 5415
Open from 7pm nightly

Standing is not allowed, nor are groups exceeding four people, but with these criteria met, Angel's Share is a wonderful place for cocktails. In fact, you might not find better classic mixes anywhere downtown. There's an extensive sake selection and delicate Japanese bar snacks too. Service is exemplary.

Nevada Smith's *soccer-oriented bar* `4 E2`
74 3rd Avenue • 212 982 2591
›› www.nevadasmiths.net Open 11am–4am daily

Diehard soccer fans, behold your Manhattan headquarters. Upstairs, jersey-wearing Europeans and a dusting of Americans sip pints while watching their favorite teams on TV. Downstairs, the scene is different, with dim lighting, polished wooden furnishings, and, on Thursdays, stand-up comedy.

B-Bar & Grill *East-West Village crossover* `4 E3`

40 East 4th Street • 212 475 2220

Open 11.30–3am daily

Barring an electrical blackout, one cannot miss the B-Bar: a neon red sign protrudes from the facade, while the patio's towering trees sparkle under a multicolored blanket of festive lights. Aside from its physical situation between New York's East and West villages, this former petrol station possesses other attributes that distinguish it as the nocturnal crossroads of the East/West divide. The fabulous outdoor patio – with its nicely spaced tables and bar – draws equal numbers of conservative West Villagers and their counterculture-embracing neighbors to the east. The dichotomy continues inside the handsome dining room and at the bar. Retro vinyl booths, wood-beamed ceilings, and mammoth framed photographs suggest a hip, East Side sensibility; yet it is executed with polish befitting a refined West 4th Street bistro.

Neighborhood allegiances aside, everybody shares in their love for B-Bar's cocktails. Take note, however: the pretty pastel hues of apple, lychee, and water-melon Martinis belie their explosive potency. Regarding the "Grill" portion of the name, B-Bar offers a varied, if somewhat uneven, American diner menu. But the crowd-pleasing, always-busy, prix-fixe brunch on the weekend brings the nighttime vibe into broad daylight: chatty crowds, outside seating when the weather's fine, and an unlimited supply of Mimosas and Bloody Marys.

Bar Veloce *Italian-style wine bar*   `4 E2`
175 2nd Avenue • 212 260 3200
>> www.barveloce.com Open from 5pm nightly

This comfortable, sleek little wine bar would not look out of place on the elegant streets of Florence. A smart menu of Italian snacks, from toasted panini to Nutella and fruit plates, gives peckish drinkers something to nibble while choosing a wine. Glasses are priced under $10, bottles up to $80.

Beauty Bar *intimate theme bar*   `4 E2`
231 East 14th Street • 212 539 1389
>> www.beautybar.com Open 5pm–4am nightly (from 7 Sat, Sun)

True to its name, the place is swathed in retro beauty-salon kitsch. East Village rockers and NYU graduate students sip potent cocktails bearing names like "Aqua Net" at the bar, while 70s glam rock and punk blare from the speakers. Check out happy hour for deals on drinks. Manicures are on offer too.

Lotus   `3 A2`
409 West 14th Street • 212 243 4420
>> www.lotusnewyork.com Open 10pm–4am Tue–Sun

It's been several years since this sleek, sexy club opened its black lacquer doors in a neighborhood best known for wholesale meat butchers, rumbling garbage trucks, and transvestite prostitutes. In so doing, Lotus helped blaze the trail that converted the Meatpacking District into a hotbed of nightlife.

Imitated throughout the city, Lotus's design is still the best, with three distinct areas for lounging upstairs, pan-Asian dining on the ground floor, and dancing below. The place exudes a subtle Eastern warmth, with a mix of blonde and cherry woods, rusty-red walls, and half-moon banquettes. The cocktail menu features signature blackberry Caipirinhas. Regulars have their preferred nights: Friday's house party GBH pulls in a serious dance crowd, while Saturday's blend of 80s pop and contemporary hip-hop draws a more mainstream, uptown element. **Adm**

Korova Milk Bar *homage to a cult film* `4 F2`
200 Avenue A • 212 254 8838
>> **www.korovamilkbar.com** Open to 4am nightly

From the rounded, swooping white script above the doorway to the geometric zebra stripes lining the entrance hall, visitors to Korova know a distinctive visual experience awaits them. The entire place is a homage to Stanley Kubrick's 1971 film about brutality and youth, *A Clockwork Orange*; indeed, the bar takes its name from the film (it was the haunt of Malcolm Macdowell's band of miscreants). Once inside, film buffs will immediately recognize many references, such as the stark white, wigged and lipsticked mannequins protruding from the walls. The cinematic homage continues with wall-mounted video monitors and curvaceous, matching black and white recliners swathed in vinyl and velvet, perched on a platform opposite the exceptionally long bar. Korova is a final destination on the East Village/Alphabet City barhopping circuit, so before midnight the spacious floor has room to spare.

After midnight, 70s punk and glam blares, while a throwback bunch of mods, punks, and stragglers recounts the night's wanderings over cheap beer, Jack Daniel's shots, and wicked vodka gimlets. For those who possess the stomach for it at such an hour, Korova's series of signature cocktails, Molokos (of course), should not be missed. The Moloko is an ice cream-based concoction, mixed with any number of liqueurs and flavorings, served in a Martini glass and kept cool in an ice-filled miniature fishbowl.

Rue B *Gallic-style retreat* `4 G2`
188 Avenue B • 212 358 1700
Open from noon Mon–Fri, from 10.30am Sat & Sun

Rue B's seductive air renders any intention of East Village barhopping pointless. The Parisian-style bar is decked out with comfy banquettes, offers respectable French wine, bistro menus, and – its *coup de grâce* – hosts live jazz with no cover charge. With all that on offer, there's no need to go anywhere else.

Uncle Ming's *cozy, crazy lounge* `4 G2`

225 Avenue B, 2nd Floor • 212 959 8506

» www.unclemings.com Open from 6pm nightly

Discreetly plying its trade above a liquor store, this unmarked lounge has the atmosphere of a party that's strictly for the in-crowd. Deep purple and pink lighting, old chandeliers, gorgeous bartenders serving strong cocktails, and DJs spinning electro beats inspire a flirtatious atmosphere among the cool clientele.

Sullivan Room *relaxed clubbing* `3 C3`

218 Sullivan Street • 212 252 2151

» www.sullivanroom.com Open from 10pm Thu–Sun

This modest, subterranean West Village jewel is one of those rare spaces in which you can feel comfortable whether you've come to dance to soulful house, lounge around with friends, or converse at the bar. A refreshing lack of attitude comes with the territory; you might even toast the DJ after his set. **Adm**

Vol de Nuit *Belgian beer & cheer* `3 C3`

148 West 4th Street • 212 982 3388

Open from 7:30pm nightly

Behind an inconspicuous door on West 4th, Vol de Nuit counts eight Belgian brews on draft – each served in its appropriate style of glass – and dozens of others in bottles. Snacks are wonderful: Belgian fries served in paper cones, and mussels paired with irresistible sauces. There's an outdoor courtyard too.

Chumley's *former speakeasy* `3 B3`

86 Bedford Street • 212 675 4449

Open from 5pm daily

"Eighty-sixed," the American bartender's code for denying service to a particularly inebriated patron, evolved from the address of this institution in the 1920s Prohibition era. Booth seating and yellowing portraits of famed writers who once sipped their pints here round out the warm, convivial pub atmosphere.

Stonewall *famous & still fabulous* `3 B3`
53 Christopher Street • 212 463 0950
Open from 2.30pm daily

When this bar's predominantly gay male clientele resisted a police raid in 1969, the ensuing riot touched off NYC's gay activist movement. Stonewall demands reverence, but it's also a fun place. Campy 60s pop music and multicolored lighting dominate the main bar, and drag queens strut their stuff nightly.

Blind Tiger Ale House *serious beers* `3 B3`
518 Hudson Street • 212 675 3848
>> www.blindtiger.citysearch.com
Open from lunchtime daily

West Village beer connoisseurs hoist their pints at the convivial Blind Tiger. No fewer than 24 microbrews chill on draft. It's one of New York's most friendly, casual places for mid-week beer drinking. Go on Wednesday evening for free cheese pairings.

White Horse Tavern *writers' haunt* `3 B3`
567 Hudson Street • 212 243 9260
Open from 11am daily

Few New York buildings, let alone bars, shelter as many literary ghosts as the White Horse Tavern. Before the West Village became a gentrified expanse of French bistros and NYU dormitories, this circa-1880 bar was a favorite spot for the neighborhood's bohemian writers to brood over 20-cent ales. But the address attained infamy in 1953, when – as legend has it – the Welsh poet and dramatist Dylan Thomas dropped dead outside, the victim of undiagnosed diabetes and untold whiskeys.

Fittingly, posters from Thomas's theatrical productions line the dark wood walls. Grandfather clocks, white porcelain horses, a pressed tin ceiling – even the bartenders' amiable rapport with afternoon regulars – evoke a bygone era. But things turn decidedly 21st-century after work and at weekends, when crowds fill the bar and adjoining dining rooms.

Cubbyhole *one for the girls* `3 B2`

281 West 12th Street • 212 243 9041
Open from mid-afternoon daily

If the suspended goldfish figurines, Chinese lanterns, and whimsical bar stools at this lesbian bar don't charm you, perhaps this will: half-price drinks until 7pm, all-you-can-drink specials on Saturday nights, and notoriously mammoth Martinis. Cubbyhole ladies are very friendly, and the mood is always casual.

Rhône *cavernous wine bar* `3 A2`

63 Gansevoort Street • 212 367 8440
>> www.rhonenyc.com Open from 5:30pm Mon–Sat

Tucked among the Meatpacking District's industrial-chic nightclubs, Rhône is an enormous wine bar with a copper bar and futuristic, lime-green recliners. Gallery owners, fashion models, and downtown professionals sip any of 30 vintages available by the glass, and nibble from French-Indochinese tasting plates.

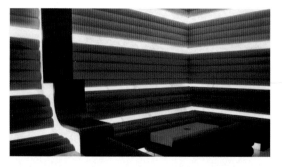

Cielo *award-winning dance club* `3 A2`

18 Little West 12th Street • 212 645 5700
>> www.cieloclub.com Open 10pm–4am Wed–Sat

Soulful house with interjected Latin grooves leave patrons little choice but to abandon their soft suede banquettes and storm the sunken dance floor. Co-owned by DJ Nicolas Matar (well known on the Ibiza scene), Cielo attracts knowledgeable clubbers and top-drawer DJs from around the world. **Adm**

Daytime Bars

When a thirst for something stronger than bottled water strikes you during midtown sightseeing, these bars make welcome stops. The daytime crowd at **Rudy's Bar & Grill** in Hell's Kitchen is as friendly as any you'll find, and Miles Davis on the jukebox makes a welcome change from the classic rock barrage of neighboring bars. Murray Hill's campy **Cabin Club at**

Pinetree Lodge has a huge back patio where potent fruit slushes are dispensed to a fun, flirty crowd. Afternoon sophistication abounds at the rooftop **Mica Bar**, within blocks of the United Nations. A parlor atmosphere pervades the **Hudson Hotel's Library Bar**, where chessboards, architecture books, and a purple-felt billiard table are all at guests' disposal. For full addresses, *see p280*.

Roxy *perennially popular nightclub*　`3 A1`
515 West 18th Street • 212 645 5156
» www.roxynyc.com Open Wed, Fri & Sat nights
Friday-night house, salsa, and hip-hop extravaganzas
tend to see this most massive of Chelsea clubs
overrun by a young clientele. By contrast, Wednesday
Roller Skating nights offer a fun, often hilarious, and
sometimes bruising reminder of disco's last days.
Saturday brings NYC's biggest gay party. **Adm**

Avalon *Chelsea club with attitude*　`3 C1`
47 West 20th Street • 212 807 7780
» www.nyavalon.com Check website for club nights
Avalon occupies hallowed ground on two counts: it's
housed in a Gothic church and is the former address
of Limelight, a legendary 1980s club that engendered
near-religious devotion among its regulars. These
days, a mixed gay and straight crowd comes to lounge
and dance to the sounds of the world's top DJs. **Adm**

Eugene *upscale schmoozing post*　`6 E5`
27 West 24th Street • 212 462 0999
» www.eugenenyc.com Open from 4pm Thu–Sat
Realized in Art Deco retro, Eugene is a spacious
supper club designed with big spending in mind.
Well-dressed Flatiron professionals nibble tuna
tartare in the cream-hued dining room, then settle
themselves onto burgundy banquettes and ottomans
in the adjacent lounge. There's dancing on weekends.

Serena *soft pink lounge*　`5 C5`
Chelsea Hotel, 222 West 23rd Street • 212 255 4646
Open from 6pm Tue–Fri, from 7pm Sat
It's had a makeover to meet fire-safety standards,
but the home of pop culture personalities hasn't lost
its touch. The Chelsea's subterranean Serena lounge
delights with its new velvet couches and pink walls
up front, and Moroccan motifs in the adjacent rooms.
Celebrity sightings are frequent.

Hiro *hotel lounge with a Japanese theme* `3 A1`

366 West 17th Street • 212 727 0212

>> www.themaritimehotel.com Open from 10pm nightly

The lounge at the Maritime Hotel is Chelsea's brooding-celebrity scene of the moment. Fashion models and rock stars sip sake, while, behind a luminescent rice paper wall, more energized guests move to 80s pop, rock remixes, and electro in Hiro's sizeable ballroom. Not famous? Try a weeknight.

Glass *receptacle for the beautiful people* `5 B5`

287 10th Avenue • 212 904 1580

Open Tue–Fri 6pm–4am, Sat 8pm–4am

An ultra-cool design and Brazilian electro rhythms draw Chelsea's gallery set to Glass like magnets. In summer, the bamboo-filled patio is the site for one of Manhattan's most exclusive people-watching scenes. Models, artists, and curators mingle over *caipiruva* cocktails, made from cachaça rum and crushed grapes.

Bungalow 8 *West Coast seduction* `5 B4`

515 West 27th Street • 212 629 3333

Open from 10pm nightly

Nightlife impresario Amy Sacco delivers a cozy, albeit exclusive, Hollywood Hills-inspired lounge to Chelsea's young style mavens. Strike your most unaffected L.A. pose – $30 glass of champagne in hand – amid swimming pool murals, quirky designer furniture, and potted palms. A digital "sunset wall" stands in for that most essential of Californian ingredients – the sun setting on the ocean.

Spirit *holistic nightlife* `5 B4`

530 West 27th Street • 212 268 9477

>> www.spiritnewyork.com Open from 10pm Fri & Sat

Eastern and Native American religions have inspired this "wellness club." Spirit has three zones: Mind, a holistic spa with massage rooms; Body, an immense dance space, where superstar DJs such as David Morales and Roger Sanchez play; and Soul, an organic restaurant, overlooking the dance floor. **Adm**

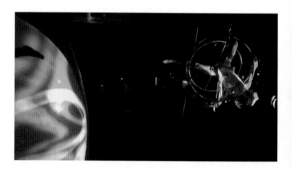

Copacabana *salsa, meréngue & samba* `5 B3`
560 West 34th Street • 212 239 2672
>> www.copacabanany.com Open 10pm–5am Tue, Fri–Sun
With its plush beige banquettes and Art Deco palm-frond motifs, the capacious Copa evokes the glamour of a 1940s supper club in Havana. Massive dance floors and a stage that can accommodate NYC's largest ensembles make for unforgettable evenings. Dress strictly to impress. **Adm**

The Ginger Man *distinguished ale house* `6 E3`
11 East 36th Street • 212 532 3740
>> www.gingermanpub.com Open from lunchtime daily
This handsome bar includes all the accoutrements of a classic pub: lustrous woods, booth seating, and hearty food. Despite the preponderance of vintage Guinness signage, it is Belgian ales and single-malt Scotches that fill the glasses of most of the gathered regulars and visitors to this watering hole.

Campbell Apartment *pricey cocktails* `6 F2`
15 Vanderbilt Avenue, Southwest Balcony,
Grand Central Terminal • 212 953 0409
Open 3pm–1am Mon–Sat, 3–10pm Sun
For all its restored Beaux Arts splendor, Grand Central Station can still be a hassle. But the sting of crowds and late trains can be swiftly soothed by the divine cocktails at Campbell Apartment. Formerly the office of 1920s railroad tycoon John W. Campbell, it looks every bit the inner sanctum of a prosperous American industrialist, with dark wood paneling, monstrous stone fireplace, and intricate, leaded glass windows.

Suited midtown professionals unwind on comfy parlor furniture or on high bar stools, tapping feet to swing and calypso rhythms. The deceptively potent libations include Prohibition Punch – a mix of passion fruit juice, cognac, Grand Marnier, and champagne. A small balcony provides more privacy for latter-day John W.s to discuss mergers and acquisitions. Note: no sneakers, jeans, or baseball caps are allowed.

Métrazur *Grand Central splendor* `6 F2`

East Balcony, Grand Central Terminal • 212 687 4600
>> www.charliepalmer.com/metrazur
Open 11:30am–3pm Mon–Fri, 5–10:30pm Mon–Sat

Métrazur packs enough panache to lure rail travelers and non-commuters alike to Grand Central's East Balcony. Smart professionals relish Charlie Palmer's beautifully crafted cocktails, such as the Riviera: Dubonnet, Grand Marnier, blood orange and lime juice.

Single Room Occupancy *discreet bar* `7 C5`

360 West 53rd Street • 212 765 6299
Open from 5pm–4am Mon–Sat

This Theater District cubbyhole might be midtown's best-kept secret. Ring the outdoor buzzer, and a member of staff will show you into a dark bar, where chic patrons sip Malbecs and full-bodied Brooklyn Monster Ale served in elegant glassware. House music pounds from the stereo.

Ava Lounge *modernist vision at the Majestic* `7 D5`

Top of Majestic Hotel, 210 West 55th Street
• 212 956 7020
>> www.avaloungenyc.com Open from 5pm daily

The 1950s Golden Age of cocktail culture is evoked here through gorgeous linear furnishings, geometric patterns on the bar, designer Martinis, and jazzy house music. The outdoor patio comes into its own in summer – the perfect place to be mesmerized by the blinking commercialism of nearby Times Square.

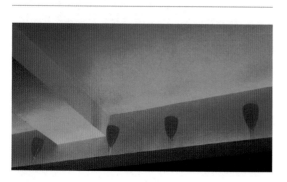

Flûte *Theater District champagne lounge* `7 D5`

205 West 54th Street • 212 265 5169
>> www.flutebar.com Open 5pm–4am Mon–Sat

Velvet couches, Belle Époque poster art, discreet alcoves, and cuddling couples create a cozy, romantic mood. Choose your bubbly from 100 bottles (18 are available by the flute). Tasting plates feature smoked salmon, tuna tartare, and foie gras. Live jazz and DJs play Thursday through Saturday.

Russian Vodka Room *for connoisseurs* `7 C5`
265 West 52nd Street • 212 307 5835
➤ **www.rvrclub.com** Open from 4pm daily

Gloss, glamour, and rampant pretension are the usual hallmarks of Manhattan lounges with extensive vodka selections. Fortunately, the Russian Vodka Room dodges this unsavory trend. The block's boisterous theater crowds rarely even notice RVR's black awning amid the twinkling lights, which means that proceedings inside the windowless lounge are intimate and relaxed. East Europeans, young and old, sit at the crescent-shaped wood bar or alcove tables, talking animatedly over music from a resident pianist.

No fewer than 50 varieties of the potent spirit fill the shelves. The curious, large glass jars you may notice above the coat rack hold luscious, home-made vodka infusions – try a bracing shot of horseradish, tangy cranberry, or mellow pear. An extensive menu of appetizing Russian delicacies, from borscht to caviar, is also available.

Baraonda *Italo-Latin festivity* `8 G2`
1439 2nd Avenue • 212 288 8555
➤ **www.baraondany.com** Open from 5.30pm Mon–Sun

Baraonda single-handedly proves that staid Upper East Siders can, in fact, party. Around midnight, the restaurant transforms into a Latin American dance house, with samba, techno, and *rock en español* compelling revelers to gulp down sangría and dance on the tables. (Skip the middling, overpriced food.)

Bemelmans Bar *cabaret & cocktails* `8 E1`
Carlyle Hotel, 35 East 76th Street • 212 744 1600
➤ **www.thecarlyle.com** Open noon–2am daily

Ludwig Bemelmans, creator of the *Madeline* children's book series, painted the exquisite zoological mural enveloping this superb uptown piano lounge. Top cabaret acts, subdued lighting, polished woods, and peerless classic cocktails set the tone for incomparably romantic evenings. Attire can be casual.

Jimmy's Uptown *jazz & more in Harlem* `11 D3`
2207 Adam Clayton Powell, Jr. Boulevard (at 130th St.)
• **212 491 4000** Open from early evening daily; also for gospel brunch Sun

Jimmy Rodriguez gives classic Southern soul food a gourmet twist (think filet mignon with horseradish grits). After dinner, the slick dining room transforms into one of Harlem's hottest clubs, with live jazz, R&B, and reggae. Local hip-hop impresarios are fans.

Frank's Lounge *DJ bar* `13 B4`
660 Fulton Street (between Lafayette & S. Elliot Sts)
• **718 625 9339**
» www.frankscocktaillounge.com Open from 5 nightly

New York's best classic 1960s soul and R&B jukebox sets the weeknight mood for nights of bonhomie among the clientele and the bar staff. Weekends are when DJs play hip-hop and soulful house, and the dance floor is jam-packed with Brooklyn's urban elite.

Zombie Hut *surprisingly refined lounge* `13 B4`
261 Smith Street (between Degraw & Douglass Sts)
• **718 855 2736**
Open from 5:30 nightly

The cartoonish name suggests tiki bar clichés such as plastic palms and grass skirts, but this intimate cocktail lounge on Brooklyn's restaurant row is a dreamier, plusher evocation of Polynesia. Young couples share potent Mai Tais by the stone fireplace, while jazzy electronic music plays. The ambience is friendly but probably not for those who are looking for a quiet couple of beers.

Ultra-colorful cocktails such as the Tiki Torch, Singapore Sling, and Scorpion Bowl are quite reasonably priced but pack a punch and (warning!) may have a tiny palm tree or a monkey floating in them. Try a pink and powerful Frozen Zombie with orange juice, rum and grenadine (to name a few of its poisons), just to kick off and you'll probably not remember much more of the evening.

Gowanus Yacht Club *local gem* `13 B4`

323 Smith Street • 718 246 1321
Open May–Oct: from mid-afternoon daily

Summer in Carroll Gardens means strolls in the park and beers at the Yacht Club. Nautical only in name, this tiny outdoor bar feels as convivial as a suburban backyard. Patio furniture, sizzling burgers and festive lights keep a hip crowd lingering long after their cheap domestic beers have been drained.

Great Lakes *graduates' gathering* `13 C4`

284 5th Avenue • 718 499 3710
Open from 6pm nightly

This spacious Park Slope favorite, with its worn couches, young, amiable crowd, and cracking indie-rock jukebox, suggests a college dormitory lounge for grown-ups. Defend your thesis anew over a Brooklyn Lager while making friends at the bar or out on the sidewalk with the banished smokers.

Bars with Views

For all the millions of dollars sunk into New York's myriad theme bars and luxe lounges, a bar with appealing views will have endless allure. **Sky Bar,** atop the Herald Square outpost of the La Quinta Inn chain, offers ample proof. The 14th-floor terrace compensates for the diminutive size of its split outdoor/indoor patio and undistinguished drinks by providing spectacular views of the Empire State Building, which literally towers above you. It's a popular gathering spot for the neighborhood's young after-work crowd.

The **Boat Basin Café** presents as rarified a setting for drinking beer and quaffing burgers as any in New York: a quirky, spacious complex, with limestone archways in its outdoor courtyard that are reminiscent of a Moorish grotto. Watch sailboats ply the Hudson from your shaded, riverfront patio table along with sociable Upper West Side couples and families. The preferred retreat among young, cosmopolitan travelers keen on seeing and being seen is the new Hotel Gansevoort's aptly named **Plunge Bar**, adjacent to the hotel's rooftop pool. Sleek patio furniture and an unfalteringly beautiful clientele are formidable distractions from the 360-degree views. The **View**, on the 47th floor of the Marriott Marquis Hotel, underwent a renovation in 2004 that removed the dance floor, but the bar still slowly revolves over Times Square. Comfy chairs and a formed mixologist make this a great spot to unwind (www.nymarriottmarquis.com/hotel/view).

As a counterpoint to all this refinement, nothing matches the gritty charm of hoisting your plastic beer cup at the weathered bar of **Ruby's** at Coney Island, where salty breezes and the boardwalk's colorful, wonderful spirit can be enjoyed free of charge. For full addresses, *see pp279–80*.

Buttermilk Bar *Brooklynite classic* `13 C5`
557 5th Avenue • 718 788 6297
Open from 6pm nightly

Operated by the same people as Great Lakes *(see p175)*, Buttermilk is remote by Park Slope standards, but worth seeking out for its hip young atmosphere. There's an excellent indie-rock jukebox, ample booth seating, and Brooklyn Brewery beers on tap. A locals' local, Buttermilk's a place to chat with Brooklynites.

Trash *gay & lesbian bar* `13 C2`
256 Grand Street • 718 599 1000
Open 5pm–4am nightly

Trash (formerly Luxx, then Toybox) has quickly established itself as the bar of choice for Williamsburg boys and girls who like to rock. Glittery vinyl booths fill with young, flirtatious singles every night, but it's at its most jam-packed on Fridays and Saturdays, when the tiny backroom is used for dancing.

Larry Lawrence *easy-going lounge* `13 C2`
295 Grand Street • 718 218 7866
Open from 6pm nightly

This bi-level Williamsburg space flaunts all the polished-wood sophistication of a Manhattan lounge, without the pretension. Downstairs, neighborhood professionals and artists sip reasonably priced Martinis and wines by the glass. Upstairs, smokers enjoy the skyward views from a garden-like atrium.

Spuyten Duyvil *Belgian beers/wicked fun* `13 C2`
359 Metropolitan Avenue • 718 963-4140
Open from 5pm nightly

A hundred different bottled beers and six rotating cask ales await beer connoisseurs at this cozy Williamsburg bar. The bright red facade hints at merriment. Inside, you'll find locals sampling rare Belgian brews, snacking on hot *soppressata* (spicy salami) sandwiches, and sharing group toasts.

Black Betty *Trashablanca* `13 C2`
366 Metropolitan Ave (at Havermeyer St.) • 718 599 0243
Open Mon–Fri 5–4, Sat & Sun 7–4

Williamsburg hipsters flock to this intimate barlounge featuring Middle Eastern decor and food in the adjacent restaurant. Think dive bar meets Arabian bordello, with pumpkin-colored walls, sofas, red velvet and beaded curtains, and tapestries. Music can be either a live band, a DJ, or from the jukebox.

Galapagos *playhouse for the arty* `13 B2`
70 North 6th Street • 718 782 5188

>> www.galapagosartspace.com Open from 6pm nightly
Almost every New York neighborhood boasts a space
where the values, styles, and habits of its residents
fuse into something emblematic. For Williamsburg –
Brooklyn's much-hyped bastion of artistic activity – it
is Galapagos. Anchoring North 6th Street's minimally
appointed bistros, cutting-edge boutiques, and two
or three remaining vacant warehouses, the venue
gives voice to local musicians, wall space to film-
makers and painters, and a great excuse for visitors
from farther afield to visit Williamsburg.

A soft magenta spotlight points out the door,
beyond which sits a huge reflecting pool and, above
it, a projection screen suspended in the air. Behind
this theatrical entrance, the performance and bar area
fills up with the neighborhood's hip young members
of Brooklyn's arts and music scene. Lushly
illuminated with ingenious spotlighting, the intimate
stage hosts everything from avant-garde rock bands
to risqué burlesque troupes – usually enthusiastically
supported by friends in the audience.

Ocularis, a weekly film series, features domestic
and international cinema. A film's director or one of
its actors is often invited along for a post-screening
discussion. Weekends bring DJs spinning electro, rock
'n' roll, soul, breakbeats, and more.

Some nights carry a cover charge, so check the
website for information about scheduled events.

streetlife

Away from the well-known tourist destinations are neighborhoods where New Yorkers shop, eat, and just hang out. To experience the variety and energy of authentic NY life, you need to visit places frequented by recent immigrants as well as born-and-bred New Yorkers. This chapter is the insider's view of where things happen for the locals – snapshots of street culture in a bubbling, bustling metropolis.

Lunchtime on Wall Street `1 D4`
Finance District frenzy

For a quintessential New York phenomenon, head to Wall Street between noon and 2pm on a weekday, and join the fast-paced business crowd for lunch. There are numerous delis and sandwich shops, including **Cosi, Pret a Manger**, the **Green Market**, and the **Amish Fine Food Market**. Be warned, though: ordering a sandwich in this high-powered financial district is not for the timid. Decide in advance what you want and be prepared to bark your order to an impatient server, who will yell "next" if you show any hesitation.

Once you've got through this experience, sit on the steps of **Federal Hall**, opposite the **Stock Exchange**. This is a good place for gazing along the concrete canyons. Alternatively, find a space in **Bowling Green Park** (south end of Broadway) or by the river in **Battery Park**. For a little calm after the lunchtime storm, **Trinity Church** (Map 1 D4) offers daily tours at 2pm, and Monday and Thursday music concerts at 1pm.

Canal Street *chopsticks & bargains* `2 E1`

A visit to New York isn't complete without a walk along the main thoroughfare of Chinatown. Canal Street is always crowded with cars and people: a jumble of languages making themselves heard within the din.

Street vendors peddle NYC T-shirts, counterfeit Rolex watches, and all manner of cheap knick-knacks. Ignore these and focus instead on the fresh produce, red bean buns, and Chinese paraphernalia in the stores on Canal St. and the quieter side streets of Bayard, Pell, and Mott. The **Chinatown Ice Cream Factory** on Bayard (No. 65) is an essential stop in summer; **HSF** (No. 46) is fantastic for dim sum. **Great NY Noodle Town** on Bowery (No. 28^1/$_2$) is another good food stop.

For an insight into the local culture and history, visit the **Museum of Chinese in the Americas**, at the intersection of Mulberry and Bayard. The **Mahayana Buddhist Temple** on Canal St. (No. 133) is another Sino-American establishment that's worth a look; with a bright yellow facade it's impossible to miss.

West 4th Street Courts on 6th Avenue `3 C3` *sport on the streets*

A simple area of asphalt by West 4th Street has become so popular for basketball that it has been officially recognized by the NYC Parks Department. Casual "pick-up" games occur year-round, and a summer tournament draws semi-pro players from around the world. Get in on the action: grab a hotdog from a street vendor, and cheer the players.

Meatpacking District *gentrified area* `3 A2`

This historic district in the westernmost pocket of West Village, just below 14th Street, is undergoing rapid change. In its 19th-century heyday, the area housed over 200 slaughterhouses and meatpacking plants. A handful of these remain, but most of the meat business has moved up to the Bronx or out of the city altogether. The former meat storage facilities – many of them listed as landmarks – are being reborn as cafés, restaurants, galleries, bars, and chic stores, and the Meatpacking District is now the hangout of models and celebrities. A shiny limousine is more often spotted than a side of beef these days. Remnants of the past can be seen, however, in architectural details. The curious metal awnings over the roads, for example, would have protected the meat as it was being moved off the trucks.

Cobbled **Gansevoort Street** was once a notorious spot for transvestite and she-male prostitutes. Diner/bistro **Florent** *(see p46)* opened on this street in 1985, pioneering the area's path to gentrification. Other established venues include **Cielo** *(see p168)*, a club where dancing is taken seriously, and French bistro **Pastis** *(see p273)*. High-end fashion boutiques **Stella McCartney** *(see p83)*, **Alexander McQueen** *(see p275)*, and **Jeffrey** *(see p85)* are steps away at 14th Street, while designer furniture is available at **Karkula Gallery** and **Vitra** *(see p276 for both)*. The former Gansevoort Docks now form part of the **Hudson River Park**. A waterside path is used by pedestrians, runners, cyclists, and roller-bladers, and leads past some scenic piers.

Tompkins Square Park Dog Run *canine romps* `4 G2`

If Fluffy isn't wearing the latest Burberry sweater, that's okay, so long as he's behaving and not sporting a spiked, pronged, or pinched collar. Toys aren't allowed either because "toys cause fights." These are some of the many rules, carefully displayed at the entrance to the dog run at Tompkins Square Park. This singular spot is the culmination of the American obsession with regulations and the New Yorker's need to give his or her dog room to promenade and socialize.

Once the preserve of drug users and prostitutes, the park is decidedly bourgeois now – the orderly dog run and its prim owners are a testament to that. Once you have gazed at the dog-walking spectacle over the fence (no people without dogs allowed in, and vice versa), stroll along 9th Street and avenues A and B. In contrast to the dog run, these roads have a funkier vibe. Notable cafés include **Itzocan** (438 E. 9th St.), and **Rue B** and **DT–UT** on Avenue B (Nos. 188 & 41, respectively).

Chelsea Flea Market & Union Square Markets *deals for steals* `3 D1`

Outdoor Market open 8am–5pm Sat & Sun • Union Square Green Market open 8am–6pm Mon, Wed, Fri & Sat • Holiday Market open from day after Thanksgiving until Christmas Eve

Chelsea's weekend flea and antiques markets are prime for finding anything from belt buckles and old buttons to botanical drawings, maps, vintage clothing, axes, and lace. The **Outdoor Market** on the northwest corner of 24th Street and 6th Avenue is a mélange of curios and furniture. **Antiques Garage** and **Antiques Annex** are geared more towards antique treasures, but also harbor a fair share of junk. Both are worth a browse; there's a $1 admission to get into the Annex. A few blocks further south, **Union Square Green Market** showcases farmers' stalls offering fruit, vegetables, fish, meat, and baked goods. During winter, the **Holiday Market** takes over – a mine of handmade jewelry, T-shirts, candles, massage oil, paintings, and hats.

Subway Passages: Grand Central to Times Square `6 F2` *underground music*

Grand Central Station and Times Square are connected by an underground Shuttle train, and the subway passages at either end of the short route are abuzz with New York energy, as bustling workers swarm through the passageways on their way to and from work. In these tunnels you'll also find excellent musicians, their performances good enough to make even the most determined commuter slow down to catch a few bars. While you may come across the occasional "rogue" performer – who'll set up and play wherever there's space – most are part of the MTA's Music Under New York program. The scheme promotes a variety of music, including jazz, Cajun, African, classical, Asian, and bluegrass. A stringent audition process held each year ensures that a high standard is maintained. Look for the authorized performers, who display an orange and black "Music Under New York" banner.

125th Street *gateway to Harlem* `11 D3`

One of the main roads in Harlem, 125th Street came to prominence during the Harlem Renaissance of the 1920s, when it became synonymous with dancing and jazz clubs. Since then the street has been the main commercial center for Harlem's predominantly black community and, over time, has provided the backdrop to civil rights activism and a creative flourishing of music, painting, literature, and drama.

Having gone through a prolonged period of economic depression and attendant crime problems, 125th street is back to being a vibrant thoroughfare again, with a mix of gentrified boutiques, mainstream chains, and street vendors. Some would argue that the soul of Harlem has moved to smaller side streets, but 125th remains the hub. For tours of Harlem, check out **Harlem Spirituals**, **Radical Walking Tours**, or **Big Apple Jazz Tours**. See if you can catch a gospel service at the Lenox Lounge *(see p149)* or some Southern-style cooking at **Amy Ruth's** *(see p267)*.

Brooklyn Heights

`13 A4`

Promenade *sublime views of Manhattan*

This is one of the best vantage points for a panorama of Manhattan. It's also a great place to enjoy a stroll – alone, hand in hand with a lover, or lead in hand with your dog. Grab an espresso at **Connecticut Muffin** on Montague (the main commercial street) and head towards the water to get onto the walkway.

A favorite spot for both locals and visitors, the promenade offers a mix of calm (despite the fact that it overlooks the Brooklyn to Queens expressway), and excitement – a thrill instilled by the awesome view of Manhattan that confronts you every time you look across the water.

The strip isn't very long, but you can combine the stroll with a perusal of Brooklyn Heights and its beautifully maintained brownstones. Back on Montague Street, there are several decent places to eat, such as **Teresa's** restaurant (No. 80), which offers tasty and authentic Polish fare alongside grilled cheese and hamburgers. Retail stores include **Heights Books** (No. 109), which specializes in second-hand publications.

Alternatively, you can take a different route from the promenade and walk along Columbia Heights to the Fulton Ferry landing, where you can buy an ice cream at the **Brooklyn Ice Cream Factory** before catching a water taxi over to Manhattan. To extend your walk further, cross via the Brooklyn Bridge.

Red Hook Food Stalls *spice & soccer*

`13 B5`

Corner of Bay and Clinton streets
Sat & Sun (end of April to first weekend in Oct)
Weekends in Red Hook's playing fields are dedicated to soccer, socializing, soaking up rays, and working one's way through as much delicious, home-cooked Latin American food as possible. Mexico, Honduras, Guatemala, and Colombia are all well represented. Try out your Spanish, and be willing to experiment.

Bedford Avenue *Williamsburg's heart* `13 C2`

Williamsburg is a compact area in north Brooklyn, packed with the accessories of bourgeois bohemia – funky cafés, hip bars, renovated lofts, fashion boutiques, and a few more trendy cafés. And Bedford Avenue is at its pulsating heart. This is an area that has changed dramatically in the last ten years, and some bemoan the arrival of Brooklyn's hip young things, who have pitched camp, placed their laptops on the counters of every café and bar in sight, and by their very presence have raised the rents. However, others are grateful for the attention the neighborhood is receiving and are happy to see some of the disused factories converted into apartments, stores, and clubs.

It is true that some of the grit may have been replaced by something funkier, lighter, and more affluent, but it is possible to find an earthy feel to the neighborhood once you look beyond the iPods and messenger bags (which you can pick up for a snip at **Brooklyn Industries**, No. 162). This is an eclectic locale, incorporating a Hasidic community in South Williamsburg, a profusion of artists, and a Polish contingent that has spilled over from Greenpoint. The Polish influence can be seen and tasted in places such as **Cukiernia** (a Polish bakery at No. 223) and **S & B Polish Restaurant** (No. 194).

The Bedford Avenue strip is most lively between North 6th and 10th streets. For a cool coffee stop, try **Verb Café** (No. 218), and watch the locals sitting at rickety wooden tables, indulging in java, listening to off-beat music, and playing checkers. The Verb is connected to a mini-mall that houses a variety of establishments, including an Internet café, the famed **Bedford Cheese Shop**, a vintage clothing store, and the bookstore **Spoonbill and Sugartown** *(see p98)*. Try **Bliss Café** (No. 191) for veggie delights, or a slice of delicious pizza at **Anna Maria's** (No. 179). Noteworthy stops are **Metaphors** (No. 195) for women's clothing and **Spacial** *(see p99)* for interior design. Check out the **Brooklyn Lager Brewery** (79 N. 11th St.), and take a free tour on Saturday (last tour 4pm) or indulge in Friday Night's Happy Hour (6–11pm).

Brighton Beach
Boardwalk *sea, sand, and snacks*

Ⓜ B, Q to Brighton Beach; F, D, Q to Coney Island/Stillwell Ave.
The Russian enclave of Brighton Beach at the south-ern tip of Brooklyn, also known as "Little Odessa," has much to offer for a day trip from Manhattan. The Brighton Beach Boardwalk is alive with Slavic lan-guages, chess games, the smell of the ocean, and a whiff of borscht wafting from one of the boardwalk cafés. For the area's best food and prices, however, go off the boardwalk and eat "inland" at **Café Glechik** (3159 Coney Island Avenue) or **Café Arbat** (306 Brighton Beach Avenue). Try the *vareniki* (similar to *pierogi* or ravioli) and drink a wholesome fruit compote. If you want to pick up snacks to take back to the waterfront, **M & I International Food Market** (249 Brighton Beach Avenue) has an impressive selection of Eastern European delicacies.

The boardwalk provides a vantage point for a lovely beach and water view. If you walk all the way along it, you'll reach Coney Island, where you can't miss the **New York Aquarium** (www.nyaquarium.com) and **Astroland** (www.astroland.com). This amusement park has the famed and rickety-looking Cyclone roller-coaster, which now has National Landmark status.

For the full Brighton Beach/Coney Island experience, have a **Nathan's Hotdog** from the original outpost on the corner of Surf and Stillwell. This is where the July 4th Hotdog Eating Championships take place. If you visit in mid- to late June, check www.coneyisland.com to find out when New York's aquatic version of Mardi Gras, the Mermaid Parade, struts down Surf Avenue.

Roosevelt Avenue *vibrancy and spice*

ⓂRoosevelt Avenue subway station is served by the
7, E, F, V, G and R trains

Roosevelt Avenue is one of the main thoroughfares
through the Queens neighborhood of Jackson Heights,
and is a veritable smorgasbord of cultures and food,
including Colombian, Chinese, Indian, Pakistani,
Korean, and Mexican. As soon as you leave the subway
station, your olfactory sense starts working overtime to
decipher the wafts of exotic ingredients that are being
mixed in various kitchens. The area may lack aesthetic
appeal, but it compensates in variety and vitality.

Along the adjacent 74th Street, you'll find stores
full of phonecards, toys, food, and confections.
For a meal try **Jackson Diner** (No. 37), or visit **Patel
Brothers Market** (Nos. 27–37) to see myriad fresh
and dried Asian spices and vegetables. Also on 74th
Street, you'll find dazzlingly intricate jewelry as well
as colorful saris and beautiful silk cloth in **Sahil Sari
Palace** (Nos. 37–55).

Arthur Avenue *a mini Little Italy*

Ⓜ4 or D subway train to Fordham Rd then No. 12 bus east;
2 or 5 subway train to Pelham Parkway then No. 12 bus west
≫ www.arthuravenuebronx.com

Another testament to the New York patchwork of ethnic
communities, Arthur Avenue, in the north Bronx, is
suffused with southern Italian traditions. The strip
offering the best in Italian produce is between 187th
Street and Crescent Avenue. Here you can find some
of the freshest and tastiest Italian food on this side of
the Atlantic. The **Egidio Pastry Shop** (622 E. 187th St.)
sells scrumptious chocolate cakes and excellent
cannoli (deep-fried tubes of pastry with a sweetened
ricotta filling), along with superb espresso. You can
buy the best home-made pasta and ravioli (rolled out
and cut right in front of you) from **Borgatti's** (632 E.
187th St.). Shops and stalls tease the senses with an
array of salamis, parmigianos, pastas, mozzarella,
and seafood. Italian is spoken widely on the street
and there's a relaxed, family-oriented vibe. *Mangia!*

havens

In New York, there's no need to leave the city limits in order to find a piece of nirvana. Along with parks and gardens, there are yoga centers, spas, churches, and tea rooms to retreat to. Vantage points at the tops of the city's towers provide inspirational views. And out at its farthest reaches – whether at Wave Hill in the Bronx or in the marshlands of Jamaica Bay – you may well discover an unexpected "wild" side to New York.

The River Project *waterside pleasures* `1 B1`

Pier 26, off West St. • 212 233 3030

»» www.riverproject.org   Open 11am–5pm daily

Just a few steps from Tribeca, this "estuarium" and research center is a perfect place to come for a deep breath or to confess to the marine gods for having just eaten sushi at neighboring Nobu *(see p46)*. Watch the boats and learn a bit about the local marine life from informative displays and the friendly volunteer staff.

Bliss SoHo *top-notch spa* `3 D4`

568 Broadway, 2nd Floor • 212 219 8970

»» www.blissworld.com

Open 9:30am–8:30pm Mon–Fri; 9:30am–6:30pm Sat

Forget about the outside world for a couple of hours, slip on a soft robe and slippers, and indulge in home-made brownies, apples, and fresh juices while you wait for your chosen treatment. Bliss has two locations in New York, but the SoHo spot – the Bliss flagship – is the one to seek out. Both men and women are pampered here, in a space reminiscent of a ship's interior. Treatments cater for the whole body, from head to toes, but the Bliss forte is facials. The trademarked Triple Oxygen Treatment and Fully Loaded facials are extremely popular with beauty-conscious New Yorkers. Alternatively, book a basic facial and add on treatments from an amazing à-la-carte menu, which offers masks, lip plumping, and capillary zapping. The changing rooms have saunas, steam rooms, and showers for further relaxation.

Angel Feet *divine foot relief* `3 B3`

77 Perry Street • 212 924 3576

Open 10am–9pm Mon, Tue, Thu & Fri, 10am–8pm Sat & Sun

As the name of this jewel-box sized basement room suggests, a reflexology session here is truly heavenly. The treatment rids feet of soreness and is given while you sit in one of two plush chairs that take up most of the intimate space. Relaxing music, candles, and a fragrant water mist for the feet add to the experience.

Jivamukti Yoga

Center *for body and spirit* 4 E3

404 Lafayette Street, 3rd floor • 212 353 0214

>> www.jivamuktiyoga.com Open 11.30am–8pm Mon–Fri,
9am–6:30 pm Sat & Sun

Calm your senses and align your posture with one of
a vast selection of hatha yoga classes, offered
throughout the day. Jivamukti, with two Manhattan
locations, has made yoga accessible to New York's
masses. You can simply drop in for a class or join an
open meditation session, but it's generally worth
calling ahead to check that space is available.

Throughout the building, the aroma of fragrant oils,
mellow music, mood lighting, and a soothing
waterfall help the process of relaxation. Massage
treatments, workshops, lectures, and yoga
demonstrations are held regularly. Take note: the
etiquette at the center dictates that shoes are to
be taken off before you enter the clean, loft-like
studio areas and changing rooms.

Wild Lily Tea Room *zen relaxation* 5 B5

511a West 22nd Street • 212 691 2258

>> www.wildlilytearoom.com Open 11am–10pm Tue–Sun

Take time out from shopping, gallery hopping, and
sightseeing at a place that takes tea very seriously.
There's no need to be stressed out by the range of
teas available; if you'd like to venture away from a
regular teabag, staff will guide you through a wide
selection of loose black tea blends, and jasmine,
ginseng, green, barley, and berry teas.

With a maximum capacity of 32 people, Wild Lily
isn't big, but the high ceilings and tiny goldfish pond
in the front create a fresh, airy, and Zen-like ambience.
As you sip your tea, enjoy the simplicity of the Japanese
decor, and the neat bento boxes, trays, and tea sets.
The food is fresh, inventive, and tasty, encompassing
traditional British fare, such as scones with clotted
cream, as well as more intriguing concoctions, such
as pea and yogurt soup, and green-tea cake. If you
feel like something stronger, sake is also available.

The Spa at the Mandarin Oriental   *luxurious respite*   `7 C4`

80 Columbus Circle at 60th St., 35th Floor • 212 805 8880
>> www.mandarinoriental.com Open 9–9 Mon–Sun

It's not cheap, but this spa is worth the expense! Splurge on wonderful body treatments, including exotically named massages such as Life Dance and Balinese Body. Herbal infusions are prepared daily by a chef (and are free), and almonds and dried fruits are offered in the Tea Lounge, which has stunning views of the Hudson River and the West Side of Manhattan. The decor is inspired by crisp Asian simplicity, elegance, and style: tiny candles line the carefully appointed hallway, and orchid buds decorate surface tops. Be sure to take advantage of the many amenities available as part of a visit to the spa, such as the Vitality Pool, the amethyst-crystal steam room (where eucalyptus oil is available to soften the skin), and the "rainforest experience" shower. Round it all off with some quality time in the Relaxing Room.

Top of the Tower @ Beekman Tower Hotel   *26th-floor calm*   `6 G1`

3 Mitchell Place, at 49th St. & 1st Ave. • 212 355 7300
Open 4pm–1am Sun–Thu, 4pm–2am Fri & Sat

A jewel of a space with wonderful views and a full cocktail menu. The calm atmosphere, unhurried service, and superb vantage point take you far away from the street-level clamor. Get a table by the window, from where the roof slopes vertiginously downward.

The Iris and B. Gerald Cantor Roof Garden   *art & leisure*   `8 E1`

The Metropolitan Museum of Art, 1000 5th Avenue, at 82nd St.
>> www.metmuseum.org Open May–late Fall: 10am–4:30 Tue–Thu & Sun, 10am–8:30pm Fri & Sat

Gorgeous views, sculpture in the foreground, and wine or cappuccino to lift your spirits. The joys of an elevated outdoor space are combined with art from the Met's collection and the whole of Central Park as a backdrop.

Conservatory Gardens at Central Park *floral sanctuary*

`10 E2`

Entrance on 5th Avenue and 105th Street • 212 360 2766
» www.centralparknyc.org Open 8am–dusk daily

Wildflowers, pruned rare roses, trimmed hedges, trees, and a thousand other floral delights are carefully arranged within these 6 acres, the most studiously tended area in Central Park. It's no wonder that New York brides scramble for permits for wedding ceremonies within these garden walls, or that school teachers are keen to bring classes for story-time sessions.

The central fountain is glorious in spring, when the wisteria that surrounds it bursts with purple, violet, pink, and white blossoms. Two more fountains are set closer to Fifth Avenue, one encircled by concentric rings of flowers. The fragrance, peace, and quiet of this garden is perfect for sitting on a bench, writing postcards, and taking time to reflect. There are free tours (rain or shine) on Saturdays from April to October; meet at Vanderbilt Gate on Fifth and 105th Street at 11am.

The Ramble at Central Park *green mazes*

`7 D2`

Enter via 5th Ave. or Central Park West between 72nd and 80th
» www.centralparknyc.org

The Ramble is the perfect place to get lost in a web of winding paths which cross 36 acres of wonderfully dense wooded areas, encompassing ponds, small bridges, and rocky outcrops. The wilderness factor in this pocket of Central Park is so great that the National Audubon Society has ranked the Ramble as one of the top 15 bird-watching sites in the whole of the U.S., putting it among National Parks such as Yosemite and geographical regions like the Everglades. If you visit early in the morning, you'll see die-hard birders at their regular spots, sporting binoculars and sipping cups of coffee or hot chocolate. The rest of the day brings a more diverse crowd, most of them with a more leisurely interest in a lunchtime stroll or a rendezvous. Note that the Central Park website refers to The Ramble within the Great Lawn section of the park.

The Rotunda
at The Pierre *traditional tea* `8 E4`

The Pierre Hotel, 2 East 61st Street • 212 838 8000
Afternoon tea served 3–5:30pm daily

This is New York's best spot for afternoon tea. The atmosphere is gracious and welcoming, with a high, domed ceiling above, and linen and fresh flowers at your table. Choose a three- or five-course tea, depending on your appetite for sandwiches and cakes.

The Cathedral Church of
St. John the Divine *glorious peace* `9 B1`

1047 Amsterdam Avenue at 112th Street • 212 316 7540
» www.stjohndivine.org Open 7–6 Mon–Sat, 1–7 Sun

Begun in 1892 but still unfinished, St. John's will be one of the largest cathedrals in the world when completed. However, its size and huge vaulted ceilings do not intimidate; rather, the church envelops you, and encourages a sense of well-being. Smaller chapels are reserved for prayer during the day, and services are held in the nave on Sunday at 11am and 6pm, with the Cathedral Choir in full voice. The organ, however, was damaged in a fire in 2001, and is awaiting repair once sufficient funds are raised.

Stained glass, intricately carved altars, and fine stonework is found throughout the cathedral, alongside modern interpretations of religious icons. These include a three-paneled, white and gold-leaf altarpiece by the late graphic designer and artist Keith Haring. As you walk down the central aisle, look up at the stunning Great Rose Window, an extraordinary creation made from over 10,000 pieces of stained glass in patterns dominated by hues of vibrant royal blue and calming indigo.

Next to the cathedral is a **Children's Sculpture Garden,** which exhibits a selection of bronze animal sculptures created by school children aged between 5 and 18. After your visit, head to the **Hungarian Pastry Shop** across the street on Amsterdam Avenue. There you can collect your thoughts, have a snack, and mingle with the erudite Columbia University set.

Wave Hill *escape to an estate*

675 West 252nd Street • 718 549 3200 • Ⓜ **Riverdale**

≫ www.wavehill.org Open Spring & Summer: 9am–5:30pm Tue–Sun (to 9pm Wed); Fall & Winter: 9am–4:30pm Tue–Sun

It's hard to believe that you're still within NYC limits (the Bronx no less) when you visit the well-situated and beautifully laid out garden and cultural center of Wave Hill. Part of Wave Hill's mission is to connect people with nature; to this end it presents impressive horticultural and art exhibits, and offers an array of environmental workshops, and musical and literary performances. Regular events include story telling, poetry readings, and chamber music and jazz concerts. T'ai chi is taught in the grounds too.

The café at Wave Hill House is a great spot, partly for the sustenance it offers, but mostly for the exceptional views. For another great view, walk along one of the paths through the white-columned pergola covered in flowering plants, and look downriver to the suspension cables of the George Washington Bridge.

Prospect Park *the lungs of Brooklyn* `13 D5`

Wollman Rink: 718 287 6215; Prospect Park Zoo: 718 399 7339; Kensington Stables: 718 972 4588

≫ www.prospectpark.org

Designed by the dynamic duo of landscape design Olmstead and Vaux (the planners of Central Park), Prospect Park is a lesser-known but equally enjoyable green playground for New Yorkers – Brooklynites in particular. It's a place to cycle, run, stroll, picnic, bird-watch, and skate, and every season has something to offer. Winter is the time for ice-skating at the Wollman Rink; summer brings colorful local festivals and concerts at the Bandshell. Prospect Park Zoo is a year-round family favorite, and other perennial attractions include horse-back riding on a track by Kensington Stables, and birding at the beautiful Audubon Center (www.prospectparkaudubon.org). Locals often use the park drive, also known as the loop, for bike riding, roller-blading, and running. Check the website for a list of seasonal events.

Brooklyn Botanic Garden *paradise* `13 D4`
1000 Washington Avenue • 718 623 7200
» www.bbg.org Open 8am–6pm Tue–Fri, 10am–6pm Sat
& Sun and hols; closes at 4:30pm Oct–Mar
Your olfactory and visual senses will be sharpened in
the wonderfully maintained BBG. A visit here may be
rewarded by bluebells in late spring or the scent of
roses in summer, while May's Cherry Blossom Festival
will transport you to the orchards of Asia *(see p16)*.

Jamaica Bay Wildlife
Refuge *an antidote to city life*
Crossbay Boulevard, Broad Channel • 718 318 4340
Ⓜ A train to Broad Channel Open sunrise to sunset daily
This wild habitat in the huge bay south of JFK airport
is where New Yorkers go to escape the intensity of the
city and delight instead in tranquillity, bird-watching,
and walking. The train takes an hour from Manhattan,
allowing you to adjust to a different pace and prepare
for another world. The journey is interesting as well:
before the train reaches Broad Channel stop, it travels
along a stretch of track surrounded by marsh and water
on either side, which heightens a sense of remoteness.

Walking to the refuge from the stop is straightforward. Go along Noel Road until you reach
Crossbay Boulevard and turn right; the refuge
entrance will be on your left after 10–15 minutes.
On the way, you'll pass waterfront houses on stilts
and wooden platforms.

The visitor center has a small but informative
interpretive area explaining the history and features
of the refuge, including the abundant wildflowers.
Jamaica Bay is a regular rest stop for migrating birds,
and teems with airborne life as thousands of shore,
land, and water birds flock to its wetlands; over 320
species have been spotted. Benches along the main
path allow you to sit, observe, and listen to bird
songs. Particularly captivating, though, is the contrast
of freshwater ponds, marshes, and wildlife set
against the distant skyline of Manhattan.

Noguchi Sculpture
Museum *intimacy, solitude, design*

32–7 Vernon Boulevard, Long Island City (entrance on
33rd Road) • 718 204 7088 • Ⓜ N & W trains to Broadway
≫ www.noguchi.org Open year round; closed Mon & Tue

Several million dollars-worth of renovation work has
ensured that this museum (which reopened in 2004
after a two-and-a-half-year closure) will continue to
inspire. It has an intimacy that's not often found in
art spaces; the renovations have not contributed to a
"blockbuster experience" in the manner of the downtown museum revamps, but rather have attempted to
refine the concrete and wood space.

This Museum is a tribute to the Japanese-American
sculptor, landscaper, and set designer Isamu
Noguchi, who established a studio in this Queens
neighborhood in 1961. Noguchi created beautiful
pieces made of materials such as wood, marble,
basalt, and metal, and his sculptures are in a
multitude of shapes and textures. The museum is

designed to eliminate distractions while you contemplate the work, allowing the art of Noguchi to be the
sole focus of attention. The space – its aesthetic a
refined, pared-back Modernism – contains several
galleries; some are exposed to the elements, others
are fully enclosed. There is also a garden, with a
majestic, fully grown *Katsura* tree and a wonderfully
subtle fountain sculpture. At its center is what
appears to be a bottomless pool.

The park is a place to reflect, to relax, and to
appreciate art without having to fight a crowd or
have museum attendants hovering over your
shoulder. There's an on-site café for light snacks,
and a store that stocks a wide range of design books
and Noguchi's trademark rice-paper lamps.

While in the area, it's also worth dropping by the
Socrates Sculpture Park, a little further north on
Vernon Boulevard. On the bank of the East River, the
park exhibits temporary installations of sculpture by
international contemporary artists.

hotels

The independent hotel scene is stronger in New York than in any other major city. More than half the hotels are not affiliated to a national or international chain, which means that they are particularly good at providing individuality, character, and style. Rooms don't come cheap, but there are deals to be had with a little planning. Check hotel and reservation agency websites to get the best deals.

ROMANTIC HIDEAWAYS

Soho House New York
29–35 9th Avenue
Enjoy the rooftop pool, soak in a generously sized tub, or romp around your private "playroom" – perfect for romantic trysts. *(See p206)*

St. Regis
2 East 55th Street
Plush and luxurious, St. Regis is a place to pamper and be pampered. Excellent bathrooms and great service. *(See p208)*

Bed & Breakfast on the Park
113 Prospect Park West, Brooklyn
This small hotel is just steps away from lovely Prospect Park. Its top-floor room has prime views and a four-poster bed. *(See p213)*

GASTRONOMIC

>> *www.in-newyorkmag.com lists hotel restaurants in the city.*

Hotel Wales
1295 Madison Avenue
The place to stay for a delicious and hearty breakfast, including fresh scones and fluffy omelets, at Sarabeth's Kitchen. *(See p213)*

The Mark
25 East 77th Street
With an extensive wine list and fine French-American cuisine, The Mark's restaurant offers a refined dining experience. *(See p211)*

Mercer Hotel
147 Mercer Street
If you can tear yourself away from the hotel's elegant rooms and deep tubs, the Mercer Kitchen is a fashionable haunt for fine dining. *(See p204)*

LIVE LIKE A LOCAL

Bevy's SoHo Loft
70 Mercer Street
With Bevy and fellow guests for company, a stay here is like sharing a spacious apartment right in the middle of SoHo. *(See p204)*

Harlem Flophouse
242 West 123rd Street
The fun, jazzy vibe of the Flophouse will instantly make you feel part of New York. Interior details evoke early 20th-century Harlem. *(See p212)*

1871 House
East 62nd Street
Many suites or studios here come with a kitchenette and fireplace, so you can pretend you've got your own pied-à-terre. *(See p210)*

Union Street B&B
405 Union Street, Brooklyn
A warm ambience and well-stocked bookshelves (and even a welcome for pet dogs) make this B&B feel like a family home. *(See p213)*

>> *www.affordablenewyorkcity.com lists B&Bs and fully furnished apartments. These offer good value for stays of over a week and even better value if you are in town for a month or more.*

BEST OF THE BARGAINS

Washington Square Hotel
103 Waverly Place
Super budget prices for clean, if flowery, rooms in a desirable Village location. Breakfast is also included in the price. *(See p205)*

Chelsea Inn
46 West 17th Street
The Chelsea Inn has low rates and kitchenettes in the rooms. It is set in a great location two blocks from Union Square. *(See p207)*

Chelsea Lodge
318 West 20th Street
A spotless lodge, with wooden floors, TVs, and shower stalls in every room. Toilets are shared, hence the bargain rates. *(See p207)*

STYLE STATEMENTS

>> Hotel prices will usually be quoted without tax. Be sure to check the figure once City and State taxes are added.

Hudson
356 West 58th Street
The spectacular courtyard, roof terrace and other lounging spaces here were created by Philippe Starck and the hotelier Ian Schrager. *(See p209)*

60 Thompson
60 Thompson Street
Comfort and style are the themes throughout. How many hotels have chairs specially designed and named for them? *(See p204)*

Morgans
237 Madison Avenue
The original "lifestyle hotel," with design touches that create a magical, understated aesthetic throughout. *(See p209)*

GREAT LOCATION

>> The hippest areas are the easy-going downtown neighbourhoods, such as SoHo and the Village, but the largest concentration of hotels is midtown, close to the theaters and department stores.

Four Seasons
57 East 57th Street
Ideal for shopping sorties on Madison Avenue – afterwards you can drop your bags and put up your feet in the luxurious spa. *(See p210)*

Abingdon Guest House
13 8th Avenue
Feel the pulse of the West Village right outside the door of these stately townhouses. Each room is individually decorated. *(See p205)*

W New York, Union Square
201 Park Avenue South
Just off Union Square, you'll be within easy walking distance of such funky neighborhoods as West Village, Chelsea, and Gramercy. *(See p207)*

Bevy's SoHo Loft *three great rooms* `3 D5`
70 Mercer Street • 212 431 8214
» www.sohobevy.com

Bevy – known to many as the "SoHo Mom" – is a real character, who relishes lively conversation with her guests. Her loft is a funky, renovated industrial space, filled with paintings and colorful fabrics. There are just three rooms, but each is characterful and spacious, with very high ceilings. Great location. **Cheap**

SoHo Grand Hotel *pet-friendly place* `3 D5`
310 West Broadway • 800 965 3000
» www.sohogrand.com

Pets are made very welcome here – indeed, if you haven't brought your own furry friend, you'll be offered a fish as a room companion. A selection of CDs is also provided, and you can buy the fish and discs if you like them. As for the 367 rooms: some are small, but all the beds are big and comfy. **Moderate**

Mercer Hotel *minimalist finesse* `3 D4`
147 Mercer Street • 212 966 6060
» www.mercerhotel.com

In a solid 1890 building near the Village, the Mercer focuses on style and service. The 62 rooms are light and minimally furnished, and the bathrooms come with large soaking tubs and Swedish Face Stockholm cosmetics. The Mercer Kitchen restaurant is worth a visit, and a fine spot for celebrity spotting. **Expensive**

60 Thompson *SoHo taste* `3 C5`
60 Thompson Street • 877 431 0400
» www.60thompson.com

60 Thompson has 100 rooms and suites, all with music and DVD systems. The setting is modern, with a sleek interior design, plush bedding, and marble bathrooms. Check out the high-backed 60 Thompson chairs, designed exclusively for the hotel by Thomas O'Brien of Aero Studios. **Expensive**

Tribeca Grand Hotel *hip & stylish* `3 C5`

2 Avenue of the Americas • 800 965 3000
» www.tribecagrand.com

Built in 2000, this hotel attracts a cool clientele. All rooms lead off from the Church Lounge, the hub of its atrium-style layout. The guest rooms match simple, modern design with top technology in the form of great sound systems and high-speed Internet access. The hotel offers the same deal on fish and CDs as its older sister, the Soho Grand *(see opposite)*. **Expensive**

Washington Square Hotel *location, location* `3 C3`

103 Waverly Place • 800 222 0418
» www.wshotel.com

This budget option is in a prime Village location, close to many attractions by foot or subway. The rooms are a little floral and frilly, but the lobby has a smart, Art Deco style. Complimentary continental breakfast makes this even better value for downtown. **Cheap**

Abingdon Guest House *Village comfort* `3 B2`

13 8th Avenue • 212 243 5384
» www.abingdonguesthouse.com

Two landmark townhouses in West Village have been converted into a guest house with nine rooms. Each room has its own style, as suggested by the names – "Martinique," "Ambassador," and so on. Prices vary according to size and decor. Light breakfasts and lunches are served at its Brewbar café. **Cheap**

Old Establishments

With an enviable location at the foot of Central Park, the **Plaza Hotel** maintains its reputation for providing the ultimate in service and comfort. The **Carlyle** on Madison Avenue has been appreciated since the 1930s for its understated elegance, superb service, and striking Art Deco design. The hotel's Café Carlyle is popular with a well-heeled Upper East Side crowd. No stranger to scandal and creativity, the **Hotel Chelsea** has a thousand stories to tell. Each room and apartment is different, and much of the building is occupied by long-stay residents. A great slice of bohemia, the Chelsea has welcomed many writers and musicians, from Mark Twain and Tennessee Williams to Bob Dylan and Sid Vicious. For individual hotel details, *see p281*.

Soho House
New York *chic hotel in the Meatpacking District*

3 A2

29–35 9th Avenue • 212 627 9800

>> www.sohohouse.com

Blink and you'll miss the entrance to Soho House – a level of discretion you'd expect of a hotel that doubles as a private members' club. Staying at the hotel gives you access to the club facilities, which include a fitness room, a private screening room, a restaurant and bar, a drawing room and library, a games room with pool table and pinball, and an elegantly comfortable club room. The Cowshed Spa offers a variety of healthy treatments and a soothing environment. The "Cowshed" products are produced by hand in the UK, home of the original, London Soho House. The prime facility, however, is the rooftop pool. Although not a place for serious laps, the pool is great for a quick dip, and the deck around it has chaise longues, umbrellas, tables, chairs, and a full bar with light snacks. The roof area is open year round, with a heated marquee in winter.

The comfortable guest rooms are classified according to size, and are labeled (in ascending order) playpen, playroom, playhouse, and playground. Mini-bars are stocked with all sorts of temptations, including Ben & Jerry's ice cream in the freezer, and chilled Martini glasses. The decor is an eclectic mix, with touches of luxury such as freestanding, rolltop bathtubs. The rooms remain functional, however, with state-of-the-art gadgets such as surround-sound entertainment systems and wireless Internet access throughout the whole building. **Expensive**

Maritime Hotel *nautical swank* `3 A1`

363 West 16th Street • 212 242 4300
>> www.themaritimehotel.com

The rooms here have a maritime theme, complete with porthole windows and an appealing blue-and-white color scheme for the bedding. Rates are reasonable, and the location is great for Chelsea and the Meatpacking District. There's 24-hour room service, a roof terrace, and a sushi bar. **Moderate**

Chelsea Lodge *fresh, clean & friendly* `3 B1`

318 West 20th Street • 800 373 1116
>> www.chelsealodge.com

Toilets are shared at this low-priced lodge, but each of the 22 refurbished rooms has wooden floors and high ceilings, and is well appointed, with a shower stall, sink, TV, and double bed. You also have the option to pay extra for a suite with more amenities. The place is bright and on a quiet side street. **Cheap**

Chelsea Inn *affordable charm* `3 C1`

46 West 17th Street • 800 640 6469
>> www.chelseainn.com

Ask for a quiet room at the back of this renovated 19th-century townhouse in a great downtown location. The budget-priced rooms all have kitchenettes and TVs, and the shared bathrooms are decorated with charming, colorful painted murals. Continental breakfast is included in the price. **Cheap**

W New York, Union Square *stylish* `3 D1`

201 Park Avenue South • 212 253 9119
>> www.whotels.com

The signature style of the "W" hotel chain involves subdued lighting and touches of purple in the otherwise minimalist white decor. Rooms are sleek, with comfy feather beds, and the service is impeccable. The dramatic lobby has a soaring staircase and areas of sand, grass, and marble. **Moderate**

Bryant Park Hotel *high-tech & colorful* `6 E2`
40 West 40th Street • 877 640 9300
>> www.bryantparkhotel.com

The plush red of the lobby desks and rug is the first thing you notice. Throughout the hotel, the simple lines of Scandinavian-inspired furniture are juxtaposed nicely with Tibetan rugs and cashmere throws. Rooms have super sound systems as well as Internet access, and the bathtubs are generously sized. **Moderate**

Royalton *theatrical style* `6 E2`
44 West 44th Street • 800 606 6090
>> www.royaltonhotel.com

In the heart of the Theater District, this Ian Schrager hotel *(see also Morgans, opposite)* has a stunning lobby that's almost like a runway. Sit on the chairs at the side and socialize, or slip into the Round Bar for cocktails and people-watching. For the best views, try to get a deal on a deluxe room or suite. **Moderate**

St. Regis *Beaux Arts beauty* `8 E5`
2 East 55th Street • 800 625 5144
>> www.stregis.com

Built in 1904 by John Jacob Astor IV, this luxurious hotel is meant to be a home away from home. The rooms even have doorbells. Original details are mixed with modern amenities, including flat-screen TVs in the bathrooms and high-speed Internet access. The hallways are wonderfully airy and bright. **Expensive**

The Peninsula *discriminating modernity* `8 E5`
700 5th Avenue at 55th Street • 800 262 9467
>> www.peninsula.com

The 1905 landmark building and deluxe, spacious rooms are as much a draw here as the ultra-modern facilities, which include Internet connections and "silent fax machines" in all the boldly colored rooms. Remote controls in the bathrooms can be used to operate speaker phones, TVs, or radios. **Expensive**

Morgans *understated sophistication* `6 E3`

237 Madison Avenue • 800 606 6090
>> www.ianschragerhotels.com

The concept of the "boutique hotel" originated at Morgans. Defined not by size (as with the grand hotels of the past) but by a unique sense of style and coolness, the hotel was an instant hit with fashion-conscious travelers. Morgans, designed in the late 1980s, recreates the ambience of an apartment house. The lobby is functional, with a small side office for the helpful and knowledgeable concierge. Decorative themes include the black-and-white checkerboard motif, reminiscent of old New York cabs, seen subtly in the elevator, in the pattern of the hallway carpets, and in the sleek stainless steel and glass bathrooms (which are also adorned with fresh flowers).

Renowned designer Andrée Putman planned the interiors, mixing materials such as raw silk, corduroy, maplewood, and formica. All rooms have grey, white, and beige color schemes, and feature banquettes and original Robert Mapplethorpe photographs – which have had to be bolted to the wall. Communal spaces include the "living room," with free computer access, and a welcoming area conducive to playing scrabble, reading, or writing.

The famed restaurant Asia de Cuba is where breakfast is served (included in the price), and Morgans Bar has a lively night scene and superb cocktails. Owner Ian Schrager has replicated his hotel philosophy with other New York establishments, including the Hudson *(below)* and the Royalton *(opposite)*. **Expensive**

Hudson *cosmopolitan, affordable & urbane* `7 C4`

356 West 58th Street • 800 606 6090
>> www.hudsonhotel.com

One thousand rooms are priced at various scales so that the surfer dude can mix with the film producer in the swanky Hudson Bar. Note that the rooms tend to be very small – the concept at this Ian Schrager hotel is that you'll spend most of your time in the beautiful and funky communal spaces. **Moderate**

Four Seasons *contemporary panache* `8 E5`
57 East 57th Street • 212 758 5700
>> www.fourseasons.com

There's nothing understated about the Four Seasons – just look at the immense lobby with its cathedral-like ceiling, marble floors, and floral arrangements as large as refrigerators. As a modern facility, the hotel was built with the savvy customer in mind. Even the most modest rooms have generous dimensions – 500 sq ft (47 sq m) rivals the floorspace of many New York studio apartments. Rooms on the top floors offer great city views, including the sweep of Central Park. The windows open to let in a bit of fresh air, and curtains can be opened from the bed with a switch. All bathrooms have Bulgari products, a glass-enclosed shower, and a deep tub that fills in 60 seconds. Other gadgets include a flat screen TV in the bathroom, and a top-quality CD player/radio. The on-site spa and fitness center offers a "floating sensory escape," perfect for defeating jetlag. **Expensive**

1871 House *country-style feel* `8 F4`
East 62nd Street • 212 756 8823
>> www.1871house.com

This beautifully renovated brownstone building is close to Central Park and an upscale shopping zone, but the quiet, leafy street makes you forget you're in the heart of the city. There's no common area for guests, but the spacious, high-ceilinged rooms, suites, and studios are ideal for lounging, and most have working fireplaces – quite a treat for a New York property. The keepers even provide duraflame logs to burn.

So long as you don't require 24-hour room service, these cozy, relaxing accommodations are a good option. The whole place is furnished with antiques and the decor is warm and homey. If you are traveling in a group of four or more, reserve the Great Room and Cottage combination; both have access to a lovely garden, the "cottage space." Some rooms have kitchenettes, but the hotel is close to many eateries. A four-night minimum is usually expected. **Moderate**

The Lowell *intimate retreat*   8 F4
28 East 63rd Street • 212 838 1400
>> www.lowellhotel.com

With 21 rooms and 47 suites, The Lowell focuses more on comfort than numbers. High-profile guests stay here to escape the paparazzi. The suites offer options such as wood-burning fireplaces, terraces, and kitchenettes. Orchids in every room are another high-quality detail, and there's an airy fitness room too. **Expensive**

Melrose *highly accommodating hotel*   8 F4
140 East 63rd Street • 212 838 5700
>> www.melrosehotelnewyork.com

Formerly the Barbizon Hotel, the Melrose has been renovated to accommodate every need of luxury-loving travelers, whether it's plush bedding, Internet access, modern gadgetry, or a well-equipped gym. It's also well situated, only three blocks from Central Park and up the street from Bloomingdales. **Moderate**

The Pierre *New York landmark*   8 E4
5th Avenue at 61st Street • 212 838 8000
>> www.fourseasons.com

A top hotel since 1930, The Pierre is a bastion of old-fashioned gentility, and is the perfect place to return to after a shopping spree at neighboring Bergdorf's. Attentive staff perform to a backdrop of chandeliers and Art Deco details. The **Rotunda** *(see p196)* is on hand for afternoon tea; Café Pierre offers full meals. **Expensive**

The Mark *Upper East Side elegance*   8 E1
25 East 77th Street • 212 744 4300
>> www.themarkhotel.com

An air of sophistication permeates the lobby and generously sized rooms of this hotel, part of the Mandarin group. Inspiration for The Mark's exquisite Neo-Classical interior is said to have come from the work of 19th-century English architect Sir John Soane. Service is thorough and professional. **Expensive**

Akwaaba Mansion *African tranquillity*

347 MacDonough Street Ⓜ Last car of A train to Utica Ave, then walk four blocks along Stuyvesant Ave • 718 455 5958 >> www.akwaaba.com

This Italianate villa is tucked away on a tree-lined street in the historic Stuyvesant Heights area. African motifs and antiques create a unique style. Some rooms include a Jacuzzi. Spend a lazy afternoon in the secluded garden, or sipping lemonade on the sun porch. **Cheap**

Harlem Flophouse *jazz-related fun*   `11 D4`

242 West 123rd Street • 212 662 0678
>> www.harlemflophouse.com

A small brass plaque is the only thing that sets the Flophouse apart from the other residences on this quiet, tree-lined brownstone block. The first thing you'll notice upon entering is the sound of jazz, drifting softly from the mantelpiece radio in the charming front room. It has been a B&B since 2000, and the owner has worked on various parts of the house to restore original details, including patterned tin ceilings, wooden moldings, and a downstairs dining room for parties.

A touch of faded glory and fresh renovation add to the appeal and charm of the four guest rooms. Each has a sink, but bathrooms are shared – a claw-foot tub in one is nicely set right under a sky light. All beds are firm, with good mattresses, and the rooms are named after notable people with either jazz or Harlem connections – often both. There are no TVs, but alarm clocks are provided. There's a smoking room in the basement and guests have access to the garden, for summer barbecues, relaxation, and reflection. Hearty and delicious breakfasts of eggs, grits, sausage, and yogurt are available at an extra charge.

The Flop House is conveniently located for subway trains and buses (the M60 can bring you right here from LaGuardia airport), and is close to the Apollo Theater *(see p148)*, Lenox Lounge *(see p149)*, and the Harlem Studio Museum *(see p119)*. The Flophouse also hosts occasional art exhibitions in the common area on the main floor. **Cheap**

Hotel Wales *classic & fresh* `10 E4`

1295 Madison Avenue • 866 925 3746
>> www.waleshotel.com

This Upper East Side boutique hotel has an intimate feel. Aveda products and fresh flowers feature in the comfortable rooms, and free coffee is available day and night. The roof deck is a great place from which to watch the buzzing city, and adjacent Sarabeth's Kitchen whips up fantastic omelets and soups. **Moderate**

Union St B&B *bohemian charm* `13 B4`

405 Union Street, Brooklyn
718 852 8406

Floral wallpaper, wooden floors, and music boxes in each of the six rooms create a charming, warm, and homey atmosphere. The continental-style breakfast includes good strong coffee. Owner Angelique is a history buff, and provides a well-stocked bookshelf of local historical books for perusal. **Cheap/Moderate**

Bed & Breakfast on the Park *Victorian time machine* `13 C5`

113 Prospect Park West • 718 499 6115
>> www.bbnyc.com

The fixtures here have been lovingly restored to maintain an ambience of Victorian gentility. Reserve the Lady Liberty Room for a four-poster bed, great city views, and exclusive access to the roof garden. Breakfast includes home-made pastries. **Moderate**

Accommodations Agencies

Hotel rates can be rather mysterious: the officially quoted "rack rate" may say one thing, but certain packages, the time of year, and discounts found on the web can give a completely different price. If you get the timing right, you can slice a lot of money off your room price. At weekends in off-peak seasons, for example, hotels often offer rooms at discounted rates. Accommodations agencies with websites to try include: **www.simply-newyork.com**, **www.a1-discount-hotels.com**, and **www.hotels.com**.

Also, if you're interested in longer stays – a duration of seven days or more – and are thinking about subletting an apartment, try **www.sublet inthecity.com**, **www.citysublets.com**, and **www.newyorkhabitat.com**.

Notes

VISITORS TO New York are treated very much the same as anyone else. While you may not be given special treatment, as long as you follow a few guidelines on personal security you'll be able to explore the city as freely as any native New Yorker. Buses and subway trains are

Visitors resting on the steps of the Metropolitan Museum of Art

reliable and cheap; there are lots of cash machines and money can be easily exchanged at banks, hotels and foreign money brokers. The wide range of prices offered by all the many hotels, restaurants and entertainment venues means your New York trip can be both fun and affordable.

SIGHTSEEING TIPS

NEW YORK'S rush hours extend from 8 to 10am, 11:30am to 1:30pm and 4:30 to 6:30pm, Monday to Friday. During these times, every form of public transportation will be crowded, and the streets will be much harder to navigate on foot.

It's worth trying to visit a cluster of sights in the same area instead of exhausting yourself rushing from one distant attraction to another. Buses are a comfortable and reliable way to get around, and you'll see the city as you travel.

It's best to avoid passing through certain areas of the city, especially at particular times *(pp220–1)*. Public toilets in bus stations should be avoided. They attract drug users and the homeless. It is best to find a large hotel, department store, coffee shop or book-store if you need a restroom.

If you need help with street directions or feel a need to get off the street, ask a policeman or find a hotel doorman. There is one on duty at the entrance to most hotels 24 hours a day.

Hotel doorman

OPENING HOURS

BUSINESS HOURS are generally from 9am to 5pm with no lunchtime closing. Only some banks close earlier, at 4pm, although some do have longer hours (8am–6pm) and open on Saturday

mornings. Many museums close on Mondays and major holidays. Some open on Tuesday or Thursday evenings during certain seasons (phone for details).

MUSEUMS

IN NEW YORK, *museum* is used as a blanket term to include institutions that offer diverse holdings. Museums either charge admission, starting at around $2, or ask for a "donation," which can be $6 to $9. There are discounts for senior citizens, students and children. The leading museums schedule free guided tours and lectures.

Museum Mile, on and near Fifth Avenue, groups a number of major museums close together. Of these, the Frick Collection and the Cooper-Hewitt are small enough to see in one or two hours, but the larger museums, the Guggenheim, Whitney, and Metropolitan, may take far longer than this.

ETIQUETTE

IT IS ILLEGAL to smoke in *any* public place or building in New York. Some restaurants now provide separate rooms for smokers, but it is best to phone ahead for details.

Business travelers need not bring a gift for their hosts. Such tokens are not expected and may even be considered improper. If you do bring something, it should be something inexpensive and

preferably representative of where you live.

Tipping is an integral part of New York life: for taxi drivers leave 10 to 15%; waiters 15 to 20%, cocktail waiters 15%, hotel room service 10% (when not added to the bill); coat check $1; hotel maids $1 or $2 per day after the first day; hotel bellhops about $1 per bag; hair stylists 15 to 20% and barbers 10 to 20%.

TOURIST INFORMATION

ADVICE ON ANY aspect of life in New York City is available from the **New York Convention and Visitors Bureau**, known as **NYC & Co**. Their 24-hour touch-tone phone service offers help outside office hours. Brochures and information kiosks can also be found at the walk-in office of the **Times Square Visitors Informa-tion Bureau**.

Hotel lobbies and museums have free literature racks, and all of the daily newspapers hold a wealth of information about what's going on where.

Useful information
NYC & Co, 810 7th Ave.
📞 *(212) 484-1222.*
W www.nycvisit.com
Times Square Information Center, 1560 Broadway.
Open: 8am–8pm daily
W www.timessquarebid.org
New York State information
W www.state.ny.us
New York City information
W www.nyc.com
On-line guide to everything in NYC: W www.jimsdeli.com

ENTERTAINMENT LISTINGS

A NUMBER of inexpensive or even free publications listing current exhibitions and leisure activities are available at newsstands, hotels or galleries throughout New York.

Among the more popular ones are *New York* magazine, *The New Yorker's* "Goings On About Town" roster and *Time Out New York*, which list offerings at the city's many museums, clubs, theaters, galleries, restaurants, cinemas, colleges and libraries, plus impending auctions. The *Village Voice* focuses on events in SoHo, TriBeCa and Greenwich Village, plus other major cultural activity in the city. *The New York Times* Friday and Sunday editions list current visual and performing arts events in their respective "Weekend" and "Arts and Leisure" sections. *Art News* is a monthly magazine that lists major art events and auctions and reviews exhibits.

There are also various free magazines. The weekly *Where* is distributed through hotel concierges and lists major museums, their opening hours, locations and any exhibitions. *Art Now/New York Gallery Guide* is released in art galleries each month. It lists current exhibitions and has useful maps showing where they are located.

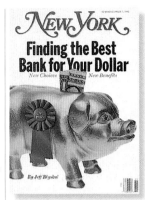

New York **magazine has weekly comprehensive entertainment listings for all of New York**

GUIDED TOURS

Whichever way you want to see New York – with the help of a pre-recorded walk or by an exciting trip in a helicopter, boat or horse-drawn carriage – organized sightseeing trips, planned by someone else, can save a lot of time, effort and often money. There are numerous companies to choose from, each providing plenty of local information.

Boat Tours

Circle Line
Sightseeing Yachts
Pier 83, W 42nd St.
((212) 563-3200.
A three-hour trip circumnavigating Manhattan.

Circle Line Statue of
Liberty Ferry
South Ferry, Battery Park.
((212) 269-5755.

Spirit of New York
W 23rd and 8th Ave.
((866) 211-3805.
Cruises include lunch or dinner.

Helicopter Tours Liberty
South Ferry.
W 34th St and
12th Ave.
((212)967 6464
Manhattan–Staten Island.

World Yacht, Inc
Pier 81 W 41st St.
((212) 630-8100.
Cruises include lunch, dinner and onboard entertainment.

Carriage Tours

59th St at Fifth Ave and
along Central Park S.
Horse-drawn carriages gather outside the Plaza Hotel. The usual itinerary takes in Central Park.

Bus Tours

Gray Line of New York
42nd St and 8th Ave.
((212) 397-2620.

Short Line
Tours/American
Sightseeing NY
166 W 46th St.
((800) 631-8405.

Bicycle Tours

Bite of the Apple Tours,
2 Columbus Circle, 59th
St & Broadway.
((212) 541-8759.
A two-hour spin around Central Park. $35 with bike rental. 10am, 1pm, and 4pm.

Walking Tours

Big Apple Greeters
1 Centre St, Suite 2035.
((212) 669-8159.
Free tours by New York natives.

Big Onion Walking Tours
PO Box 250201,
Columbia University.
((212) 439-1090.
Historical and ethnic.

Harlem Spirituals, Inc.
690 8th Ave.
((212) 391 3900.

Harlem's history and culture. Apr–Oct only.
Heritage Trails
Four free do-it-yourself historical trails begin at Federal Hall; brochures at Federal Hall.

Museum of the City of
New York
103rd St and Fifth Ave.
((212) 534-1672.
Architecture and history.

NBC Studio Tour
30 Rockefeller Plaza.
((212) 664-7174.

92nd Street Y
1395 Lexington Ave.
((212) 415 5500.
Culture and history.

Talk-a-Walk
30 Waterside Plaza.
((212) 686-0356.
Recorded itineraries.

Carriage ride in Central Park

DISABLED TRAVELERS

D ISABLED PEOPLE may find New York a challenging city. Only 21 of Manhattan's subway stations are wheel-chair-accessible and, while all buses are equipped for wheelchair access, some major boarding areas are not.

Many hotels, restaurants, and tourist attractions are equipped for disabled visitors, but it is wise to check. Also ask about accessibility to rest rooms.

Some museums offer tours for deaf, blind, or disabled people, and all Broadway theaters have devices for the hearing impaired. An excellent resource is *Access Guide to New York City*, available from the **Mayor's Office for People with Disabilities**.

Useful information

The Mayor's Office for People with Disabilities. **[** *(212) 788-2830* *www. nyc.gov/mopd*

A New York city bus "kneeling" to help the elderly board

CUSTOMS AND IMMIGRATION

C ITIZENS OF Britain, New Zealand, Australia, and 26 other countries do not need visas if they are staying in the US for 90 days or less. Canadians need only proof of citizenship and a photo ID. Students do need proper visas. All travelers need round-trip or onward passage tickets and must show proof they have $500 or more. Check with a US embassy or travel agent if in doubt.

Customs allowances per person when you enter the US are 200 cigarettes, 50 cigars or 4.4 pounds (2 kilograms) of tobacco; no more than 2 pints (1 liter) of alcohol; gifts worth no more than $100; no meat or meat products (even in cans), seeds, growing plants or fresh fruit.

Upon arrival at one of New York's airports, follow signs stating "other than American passports" to immigration counters where your passport will then be inspected and stamped. Once you have reclaimed your baggage from the appropriate area (again, follow the signs), you will be approached by a Customs officer. He or she will examine the Customs declaration you should have received and filled in on your flight and direct you either toward the exit or to a Customs inspector who will then search your luggage. According to US Customs officials, only 5% of all travelers will have to have their luggage searched. There are no red or green Customs channels – you're cleared and free to go once the Customs officer has seen your fully completed declaration.

STUDENT TRAVELERS

M ANY MUSEUMS and theaters allow students a discount on admission. To receive this, however, you will need to carry proof of your student status at all times.

An International Student ID Card can be purchased quite cheaply, provided you have the right credentials, from the **Council Travel**, which has two branches in New York. At the same time, ask for a copy of the *ISIC Student Handbook*. This invaluable booklet identifies places and services throughout the US that offer a range of discounts to card holders. Included are selected accommo- dations, various museums, the- aters, tours, attractions, nightclubs and restaurants.

Although it is normally extremely difficult to obtain permission to work in the US, students are an exception to this rule, being eligible to work as part of exchange programs, or as interns. Any branch of the Student Travel Association in the UK, Australia or New Zealand will be able to help you with details of working holidays in New York. In London, contact the **Council on International Educational Exchange**.

STUDENT INFORMATION

Bunac Summer Camps
P.O. Box 430, Southberg.
[*(203) 264-0901.*
Summer only.

Council on International Educational Exchange
633 3rd Ave.
[*(212) 822-2600.*

52 Poland St, London W1V 4JQ
[*020 7478-2000.*

STA Travel
10 Downing Street.
[*(212) 627 3111, (800) 781 4040.*

CONVERSION CHART

Bear in mind that 1 US pint (0.5 liter) is a smaller measure than 1 UK pint (0.6 liter).

Imperial system:
1 inch = 2.5 centimeters
1 foot = 30 centimeters
1 mile = 1.6 kilometers
1 ounce = 28 grams
1 pound = 454 grams
1 US pint = 0.47 liter
1 US gallon = 3.8 liters

Metric system:
1 millimeter = 0.04 inch
1 centimeter = 0.4 inch
1 meter = 3 feet 3 inches
1 kilometer = 0.6 mile
1 gram = 0.04 ounce

International Student ID Card

New York daily newspapers

A newspaper vending machine

NEWSPAPERS, TELEVISION AND RADIO

YOU CAN BUY foreign newspapers, usually the previous day's issue, at **Universal News**, airports, hotels and newsstands near international business areas like the World Financial Center or Wall Street.

TV program schedules can be found in the weekly *TV Guide* magazine and the television section of the Sunday edition of *The New York Times*.

The choice of TV stations available in New York is vast. CBS operates on channel 2, NBC on channel 4, ABC on channel 7 and WNYW (Fox) on channel 5. PBS offers cultural and educational fare, including some vintage BBC programs, on channel 13. Cable TV offers everything from the Arts and Entertainment Network (channel 16) to public access programs.

AM radio stations include WCBS News (880AM) and WFAN Sports (660AM). Some FM stations are WNEW rock (102.7FM), WBGO jazz (88.3FM) and WQXR classical (96.3FM).

Information Universal News, 234 W 42 **C** *(212) 221-1809.*

ELECTRICAL APPLIANCES

ALL AMERICAN electric current flows at a standardized 110 to 120 volts AC (alternating current). You will need to bring an adapter plug and a voltage convertor that fits standard US electrical outlets. US plugs have two flat prongs.

Most modern New York hotels provide wall-mounted electric hair dryers in bathrooms. In addition, some hotels have wall plugs capable of powering both 110- and 220-volt electric shavers, but little else – not even radios. It can, in fact, be dangerous to connect anything more powerful. If you bring along sophisticated electrical appliances with you, be certain to take a battery pack as well. You will also need an adapter to recharge your spare batteries.

Few New York hotel rooms provide irons or coffee-makers. However, room service should be able to provide you with an iron upon request.

Standard plug

EMBASSIES AND CONSULATES

Australia
150 E 42nd St.
C *(212) 351-6500.*
W www.australianyc.org

Britain
845 Third Ave.
C *(212) 745-0200.*
W www.britainusa.com/ny

Canada
1251 Sixth Ave at 50th St.
C *(212) 596-1628.*
W www.canada-ny.org

Ireland
345 Park Ave.
C *(212) 319-2555.*
W www.irelandemb.org

New Zealand
37 Observatory Circle, NW, Washington, DC 20008.
C *(202) 328-4800.*
W www.nzemb.org

RELIGIOUS SERVICES

THERE ARE SOME 4,000 places of worship in New York, catering to almost any faith. Most hotels have lists of local organizations and service times. Among the leading churches and temples are:

Baptist
Riverside Church
122nd St at Riverside Dr.
C *(212) 870-6700.*

Catholic
St. Patrick's Cathedral
Fifth Ave at 50th St.
C *(212) 753-2261.*

Episcopal
St. Bartholomew's
109 E 50th St.
C *(212) 378-0200.*

Jewish
Reform
Temple Emanu-El
Fifth Ave at 65th St.
C *(212) 744-1400.*

Orthodox
Fifth Avenue Synagogue
5 E 62nd St.
C *(212) 838-2122.*

Lutheran
St. Peter's
619 Lexington Ave.
C *(212) 935-2200.*

Methodist
Christ Church United Methodist
520 Park Ave.
C *(212) 838-3036.*

Riverside Church

Personal Security and Health

Police badge

IN 1998, NEW YORK was rated the safest among large US cities with a population of more than one million. This ranks New York 166th among cities with population of over one hundred thousand. The city's police force concentrates on foot and bicycle patrols in tourist areas, and security has been beefed up in midtown, in the transportation system and at airports. While there are places where any traveler would be foolish to tread after dark – and sometimes in daylight – if you keep your wits about you and stick to the following guidelines, you should enjoy a trouble-free visit.

New York City police patrol using a range of transportation

LAW ENFORCEMENT

THE NEW YORK police department has around-the-clock foot, horse, bike and car patrols. These are concentrated in specific areas at critical times – for instance, the theater district during show times. There are police who ride the subways and buses, and the recent dramatic drop in crime statistics reflects this.

You may also see youths wearing red berets. As their T-shirts proclaim, they are Guardian Angels. Always unarmed, these safety patrols "police" the subways and midtown streets. Although tolerated by the police and often a welcome sight, they have no official powers.

GUIDELINES ON SAFETY

UNDER THE LEADERSHIP of former mayor Rudolph Giuliani, New York became a relatively safe place to roam. Common sense still rules, however, so be alert and walk as if you know where you're going. Avoid eye contact and confrontations with down-and-outs. If someone asks you for money, be careful and do not be drawn into conversation.

Avoid deserted streets. At night, if you can't afford a taxi, try to travel with a group and keep away from the Lower East Side, Chinatown, midtown west of Broadway (except Lincoln Center and Times Square) and any place off the beaten path. The Financial District (except for the World Financial Center) is deserted after business hours, and some TriBeCa and SoHo streets can be risky after dark.

Parks are often used for drug dealing. They are safest when there is a crowd for a rally, concert or other event, although you should still take precautions to avoid being pick-pocketed. If you want to go for a jog, ask your hotel concierge for a map of safe routes and follow his or her advice. When walking in the park or street, keep your wallet in an inconspicuous place and have enough change handy for phone calls and bus fares. It's best not to have to dig into your purse or wallet while standing in line. Never stop to count your money on the street, and be aware of strangers watching at bank machines. Defeat purse snatchers by carrying your bag with the clasp facing toward you and the shoulder strap across your body.

Leave valuable jewelry at home or stored at your hotel; do not allow anyone except hotel and airport personnel to carry your luggage or parcels; and stow your valuables and camera in a locked suitcase or closet safe when you leave your hotel room.

Mounted police officers patrolling the streets to keep the city safe

LOST AND FOUND

THE CHANCES are poor of recovering anything lost in New York City. There is no city-wide lost and found. The lost-and-found rooms at Grand Central and Penn Station, however, are well-run with helpful staff. Most taxi and transport firms also have lost and found departments.

In the event of loss or theft, report all missing items to the police and make sure you get a copy of the police report for

As a general rule, be alert when you walk down the street

Cap and badge worn by city police

your insurance claim. Keep a record of your valuables' serial numbers and receipts as proof of possession.

Useful Information

Lost and Found Offices

Bus and subway services
☎ (212) 712-4500.

Taxis
☎ (212) 692-8294.

Stolen or Lost Credit Cards

American Express
☎ (800) 333 AMEX (free).

Diners Club
☎ (800) 234-6377 (free).

JCB
☎ (800) 366-4522 (free).

MasterCard
☎ (800) 627-8372 (free).

VISA
☎ (800) 336-8472 (free).

Travel Insurance

T RAVEL INSURANCE is highly recommended, mainly because of the high cost of medical care. There are many types of coverage, with prices dependent on the length of your trip and the number of people covered on the policy.

Among the most important features are: accidental death, dismemberment, emergency medical and dental care, trip cancellation, and baggage and travel document loss. There are many policies that include all these items. Your travel agent or insurance company should recommend a suitable policy.

Medical Treatment

B E PREPARED to undergo an expensive experience: some of the city's practitioners and facilities are among the best around, and medical fees in the US are unregulated. Be sure to protect yourself well with insurance. A few physicians and dentists may accept credit cards, but they are much more likely to want payment in cash or traveler's checks. Hospitals accept most credit cards *(see p222)*.

A 24-hour pharmacy, one of several in the city

Emergencies

I N THE EVENT of your being involved in a medical emergency, proceed at once to a **Hospital Emergency Room**. Should you need an ambulance, telephone 911 and one will be sent. If your medical insurance is properly in order, you won't have to worry about costs.

Unless you are impoverished, it is better to avoid the city-owned hospitals listed in the telephone book Blue Pages. Instead, choose one of the many private hospitals listed in the Yellow Pages. Dial 411 and ask the operator to give you the number of the nearest public or private hospital. Other options include asking your hotel to call a doctor or dentist to visit you in your room, or finding one yourself through the **NY Hotel Urgent Medical Services**, **Dial-A-Doctor** or **NYU Dental Care**. For more general advice and information call **Travelers' Aid**, a national organization geared to helping travelers.

Crisis Information

All Emergencies
☎ 911 (or 0). This alerts police, fire and medical services.

Crime Victims Hot Line
☎ (212) 577-7777.

Dial-A-Doctor
☎ (212) 971-9692.

Hospital Emergency Rooms
St. Vincent's, 11th St and Seventh Ave.
☎ (212) 604-7998.

St. Luke's Roosevelt.
58th St and Ninth Ave.
☎ (212) 523-6800.

National Organization for Women (NOW)
☎ (212) 627-9895.

NY Hotel Urgent Medical Services
☎ (212) 737-1212.

NYU Dental Care
345 E 24th St/1st Ave.
☎ (212) 998-9800
(9am–6:30pm Mon–Thu, 9am–4pm Fri), (212) 998-9828 (weekends and after 9pm).

Pharmacy (24-hour)
Rite Aid, 50th St./8th Ave.
☎ (212) 247-8384.

Poison Control Center
☎ (212) 764-7667.

Sex Crimes Report Line
☎ (212) 267-7273.

Travelers' Aid
JFK Airport, Terminal 410.
☎ (718) 656-4870.

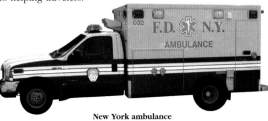

New York ambulance

Banking and Currency

N EW YORK IS THE NATION's banking center. It has a wealth of local, regional and major national banks, plus some retail branches of the leading foreign banks. Fleet Bank and Barclays are well represented in New York; the banks of Australia, Canada, Ireland, Scotland, Tokyo, and Turkey all have offices or branches.

BANKING

N EW YORK banks are generally open weekdays from 9am to 3pm. There are, however, a number of banks that open earlier or close late evening to suit commuters' needs. Tellers are behind a counter. At most banks, all the tellers will cash traveler's checks and exchange your foreign currency.

Automated teller machine (ATM)

AUTOMATED TELLER MACHINES

A CONVENIENT development in banking has been the introduction of the automated teller machine (ATM). These are found in nearly all bank lobbies and enable you to obtain American currency 24 hours a day by electronically tapping into your own bank account. ATMs usually issue American banknotes in $20 denominations.

Before you leave for New York, check with your bank about which New York City banks and ATM systems will accept your bank card and what fees and commissions will be charged on each transaction. Most ATM machines are in either the Cirrus or Plus network. They accept various US bank cards, MasterCard and VISA cards and certain others. Among the many advantages of ATMs is the swift, secure exchange of your money at the wholesale rate used between the banks when they make their million-dollar deals.

On a more cautionary note, be aware of your surroundings when using an unlocked ATM. It is best to use them only in daylight hours or when the streets are crowded.

CREDIT CARDS

M ASTERCARD, American Express, VISA, JCB and Diners Card are widely accepted throughout the United States, regardless of which company or bank issues them. These cards can also be used to obtain cash advances from various ATM machines. They may also be upgraded to confer higher spending limits. In the US you can use a credit card to pay for nearly everything imaginable, from groceries to restaurant and hotel bills, and telephone orders for movie and theater tickets. Major expenses such as tours, travel packages and expensive rentals are all best paid for by credit card. Try to avoid carrying huge sums of money around with you.

CASHING CHECKS

D OLLAR TRAVELER's checks issued by American Express and Thomas Cook are widely accepted without a fee by most of New York's department stores, shops, hotels and restaurants. Traveler's checks in other currencies, including sterling, are not universally accepted. They can usually be

Foreign currency exchange counter at Chequepoint USA

exchanged by your hotel cashier, but may require a visit to a bank. Exchange rates are printed daily in the *New York Times* and *Wall Street Journal*, and may be posted in bank windows. American Express checks are exchanged without a fee at American Express offices. Major hotels have cashiers to exchange traveler's checks.

Foreign exchange brokers are few. Among the most solidly established are **Travelex Currency Services Inc.** and **American Express**. The ones listed on the opposite page have late hours. Others are listed in the city's telephone Yellow Pages under *Foreign Money Brokers*. Expect to pay a fee, which will vary widely from one place to the next, plus a commission.

Chase Manhattan Bank offers exchange in more than 400 locations and there are scores of hole-in-the-wall check-cashing shops in Manhattan. They are listed in the Yellow Pages classified section. They may not be willing to cash your traveler's checks though, and they are very unlikely to accept or cash foreign checks.

MONEY WIRES

I N EMERGENCIES you can arrange to have money wired to you through Moneygram or Western Union.

Moneygram
C *(800) 926 9400*

Western Union
C *(800) 225 5227*

Coins

American coins come in 50-, 25-, 10-, 5- and 1-cent pieces. The new gold-tone $1 coins are now in circulation as are the State quarters, which feature an historical scene on one side. Each value of coin has a popular name: 25-cent pieces are called quarters, 10-cent pieces are called dimes, 5-cent pieces called nickels and 1-cent pieces called pennies.

**25- cent coin
(a quarter)**

**10- cent coin
(a dime)**

**5- cent coin
(a nickel)**

**1- cent coin
(a penny)**

**A one-dollar coin
or 'buck'**

Bank Notes (Bills)

Units of currency in the United States are dollars and cents. There are 100 cents to a dollar. Notes come in $1, $5, $10, $20, $50 and $100s. All bills are green, so check the amount carefully. The new $20 and $50 bills with new security features are now in circulation; they have larger numbers when compared to the old notes.

FINANCIAL SERVICES

American Express
822 Lexington Ave.
☎ *(212) 758-6510.* ◐ *9am–6pm Mon–Fri, 10am–4pm Sat.*
Helpline ☎ *(800) 333 AMEX*

Choice Forex
Grand Central Terminal.
☎ *(212) 661-7600.*
◐ *7am–9pm Mon–Fri, 10am–6pm Sat & Sun.*

Cirrus/MasterCard
☎ *(800) 424-7787*

VISA Plus
☎ *(800) 843-7587*

Travelex
1590 Broadway.
☎ *(212) 265-6063.*
1271 Broadway
☎ *(212) 679-48773* ◐ *9am–7pm Mon–Sat, 9am–5pm Sun.*
Also at: 317 Madison Ave, 510 and 29 Broadway ◐ *9am–5pm Mon–Sun.*
☎ *(800) CURRENCY.*

1- dollar bill ($1)

5- dollar bill ($5)

10- dollar bill ($50)

20- dollar bill ($20)

50- dollar bill ($50)

100- dollar bill ($100)

Using New York's Phones

Sign for public payphones

PUBLIC PAY PHONES can be found at many street corners, in hotel and office lobbies, restaurants, bars, theaters, and department stores. Few use credit cards, but you can now buy prepaid phone cards. Most phones are coin-operated and take 5-, 10- and 25-cent coins. In 2003 Neptune 800 internet payphones were introduced to the streets of New York. These have a color monitor, keyboard, and webcam, and offer customers internet access at 25 cents per minute.

NEW YORK TIME

New York is on Eastern Standard Time. When making international calls, calculate the time in the country you are calling. For the UK add 5 hours; for Australia add 15 hours; and for New Zealand add 17 hours.

PUBLIC TELEPHONES

THE STANDARD pay phone has a hand receiver and 12-button key pad and is pillar- or wall-mounted. In some locations the pay phone may belong to an independent company. The independents are often more expensive and less reliable. Regulations require each public pay phone to post information about charges, toll-free numbers and how to make calls using other carriers. Look for the

Independently operated pay phone

Verizon logo on the box to be sure the phone will reach all numbers at standard rates. To complain about service, call the **Public Service Commission**.

Useful information
Public Service Commission ((800) 342-3355 (tollfree).
To check e-mail
Times Square Information Center, 1560 Broadway, NY Computer Cafe, 247 E 57th St. ((212) 872-1704; many New York Public Libraries have Internet desks, but there is often a time limit for use.

PAY PHONE CHARGES

WITHIN the New York boroughs, the standard charge, around 25 cents, buys three minutes' talking time. If your call lasts longer, the operator will request additional payment.

Many newsstands now sell prepaid phone cards for long-distance calls; they can be bought in $5, $10, and $25 amounts. The cards offer substantial savings compared to standard rates. However, the calls are connected over the Internet and so the sound quality may not be as good as calls using a standard carrier. International long-distance rates for calls

USING A COIN-OPERATED PHONE

1 Lift the receiver.

3 Dial or press the number.

Coins
Make sure you have the correct coins available before you dial.

5 cents

10 cents

25 cents

2 Insert the necessary coin or coins. The coin drops as soon as you insert it.

4 If you do not want to complete your call or it does not get through, retrieve the coin(s) by pressing the coin return.

5 If the call is answered and you talk longer than the allotted three minutes, the operator will interrupt and ask you to deposit more coins. Pay phones do not give change.

A typical public pay phone stand

dialed direct vary from country to country. For calls to the UK, the dis-count rate starts at 1pm, then drops to an economy rate from 6pm until 7am the next day.

USEFUL NUMBERS

Directory Inquiries
☎ *411; 10-10-9000.*

US Post Office
☎ *(800) ASK USPS.*

Operator Assistance
☎ *0.*

Speaking Clock
☎ *(212) 976-1616.*

International Directory Inquiries
☎ *00.*

REACHING THE RIGHT NUMBER
• Five area codes are used in New York: 212 , 917, 646 for Manhattan; the other boroughs use 718 and 347. Calls to 800, 888, and 877 numbers are free.
• To call a number outside your own area, first dial 1. For example, to dial Queens from Manhattan dial 1 (718) (number). To call inside your area, dial the area code first.
• To call long distance from a pay phone: dial 0 followed by the area code and then the number. The operator will answer and tell you how much money you need to deposit.
• To make an international direct call: dial 011 followed by the country code (New Zealand: 64; Australia: 61; UK: 44), then the city or area code (minus the first 0) and the local number.
• To make an international call via the operator: dial 01 followed by the country code, the city code (minus the first 0) and then the local number.
• International Directory Inquiries are on 00. International operator assistance is on 01.
• **In an emergency, phone 911.**

Sending A Letter

US postal service logo

APART FROM post offices, letters can be mailed at your hotel concierge desk (which usually also sells stamps); in letter slots in office building lobbies; in air, rail and bus terminals; and in the occasional street mailbox. These are always painted blue, or red, white and blue. Mail in most mailboxes is not picked up on weekends.

POSTAL SERVICES

THE CITY'S main **General Post Office** is open 24 hours a day. Stamps can be bought here or from branch offices (a handy one is in the Empire State Building) or from coin-operated machines in pharmacies, department stores and bus and train stations. All letters go first class.

The post office offers three special delivery services: **Express Mail** service for next-day delivery, **Priority Mail** service for two-day delivery, and **International Express Mail** for overseas. Priority Mail will also pick up letters on weekdays for an extra charge. Private express mail can be arranged through

Colorful US stamps

hotel concierges or with one of the delivery services listed in the telephone book.
Useful information
General Post Office, 421 8th Ave.
☎ *(212) 967-8585.*
☎ *(800) 222-1811* Priority and Express Mail.
☎ *(800) 463-3339* FedEx.
☎ *(800) 225-5345* DHL.
☎ *(800) 782-7892* UPS.
Internet guides
W www.bigyellow.com
W www.usps.com

HELD MAIL

MAIL will be held for you for 30 days at the General Post Office's General Delivery window. Mail can be sent to any local post office by giving the zip code or name. Address mail with: Name, General Delivery, US Post Office, New York, NY 10001.

Express Mail   **Priority Mail**

Mailboxes
Mailboxes can be few and far between on New York streets, and it may be easier to find a post office. Instructions on how to use each mailbox are written on the box. If you use Express or Priority services, weigh your letters at a post office to figure out the postage needed.

Standard mailbox

MANY INTERNATIONAL airlines have direct flights to New York. It is also very well served by charter and domestic services. Price wars between airlines have reduced fares, and domestic flights now prove a viable alternative to bus and train tickets; group tour package prices are often

Grand Central Terminal

unbeatable. The *QM2* is one of several cruise ships that dock in the city. Long-distance trains serving New York are clean and comfortable. Interstate and long distance buses have air-conditioning, video screens and on-board toilets. For information on arriving in New York see the map on pages 230–1.

AIR TRAVEL

NEW YORK CAN be reached by air direct from most major cities. The flight from London takes about eight hours. However, there are no direct flights from Australia or New Zealand. Instead, the airlines fly to the West coast, which takes around 14 hours, land, refuel and then continue on to New York.

Among the main carriers to New York are **Air Canada**, **Delta**, **Continental**, **British Airways**, **American Airlines**, **Virgin Atlantic** and **United Airlines**. All international flights arrive at Newark or JFK airports.

APEX (Advance Purchase Excursion) tickets for the scheduled airlines are usually the cheapest return fares apart from package tours. But they must be bought in advance and are valid for a stay of 7 to 30 days. Some airlines offer cheaper fares if you limit your stay to specified periods. Senior citizens may also receive discounts on some flights.

AIRLINE NUMBERS

Air Canada **C** *(888) 247-2262.*
W www.aircanada.ca

American Airlines **C** *(800) 433-7300.*
W www.aa.com

British Airways **C** *(800) AIRWAYS.*
W www.british-airways.com

Continental **C** *(800) 231-0856.*
W www.flycontinental.com

Delta **C** *(800) 241-4141.*
W www. delta.com

United Airlines **C** *(800) 241-6522*
W www.united.com

Virgin Atlantic **C** *(800) 862-8621*
W www.virgin-atlantic.com

OCEAN TRAVEL

NEW YORK IS a regular port of call for many cruise liners, in addition to the *QM2*, which docks there, via Southampton, 25 times a year. You can also take the *QM2* from New York to Australia and New Zealand. Ocean travel offers an expensive but

Long-distance Greyhound bus

relaxing way of traveling to New York. Ships dock at the Hudson River piers in midtown Manhattan.

LONG-DISTANCE BUSES

ALL LONG-DISTANCE buses such as **Greyhound Lines** arrive in the city at the **Port Authority Bus Terminal**. Buses from here also connect with the three airports. With over 6,000 buses arriving and leaving daily and carrying some 172,000 passengers, the atmosphere is chaotic. Many hotels are also accessible directly from the terminal.
Useful information Greyhound Bus Lines **C** *(800) 231-2222. (24 hrs).* **W** www.greyhound.com
Port Authority Bus Terminal. W 40th St and Eighth Ave.
C *(212) 564-8484 (24 hrs).*
W www.panynj.gov

TRAIN TRAVEL

AMTRAK TRAINS from Canada, upstate New York, southern, northeastern and western states all stop at Penn Station. Metro-North lines from upstate New York and Connecticut arrive at Grand Central Terminal.

Ocean liner anchored in Manhattan

New York Airports

THE THREE MAIN airports (Newark, JFK and La Guardia) are all well connected to central Manhattan. Look for uniformed "skycaps" – scarlet-capped porters wearing distinctive badges, who will help you with your luggage. Never trust anyone else to help carry your bags – you may never see them again. Taxi dispatchers will help you into a licensed taxi at the taxi area.

GETTING INTO MANHATTAN

THE GROUND Transportation center at each airport will give you information on the ways you can continue your trip. The most useful services, operating from LaGuardia and JFK, are the **New York Airport Service** and **Super Shuttle**. The former stops at Grand Central; the latter will drop you anywhere in Manhattan. New Jersey Transit buses and **Olympia Airport Express** also go to and from each airport into the city. The fare on the Olympia buses is one of the best bargains.

Shared vehicle rides are offered at JFK and LaGuardia by **Classic Airport Share Ride** and **Connecticut Limo**. You can sometimes share a taxi or one of the independent (gypsy) cabs into Manhattan. For the price of a subway ride, the "A" line connects with a shuttle bus and takes passengers to

Taxi dispatcher

and from JFK. The M60 city bus also goes to and from LaGuardia. Most of the car rental firms have courtesy telephones at the baggage-claim areas. Telephone numbers and web addresses for your advance reservations are listed on page 234.

BUS COMPANIES

New York Airport Service (718) 875-8200.

Classic Limousine (800) 666-4949. W www.classictrans.com

Super Shuttle 212-BLUE VAN. W www.supershuttle.com

Olympia Airport Express (212) 964-6233. W www.olympiabus.com

Connecticut Limo (800) 472-5466. W www.ctlimo.com

LA GUARDIA (LGA)

PRINCIPALLY SERVING business travelers, La Guardia lies 8 miles (13 km) east of Manhattan on the north side of Long Island in Queens.

Upon arrival, you can rent luggage trolleys from the baggage-claim area next to the luggage carousels. Skycaps are on hand to assist you. Baggage can also be left in the Tele-Trip business center on the departure level. Foreign exchange desks are located around the Central Terminal.

Uniformed taxi dispatchers at the airport are on duty at peak hours. Only use yellow taxis licensed by the city. The cost of tolls, plus a small surcharge after 8pm and all day Sunday, will be added to the fare shown on the meter (about $20–$30 to midtown).

Useful information Airport Information Service (718) 533-3400. W www.laguardiaairport.com W www.panynj.gov

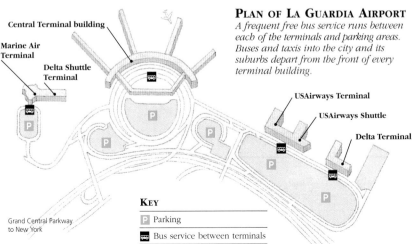
Transatlantic jet

PLAN OF LA GUARDIA AIRPORT
A frequent free bus service runs between each of the terminals and parking areas. Buses and taxis into the city and its suburbs depart from the front of every terminal building.

Central Terminal building

Marine Air Terminal

Delta Shuttle Terminal

USAirways Terminal

USAirways Shuttle

Delta Terminal

Grand Central Parkway to New York

KEY

P Parking

Bus service between terminals

JFK Airport

NEW YORK'S main airport, JFK, is 15 miles (24 km) southeast of Manhattan, in the borough of Queens. American Airlines, British Airways, Delta, Continental, and United have their own arrivals buildings, with customs and immigration facilities. Other international airlines use Terminals 1, 5, and 6. A $10 billion airport expansion includes a new terminal for American Airlines.

Luggage trolleys are free on

Main Hall at the International Arrivals Building, JFK

Airport information signs at JFK

arrival in the meeting area. Foreign exchange offices are located in all terminals.

Transportation to Manhattan can be arranged 24 hours a day at the Ground Transportation desk on the ground level near the baggage-claim. Courtesy phones are provided by car rental companies. Most have shuttle service to their rental offices. Taxis wait outside terminals. A trip to Manhattan takes up to an hour; there is a flat fee of $45 plus tolls. The New York Airport Service bus is reliable, safe, and operates

24 hours. For early morning flights there are hotels near the airport. Hotels can be booked at the Meegan Services desk.

A light-rail system, AirTrain JFK, began service to the Howard Beach terminal at the end of 2002, and started service to Jamaica Airtrain terminal in 2003, providing direct onward connections to the city subway.

USEFUL ADDRESSES

Airport Information Service
ⓘ *(718) 244-4444.*

Best Western JFK Airport
138–10 135th Ave, Queens.
ⓒ *(718) 322-8700.*

Holiday Inn JFK
144–02 135th Ave, Queens.
ⓒ *(718) 659-0200.*

✈ Helicopter Flight Services ⓒ
(212) 355-0801. Ⓦ
www.heliny.com; Liberty
Helicopters ⓒ *(888) 692-4354.*

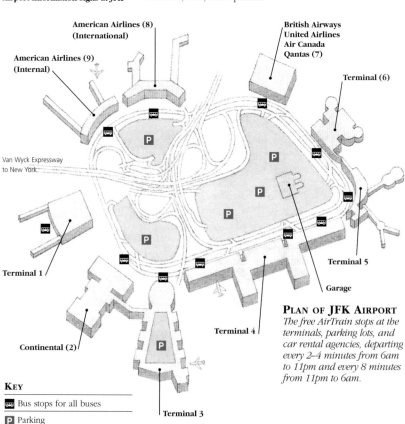

American Airlines (8)
(International)

American Airlines (9)
(Internal)

British Airways
United Airlines
Air Canada
Qantas (7)

Terminal (6)

Van Wyck Expressway
to New York

Terminal 1

Continental (2)

Terminal 5

Garage

Terminal 4

Terminal 3

PLAN OF JFK AIRPORT
The free AirTrain stops at the terminals, parking lots, and car rental agencies, departing every 2–4 minutes from 6am to 11pm and every 8 minutes from 11pm to 6am.

KEY

🚌 Bus stops for all buses

🅿 Parking

NEWARK AIRPORT

Bus terminal at Newark Airport

KEY

P Parking

🚌 Bus stop

— Newark AirTrain

PLAN OF NEWARK AIRPORT

The free AirTrain services connect the terminals and parking lots. Every 3–4 minutes from 5am to midnight and every 10–24 minutes from midnight to 5am. The journey time between terminals is 7–11 minutes.

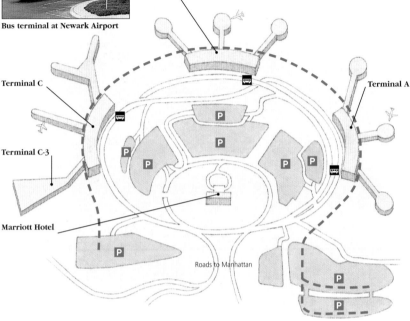

Terminal B
(International Arrivals)

Terminal C

Terminal A

Terminal C-3

Marriott Hotel

Roads to Manhattan

Newark, New York's second largest international airport, is about 16 miles (26 km) southwest of Manhattan, in New Jersey.

Most international flights arrive at Terminal "B." Baggage trolleys are free for arriving international passengers. There is no baggage room. Foreign exchange desks are available in each terminal.

The Ground Transportation services desk, open 24 hours a day, is next to the baggage-claim area. Courtesy phones are provided by limousine and car rental firms. Many of these have a free shuttle service to their rental offices.

There are taxi stands located outside most arrival areas. Uniformed taxi dispatchers will also help you hail a cab. Never accept a ride into town from anyone who approaches you in the terminal: they may not have insurance and could charge an outrageous fare. The trip into Manhattan takes

about 40–60 minutes and will cost you up to $50.

Buses to Manhattan can take 40 minutes to over an hour, but cost about $12. Electronic boards around the terminal list departure times. AirTrain Newark (www.airtrain newark.com) connects you to the NJ Transit and Amtrak trains; it then continues to New York Penn Street. The 25-minute journey costs $11.55.

Hotels can be booked on arrival through the courtesy phones that are linked directly to various Manhattan

hotels. At Newark, these are located in all the terminals.

USEFUL ADDRESSES

Port Authority at Newark Airport
📞 *(888) 397-4636.*
🌐 www.newarkairport.com

Holiday Inn International
1000 Spring St, Elizabeth, N J.
📞 *(800) 465-4329.*

Marriott Hotel
Newark Airport grounds.
📞 *(800) 228-9290.*

Arrival and departure monitors at Newark Airport

Arriving in New York

THIS MAP SHOWS the links between New York's three airports and the center of Manhattan. It also illustrates rail connections linking New York to the rest of the United States and Canada. Travel information, including travel times for subway, bus, rail and helicopter services, is listed in each information box. The passenger ship terminal, New York's key point of arrival for the flood of post-war immigrants, is located a short distance from the center of Manhattan. Port Authority Bus Terminal, on the West Side, provides services across the city.

Ships at the passenger terminal

PASSENGER SHIP TERMINAL
Piers 88–92 for QM2 and other cruise ship arrivals and departures.

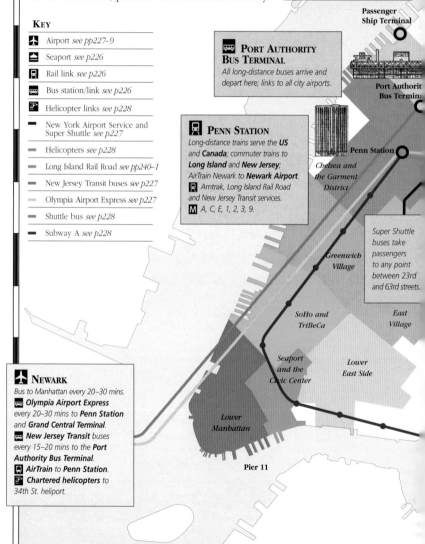

KEY

✈	Airport see pp227–9
⚓	Seaport see p226
🚊	Rail link see p226
🚌	Bus station/link see p226
🚁	Helicopter links see p228
▬	New York Airport Service and Super Shuttle see p227
▬	Helicopters see p228
▬	Long Island Rail Road see pp240–1
▬	New Jersey Transit buses see p227
▬	Olympia Airport Express see p227
▬	Shuttle bus see p228
▬	Subway A see p228

Passenger Ship Terminal

🚌 PORT AUTHORITY BUS TERMINAL
All long-distance buses arrive and depart here; links to all city airports.

Port Authority Bus Terminal

🚊 PENN STATION
Long-distance trains serve the **US** and **Canada**; commuter trains to **Long Island** and **New Jersey**; AirTrain Newark to **Newark Airport**.
🚊 Amtrak, Long Island Rail Road and New Jersey Transit services.
Ⓜ A, C, E, 1, 2, 3, 9.

Penn Station

Chelsea and the Garment District

Greenwich Village

Super Shuttle buses take passengers to any point between 23rd and 63rd streets.

SoHo and TriBeCa

East Village

Seaport and the Civic Center

Lower East Side

✈ NEWARK
Bus to Manhattan every 20–30 mins.
🚌 **Olympia Airport Express** every 20–30 mins to **Penn Station** and **Grand Central Terminal**.
🚌 **New Jersey Transit** buses every 15–20 mins to the **Port Authority Bus Terminal**.
🚊 AirTrain to **Penn Station**.
🚁 **Chartered helicopters** to 34th St. heliport.

Lower Manhattan

Pier 11

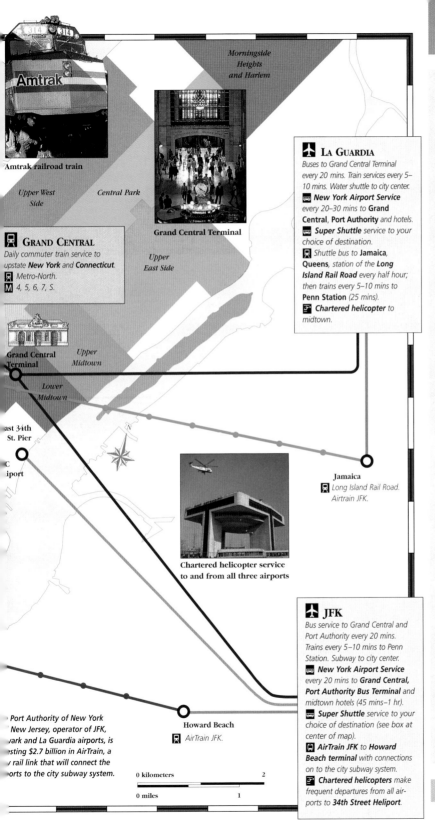

Amtrak railroad train

Morningside
Heights
and Harlem

Upper West
Side

Central Park

Grand Central Terminal

🚆 GRAND CENTRAL

Daily commuter train service to
upstate **New York** and **Connecticut**.
🚆 Metro-North.
Ⓜ 4, 5, 6, 7, S.

Upper
East Side

Grand Central
Terminal

Upper
Midtown

Lower
Midtown

ast 34th
St. Pier

C
iport

N

✈ LA GUARDIA

Buses to Grand Central Terminal
every 20 mins. Train services every 5–
10 mins. Water shuttle to city center.
🚌 **New York Airport Service**
every 20–30 mins to **Grand
Central**, **Port Authority** and hotels.
🚐 **Super Shuttle** service to your
choice of destination.
🚌 Shuttle bus to **Jamaica**,
Queens, station of the **Long
Island Rail Road** every half hour;
then trains every 5–10 mins to
Penn Station (25 mins).
🚁 **Chartered helicopter** to
midtown.

Jamaica
🚆 Long Island Rail Road.
Airtrain JFK.

Chartered helicopter service
to and from all three airports

✈ JFK

Bus service to Grand Central and
Port Authority every 20 mins.
Trains every 5–10 mins to Penn
Station. Subway to city center.
🚌 **New York Airport Service**
every 20 mins to **Grand Central**,
Port Authority Bus Terminal and
midtown hotels (45 mins–1 hr).
🚐 **Super Shuttle** service to your
choice of destination (see box at
center of map).
🚆 **AirTrain JFK** to **Howard
Beach terminal** with connections
on to the city subway system.
🚁 **Chartered helicopters** make
frequent departures from all air-
ports to **34th Street Heliport**.

Howard Beach
🚆 AirTrain JFK.

Port Authority of New York
New Jersey, operator of JFK,
ark and La Guardia airports, is
esting $2.7 billion in AirTrain, a
rail link that will connect the
orts to the city subway system.

0 kilometers   2

0 miles   1

Notes

WITH OVER SIX thousand miles of streets, walking around New York could prove difficult. But the city is a network of districts and many of the major sites can be visited area by area. Taxis are best for door-to-door transit but can be held up in traffic jams, especially during rush hours. The city's bus service is reliable and cheap but often slow. Subways are quick, reliable and cheap, and make stops throughout central Manhattan. There are weekly and day passes that are valid for all public transportation. These are the best value when visiting the sights of the city.

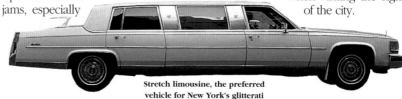

Stretch limousine, the preferred vehicle for New York's glitterati

NEGOTIATING THE AVENUES AND STREETS

MANHATTAN'S avenues run approximately north to south; its streets (except in the older areas) run east to west. Fifth Avenue is used to divide East and West Street addresses; Five West 40th Street is, for example, a few doors west of Fifth Avenue on 40th Street, and Five East 40th is a few doors to the east.

Most streets in midtown are one-way. In general, traffic is eastbound on even-numbered streets and westbound on odd-numbered streets. Avenues also tend to be one-way, alternating northbound or southbound. First, Third (above 23rd Street), Madison, Eighth, Avenue of the Americas (6th Ave) and Tenth avenues, are all northbound, while Second, Lexington, Fifth, Seventh, and Ninth avenues and Broadway below 59th Street are southbound. There is two-way traffic on York, Park, Eleventh and Twelfth avenues and Broadway above 60th Street.

Although most city blocks north of Houston Street are rectangular, they are not very uniform: east–west blocks are three or even four times longer than north–south blocks.

Certain streets have more than one name, for instance, Avenue of the Americas is also Sixth Avenue. Note too that Park Avenue South is not the same as Park Avenue. Many intersections and plazas have titles commemorating people or events. The maps in this guide use the names most often used by New Yorkers.

Rush-hour gridlock in Manhattan

FINDING AN ADDRESS

A useful formula has been devised to help pinpoint any **Avenue Address**. By dropping the last digit of the address, dividing the remainder by 2, then adding or subtracting the **Key Number** given here, you will discover the nearest cross street. For example: To find No. 826 Lexington Avenue, first you have to drop the 6; divide 82 by 2, which is 41; then add **22** (the key number). Therefore, the nearest cross street is 63rd Street.

MADISON AVENUE

A road sign for Madison Avenue positioned at an intersection with a street

Avenue Address	Key Number	Avenue Address	Key Number
1st Ave	+3	9th Ave	+13
2nd Ave	+3	10th Ave	+14
3rd Ave	+10	Amsterdam Ave	+60
4th Ave	+8	Audubon Ave	+165
5th Ave, up to 200	+13	Broadway above	
5th Ave, up to 400	+16	23rd St	-30
5th Ave, up to 600	+18	Central Park W, divide	
5th Ave, up to 775	+20	full number by 10 +60	
5th Ave 775–1286,		Columbus Ave	+60
do not divide by 2	-18	Convent Ave	+127
5th Ave, up to 1500	+45	Lenox Ave	+110
5th Ave, up to 2000	+24	Lexington Ave	+22
(6th) Ave of the		Madison Ave	+26
Americas	-12	Park Ave	+35
7th Ave below		Park Ave South	+08
110th St	+12	Riverside Drive, divide	
7th Ave above		full number by 10 +72	
110th St	+20	St Nicholas Ave	+110
8th Ave	+10	West End Ave	+60

PLANNING YOUR JOURNEY

THE STREETS and sidewalks are busiest during the rush hours – 8 to 10am, 11:30am to 1:30pm and 4:30 to 6:30pm, Monday to Friday. Throughout these periods it is better to face the crowds on foot than attempt any journey by bus, taxi or subway. At other times of day and during certain holiday periods, the traffic is often much lighter and you should reach your destination quickly.

There are, of course, a few exceptions. Fifth Avenue should always be avoided on parade days (St. Patrick's Day and Thanksgiving Day are the worst). Celebrity visits or one of the regular demonstrations at City Hall can cause major disruption to the traffic. The area around Seventh Avenue, south of 42nd Street, is likely to be busy during the day with the truck and handcart traffic of New York's garment industry.

WALKING

MOST INTERSECTIONS between avenues and streets have lampposts with name-markers and electric traffic signals. The traffic lights show red (stop) and green (go) for vehicles and "Walk–Don't Walk" for pedestrians. Most New Yorkers, however, rely on their own judgment rather than on the numerous "Walk" signs.

Remember that vehicles keep to the right. There are no

Pedestrian crossing

Do not cross the street

You may cross the street

Staten Island Ferry leaving Battery Park

Circle Line tour boat

cautionary "Look Left" signs to alert you to the direction of oncoming traffic. There are, however, numerous one-way streets, so it's best to look both ways before you cross. Beware, too, of cars, trucks and taxis turning the corner behind you as you start to cross the street.

There are pedestrian crossings at some intersections. These are officially designated pedestrian crossing points (at Rockefeller Center for instance) and are closely monitored by the police. The city has a few underground walkways for pedestrians in Central Park.

WATER TAXI

THE NEW YORK water taxi arrived in 2002 and runs from East 90th Street Pier to Pier 84. Visit www.nywatertaxi.com for more information.

FERRIES

There are two ferries of interest to visitors (see also p217): the Circle Line runs a ferry to the Statue of Liberty and Ellis Island several times each day from Battery Park at the southern tip of Manhattan – [W] www.circleline.com. The 24-hour Staten Island ferry from Battery Park travels the channel and offers splendid views of lower Manhattan, the Statue of Liberty, Ellis Island, the bridges and Governors Island. The round trip is the best bargain in New York; it's free.

CYCLING

CYCLING IN THE city is safest on the park pathways (Central Park and along the East and Hudson rivers) in daylight hours. You can rent bikes at Columbus Circle or the Loeb Boathouse in Central Park.
Useful information
Central Park Bike Rental, 2 Columbus Circle.
[C] (212) 541-8759.
[W] www.centralparkbiketour.com

Cyclist in Central Park

Driving in New York

HEAVY TRAFFIC AND EXPENSIVE rental cars make driving in New York a frustrating experience. You must wear a seat belt. The speed limit is 30 mph (48 km/h) – which is difficult to exceed because of Manhattan's potholes and traffic. Most streets are one-way, and there are traffic lights at every corner. Driving is on the right.

Busy traffic heading down Sixth Avenue

RENTING A CAR

TO RENT A CAR you must be at least 25 years old, or pay a surcharge. You will need a valid driver's license (for foreign visitors an International Driver's License is useful), a passport, and a credit card or you will have to pay a deposit.

Unless you are adequately covered by your own insurance policy, you should also take out damage and liability protection, as personal injury lawsuits are very common. Refill with gas before you return the car or you'll pay double the normal price for fuel. It is cheaper to rent a car in the city than at the airports.

TRAFFIC SIGNS

Black-and-white markings on many street crossings mean that pedestrians have right of way. At intersections, they indicate that traffic should keep out when the light is red. Unlike the rest of New York State, you can never turn right on a red light unless there is a sign indicating otherwise.

Traffic flows in a single direction

PARKING

PARKING IN Manhattan is difficult and costly. Parking areas and parking garages post their rates at the entrance. Some hotels include parking charges in their room rates.

In some areas there are meters at the curb for short-term (20–60 minutes) parking. Don't be tempted to park at out-of-order meters – you may receive a parking ticket. Yellow street and curb markings mean no parking.

"Alternate-side" parking applies on most of the city's side streets. Cars may usually be left all day and night but must be moved to the other side of the street before 8am the next day. For specific information call the **Transportation Department**.

PENALTIES

IF YOU RECEIVE a parking ticket, you have seven days to pay the required fine or to appeal against it. If you have any queries about your ticket call the **Parking Violations Bureau** between 8:30am and 7pm on any weekday.

New York's tow-away crews are extremely active, and one-third of cars towed suffer damage. If you cannot find your car at its parking place, first of all call the traffic department's tow-away office. The pound is open 24 hours a day, Monday to Saturday. You can redeem your car for a hefty fine of $150, plus $10 per day storage fee. Traveler's checks, certified checks, money orders and cash are all accepted. There is an ATM machine *(see p222)* on the premises. If you have rented the car, the contract must be produced, and only the authorized driver may redeem the car. If the car is not at the pound, report it to the police.

Useful information
Police emergencies only 911;
Parking Violations Bureau (718) 802-3636; Traffic Dept, Tow Pound, Pier 76, W 38th St and 12th Ave; uptown at the 207th St. Pound (212) 788-7800;
Transportation Dept 311.

BRIDGE TOLLS

MOST MAJOR access routes in and out of New York City levy tolls. These vary in price from $1.50 for some of the smaller bridges, to $6.00 for the George Washington Bridge between New York and New Jersey. The bridges of the Triborough Bridge Authority charge $3.50 each way. All tolls must be paid in cash. Avoid E-Z Pass lanes, marked with purple signs, which are only for holders of pre-paid passes.

CAR RENTAL AGENCIES

IF YOU NEED TO rent a car while in New York, agencies are listed in the telephone directory under *Automobile Renting*. The major rental companies include:

Avis (800) 331-1212.
W www.avis.com

Budget (800) 527-0700.
W www.drivebudget.com

Dollar (800) 800-4000.
W www.dollar.com

Hertz (800) 654-3131.
W www.hertz.com

National (800) CAR RENT.
W www.nationalcar.com

Entry prohibited

50 mph (80 km/h) speed limit

Give way to all vehicles

Stop at intersection

New York's Taxis

New York taxi cab

Aᴸᴸ ʟɪᴄᴇɴsᴇᴅ ᴛᴀxɪ cabs are yellow. If their roof numbers are lit up, they are available and can be flagged down. Occupied cabs have their top lights switched off. Taxis that are not on duty have their "Off-Duty" sign lit. Only licensed cabs are authorized to pick up people who hail them from the street; accepting a ride from anyone else can be dangerous and expensive.

TAKING A CAB

Tʜᴇʀᴇ ᴀʀᴇ more than 12,000 Yellow Cabs in New York. Each one has a meter, and many can issue printed receipts. A taxi can carry up to four passengers with a single fare covering everyone on board.

Taxi stands are scarce; hotels, Penn Station and Grand Central Terminal are by far the best places to seek cabs.

Licensed taxis undergo periodic inspections and are insured against accidents and losses. Non-licensed or "gypsy" cabs are unlikely to have these safeguards, and are not recommended.

Once the cab driver accepts a passenger the meter starts ticking at $2.50. The fare increases 40 cents after each additional 292 yards (267 meters) or every 120 seconds of waiting time. There is an additional 50-cent charge between 8pm and 6am, and a $1 charge between 4pm and 8pm on weekdays.

A few drivers now accept credit cards but most will want to be paid in cash. Tip the driver about 15%.

Cab driving is a traditional occupation of newly arrived immigrants and, as such, communication can be a problem. Although owners of licensed cabs must pass exams in

```
I ♥ NEW YORK
TRIP#    004653
09:11AM 11-15-92
MEDALLION# 6N64
DIST        2.30
FARE $      6.00
TLC:212-221-TAXI
```

A printed receipt available from most taxi cabs

English comprehension and the layout of the city, they will not necessarily understand either. Make sure your driver understands exactly where you want to go before you start your ride.

By law, a driver must take you anywhere in the city unless the off-duty sign is lit and the roof light is off. The driver should not ask you your destination until after you've sat down, and must follow your requests not to smoke, to open or close a window, and to pick up or drop off passengers as you direct. If he or she doesn't comply you can report them to the **Taxi & Limousine Commission**.

Each yellow cab displays the driver's photograph and registered number next to the meter. Drivers can be sullen, or try to overcharge or not cooperate with some of your requests. Make a note of the driver's number or the license or receipt number (if you have requested one), and report it to the Commission.

Yellow taxi cabs dominating one of the city's avenues

TAXI NUMBERS

Taxi & Limousine Commission
☎ *311*

Lost and Found
☎ *311*

If you would prefer to use a taxi that has been radio-dispatched, rather than hailing one on the street, call:

Allstate Car & Limousine
☎ *(800) 453-4099 (toll free).*

Chris Limousines
☎ *(718) 356-3232.*

Tri-State and Limo Service
☎ *(212) 777-7171.*

Notes

A meter will display your fare as it mounts up. Additional costs are then shown separately.

The roof-light illuminates the cab's number as well as the driver's "Off-Duty" sign.

Traveling by Bus

The city's more than 4,000 blue-and-white buses cover more than 200 routes in the five boroughs. Many run 24 hours a day, every day. The buses are modern, clean and air-conditioned. Traveling by bus is a good way to take in many of New York's sights. Buses are also considered safe and tend not to get crowded. Smoking is forbidden on all public buses, and animals except service animals (guide dogs) are not allowed.

Fare

You can pay the fare on a bus using a MetroCard or exact change (these must be in coins only). Bus drivers cannot make change, and fare boxes do not accept dollar bills, half dollars or pennies. You can buy the MetroCard at any subway station booth.

If you are need to take more than one bus to reach your destination, you are eligible for a free transfer. If you pay your bus fare with a MetroCard, a free bus-to-subway, subway-to-local bus, or local bus-to-bus transfer is electronically placed on the card. If you pay with exact change, be sure to ask the driver for a transfer ticket when you pay.

There are discount fares for senior citizens and the disabled. All buses can "kneel," which helps elderly people to board *(see p218)*, and they are also accessible to wheelchairs via a lift at the rear or front.

Recognizing Your Bus

Each bus stop serves more than one route, so look for the route number posted on the lighted strip above the windshield on the front of the bus. Ask the driver if he or she will be stopping at your destination or close to it.

Exit the bus through the double doors toward the rear.

Riding the Bus

Buses will stop only at the designated bus stops. They follow north–south routes on the major avenues, stopping every two or three blocks. Crosstown buses, running east–west, stop at every block *(see p232)*. Many routes run a 24-hour daily service, which becomes a lot less frequent during the evening and at night; other bus services operate only during the peak hours of 7am to 10pm.

Bus stops are marked by red, white and blue signs and yellow paint along the curb. Most also have bus shelters. A route map and schedule is posted at each stop. When you have identified your bus, enter at the front door and present your MetroCard or put your change in the fare box. Request a transfer if you will be changing to another bus. The majority of New York's bus drivers are very friendly and will call out your stop if you

The fare box is just inside the entrance doors, next to the driver.

Bus stops often have three-sided, glass-walled shelters.

This bus map shows the route and main stopping-off points for route M15.

ask them to. To request a stop when traveling on the bus, press the yellow or black vertical call strip between the windows. A "Stop Requested" sign near the driver will then light up. If the bus is crowded, it is worth starting to move toward the exit door when you are a few blocks from your stop.

Leave through the double door located toward the rear of the bus. The driver will activate the door release as soon as the bus has stopped, but you then have to push the yellow stripe on the door, not the door itself. This automatically opens the door and keeps it open.

Route numbers appear on the front and side of the bus.

Enter the bus through the doors at the front.

LONG-DISTANCE & COMMUTER BUSES

BUSES TO THE rest of the US and Canada leave from the **Port Authority Bus Terminal**. Another terminal, at the Manhattan end of the George Washington Bridge, is for local buses to northern New Jersey and New York's Rockland County.

Bus tickets at Port Authority are on sale in the main concourse. The long-distance bus companies, Greyhound, Peter Pan, and Adirondack and the commuter Short Line and NJ Transit have their own ticket counters. There are no reservations taken on any of these bus lines.

There are bathrooms open from 6am to 10pm, but caution is advised. The homeless congregate in Port Authority.

A Greyhound bus arriving in New York en route to Port Authority

BUS INFORMATION

Route Maps
Available from MTA, 370 Jay St, Brooklyn, NY 11201 or NYC Visitors Center, 810 7th Ave (212-484-1222).
MTA Travel Information
📞 *(718) 330-1234 (24 hrs).*
🌐 *www.mta.info*

Port Authority Bus Terminal
West 40th St and Eighth Ave.
📞 *(212) 564-8484.*
🌐 *www.panynj.gov*

George Washington Bridge Terminal
178th St. and Broadway. 📞 *(800) 221 9903.* 🌐 *www.panynj.gov*

Lost Property
📞 *(212) 712-4500.*

SIGHTSEEING BY BUS
For a pleasant and cheap alternative to a tour bus, hop on a city bus and see New York with the New Yorkers. Bus routes M1 and M6 down Fifth and Seventh Avenues to the Battery, returning north via the Wall Street area, Madison Avenue, and Sixth Avenue. Route M5 gives fine views of the Hudson River as buses travel north on Riverside Drive to the George Washington Bridge at 178th Street. Route M104 travels from the United Nations at First Avenue across 42nd Street, through Times Square, then follows Broadway north by Lincoln Center to Columbia University at 125th Street.

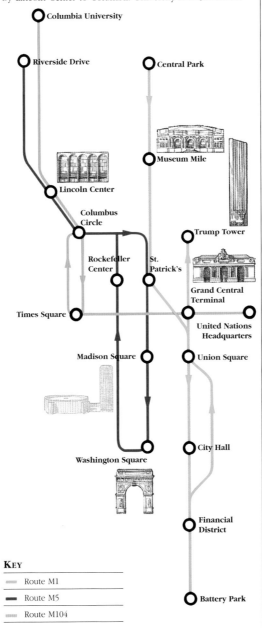

KEY

▬	Route M1
▬	Route M5
▬	Route M104

Using the Subway

New York subway logo

THE SUBWAY is the quickest and most reliable way to travel in the city. The vast system extends over 233 route miles (375 km) and has 468 stations. Most routes operate 24 hours a day throughout the year. Night services are less frequent, and fewer trains run on weekends. In the past few years the subway system has been completely upgraded, and the trains are now air-conditioned, well lit, safer and more comfortable.

USING THE SUBWAY

Many subway entrances are marked by illuminated spheres: green where the station booth is manned around the clock; red means that there is restricted entry. The stations are marked by a sign bearing the name of the station and the numbers or letters of the routes passing through it.

The subway system runs 24 hours a day, but not all sections of all routes operate at all times. The basic service tends to run from 6:30am to midnight. Generally, trains run every 2 to 5 minutes during rush hour; every 5 to 10 minutes through the day; every 5 to 15 minutes in the evening; and every 20 minutes from midnight to 6:30am.

Bear in mind that there are two types of trains. Local trains stop at all stations, and express trains are faster and skip many of the less major stops. Whether a train is local or express is indicated on the outside of each subway car. If you are boarding an express train ensure that it stops at the station where you intend to get off. Local and express stations are distinguished on every subway map.

THE SUBWAY SYSTEM

The New York City system covers Manhattan, the Bronx, Brooklyn, and Queens. Twenty-six subway lines, more than any other system in the world, serve 468 stations. Each line is identified by a color and a letter or number. Route four is on the green line and is labelled on maps and in stations with a four in a green circle. The train on route four, the Lexington Avenue Express, runs between Woodlawn and Utica Avenue stations. Other trains (routes five and six) run along the green line. The four, five, and six routes converge in Manhattan, but vary considerably through the outer boroughs.

You will find a Customer Information bulletin board near the main booth in every station. The maps posted here have a comprehensive guide that explains the trains and timetable of each route.

Local, express stops, and interchange points are identified on the map. The letters and numbers below the station names indicate which routes serve that particular station. A letter or number in heavy type indicates that trains on that route stop there from 6am to midnight; letters in lighter type mean that the route is served by a part-time service only; a boxed letter or number shows the last stop on the line.

This station's green sphere shows that it is staffed continuously

SUBWAY FARE

The fare is $2 no matter how far you travel. The MetroCard, a pass with an electronic strip that you can either top-up with credit or treat as a transit pass, has replaced tokens as the main means of paying subway fares. The MetroCard is also valid on the city's buses.

The one-day FunPass for $7 and the 7-day Unlimited Ride MetroCard for $24 allow unlimited travel on both subways and buses. Alternatively, you can put from $4 to $80 of credit on a MetroCard. For any amount over $10, you will receive a 20% bonus. So, if you put $10 on your pass, you will receive 6 journeys for the price of five; for $20, you will receive 12 rides for the price of 10. MetroCard is sold at 3,500 locations, many of them convenience stores, around the city. You can buy a MetroCard or top up your existing one at vending machines found in subway stations. They accept cash, credit cards and debit cards.

SAFETY ON THE SUBWAY

In general, the safest, but most crowded, times to travel are between the rush hours of 9am to 4:30pm. Use common sense, stand in the "Off-Hour Waiting Area" on the platforms, and always be sure of where you are going when you use the subway. It is safe to travel to outer boroughs, although it is not a good idea for anyone to travel alone after 10pm. Use the central cars and avoid all cyc contact with any unsavory characters.

In an emergency, contact either the station agent in the station booth or a member of the train crew in either the first car or in the middle of the train.

Subway information
Travel information
Tel (718) 330-1234 or for
non-English speakers (718) 330-4847
Metrocard Customer Service
Tel (212) 638-7622.
www.mta.info

MAKING A TRIP BY SUBWAY

Subways run north–south up and down the city on Lexington Avenue, 6th Avenue, 7th Avenue/Broadway and 8th Avenue. The N, R, E, F, V, and W trains to Queens run east to west.

1 There is a map of the subway system on the back inside cover of this book. Large-scale maps are also positioned in prominent areas in every station. Maps are also available at www.mta.info

Subway map

Booth with agent

2 Buy a MetroCard or token from a station subway booth or vending machine. The machines accept most credit cards and bills up to $50 but not pennies. You can also refill your MetroCard.

3 Use the card or token to pass through the turnstile onto the platform.

Entry turnstile

4 Follow the directions for the train you want. For safety, stay in sight of the booth as you wait for your train; at night, stay in one of the yellow off-hours waiting areas.

Off-hours waiting area

5 Each train displays its route number or letter in the appropriate color and the names of the terminal stations.

Route indicator

6 Once aboard, you will find a system map next to the door on each side of the car. Newer trains have electronic ones that light up overhead. Stops are announced on the public address system, and you will see station names at each platform. The doors are operated by the conductor. For safety, be sure to enter a well-populated car.

7 After leaving the train, look for signs giving directions to the exit. If you need to change trains, just follow the signs to the connecting platforms.

Traveling by Train

NEW YORK HAS TWO main train stations. Grand Central Terminal is served by commuter trains from New York's suburbs and Connecticut, while Pennsylvania (Penn) Station is the terminal for long-distance services from the rest of the US and also Canada. Most commuter trains have no buffet cars on board, so it's best to buy any food and drink you want before boarding the train. Seat reservations are available only on the long-distance intercity services.

An Amtrak train

GRAND CENTRAL TERMINAL

GRAND CENTRAL Terminal on Park Avenue between 41st and 42nd streets is the main terminal for **Metro-North Railroad** trains (Hudson, New Haven and Harlem lines), which run north and east of New York and serve southwest Connecticut and Westchester, Dutchess, and Putnam counties.
From Grand Central you might travel by train to such destinations as the Bronx Zoo, the New York Botanical

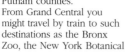

Long Island Rail Road logo

Garden and President Franklin D. Roosevelt's Hyde Park estate.
The 4, 5 and 6 trains on the green (Lexington) line and number 7 on the purple (Flushing) line serve Grand Central subway station, below the main terminal. A shuttle service links Grand Central to Times Square. Many bus lines stop at Grand Central.

PENN STATION

PENN STATION, between Seventh and Eighth avenues and from 31st to 33rd streets, is a modern terminal that was rebuilt in 1963 underneath the Madison Square Garden complex.
Commuter trains, New Jersey Transit trains and **Amtrak** trains from Canada and other parts of the US terminate at this station. There are no luggage trolleys, but redcap porters will help.
You will find taxis at street level. Buses run downtown on Seventh Avenue and uptown on Eighth Avenue. The blue (8th Avenue) subway lines, A, C, and E run on the Eighth Avenue side of the station; the red (Broadway) lines, 1, 2, 3 and 9 run on the Seventh Avenue side of the station. The ticket counters and waiting rooms are one level below; the trains leave from an even lower level.
From Penn Station, you could head out to New Jersey and Long Island or venture farther on Amtrak trains to

Canada, Philadelphia or Washington. Also in Penn Station are ticket offices and departure points of the **Long Island Rail Road (LIRR)**, mainly a commuter line, but with trains to such Long Island resorts, as the Hamptons, Montauk Point, and Fire Island.

PATH TRAINS

PATH TRAINS operate round the clock between New Jersey stations (Harrison, Hoboken, Jersey City and Newark) and Penn Station in Manhattan. They also stop at Christopher Street, the World Trade Center, 9th, 14th, 23rd and 33rd Streets and Avenue of the Americas (6th Avenue).

LIRR train at Penn Station

AMTRAK

AMTRAK IS THE US national railroad passenger service linking New York with other US cities and Canada. Some Amtrak trains have cars with reclining seats; others have dining facilities and lounge cars. Sleeper cars are available on all long-distance routes. The new express trains operate on certain Amtrak routes, such as the **Acela** between Boston and Washington via New York.
Tickets can be bought at Penn Station, as well as from Amtrak Travel Centers. Buy your ticket before getting on the train as there is a penalty for buying tickets on board. Senior citizens receive a 15% discount; the conductor will ask for proof of age. There are no student discounts. Seat reservations made by phone with a credit card need to be made at least 10 days in advance of travel if you want the tickets mailed to you.
Amtrak also offers a Great American Vacations package and various promotional fares during the year. Ask for information when you book.

Grand Central Terminal

Information board at Penn Station

TICKETS AND TRAVEL

TICKETING AREAS at all train stations are well lit and generally crowded at all times of the day. Ticket offices will accept most credit cards, as well as cash. There are a variety of ticket types, most based on a one-way fare; a return fare is twice the single fare. If you are planning a number of trips, Metro-North and LIRR offer weekly and off-peak passes that will save you money.

Train times, destination and gate numbers are continually updated on numerous large information boards. Watch for signs indicating the major interim stops and transfer points, listed next to the gate for departing trains. Wait for the opening of the gate posted for your train. Metro-North and LIRR cars are all one class, and have no reserved seating, Amtrak trains offer both services. The conductor will ask to see your ticket after the train has left the station.

Penn Station and Grand Central Terminal have good facilities, including bathrooms, banks, shops, bars and restaurants.

TRAIN INFORMATION

Amtrak Travel Centers
C *(800) USA-RAIL or (800) 872-7245.* **W** *www.amtrak.com*

Acela
C *(800) 523-8720.*
W *www.amtrak.com*

Long Island Rail Road
(LIRR) **C** *(718) 217-LIRR (Information).*
C *(212) 643 5228 (Lost property).*
W *www.mta.info*

Metro-North
C *(212) 532-4900 (Information).*
C *(212) 340-2555 (Lost property).*
W *www.mta.info*

PATH Trains
C *(800) 234-7284.*
W *www.panynj.com*

DAY TRIPS BY TRAIN

There are some beautiful places outside New York city, which, if your time allows, are well worth a visit. Below is a list of some recommended sights within 125 miles (200 km) of New York city center. For further details, call the New York Convention and Visitors Bureau *(see p216)*.

Phillipsburg Manor, Tarrytown

Stony Brook
Peaceful north shore village. Entrance to the Three Villages historic district.
🚉 *58 miles (93 km) east. Long Island Rail Road from Penn Station. 2 hrs.*

The Hamptons
Chic bars and boutiques in a weathered, historic setting. The Beverly Hills of Long Island.
🚉 *100 miles (161 km) east. Long Island Rail Road from Penn Station. 2 hrs, 50 min.*

Montauk Point
State park on the easternmost tip of Long Island; windswept ocean views.
🚉 *120 miles (193 km). LIRR from Penn Station. 3 hrs.*

Westbury House, Old Westbury
John Phipps's 1906 re-creation of a Charles II mansion with exquisite English formal gardens.
🚉 *24 miles (39 km) east. Long Island Rail Road from Penn Station. 40 min.*

Tarrytown
Washington Irving's home "Sunnyside" and Jay Gould's mansion.
🚉 *25 miles (40 km) north. Metro-North from Grand Central, then taxi. 40–50 min.*

Hyde Park
Springwood estate of Franklin D. Roosevelt and the Vanderbilt mansion.
🚉 *74 miles (119 km) north. Metro-North from Grand Central to Poughkeepsie, then bus. 2 hrs.*

New Haven, Connecticut
Home of Yale University.
🚉 *74 miles (119 km). Metro-North from Grand Central Terminal. 1 hr, 46 min.*

Hartford, Connecticut
Mark Twain's riverboat-style house, Atheneum Museum and Old State House.
🚉 *112 miles (180 km) north. Amtrak from Penn Station. 2 hrs, 45 min.*

Winterthur, Delaware
Henry du Pont's collection of Early American art, museum and gardens.
🚉 *116 miles (187 km) south. Amtrak from Penn Station to Wilmington, then bus to Winterthur. 2 hrs.*

Yale University in New Haven, Connecticut

New York Street Finder

Almost every listing in this guide includes a (boxed) page and grid reference to the maps in this section. The few entries that fall outside the area covered by these maps give transport details instead. Maps 1 to 12 cover the whole of Manhattan, while Brooklyn is shown on Map 13. An index of the street names follows on *pp257–9*.

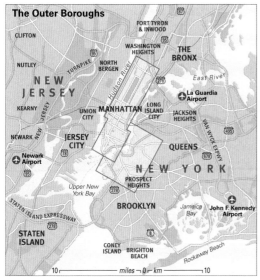

The Outer Boroughs

Key to Street Finder

▨ Sight/public building	⊗ Post office
Ⓜ Subway station	Ⓟ Parking
Ⓡ Railroad station	⊨ Railroad line
⊜ Ferry terminal	▥ Pedestrian street
⊜ Bus terminal	▨ Expressway
⊕ Heliport	
⊜ Aerial tramway	**Scale of maps 1–12**
ⓘ Tourist information office	0 meters ▭ 500
⊕ Hospital with emergency room	0 yards ▭ 500
⊜ Police station	**Scale of map 13**
⊕ Church	0 kilometers ▭ 1
⊙ Synagogue	0 miles ▭ 1

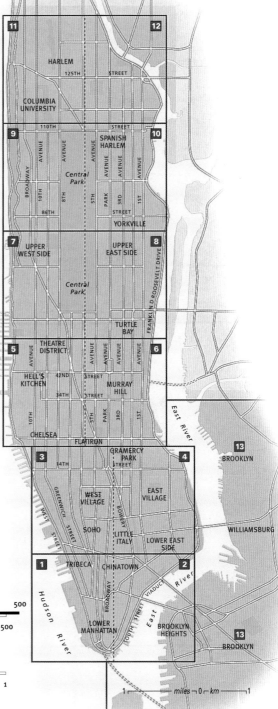

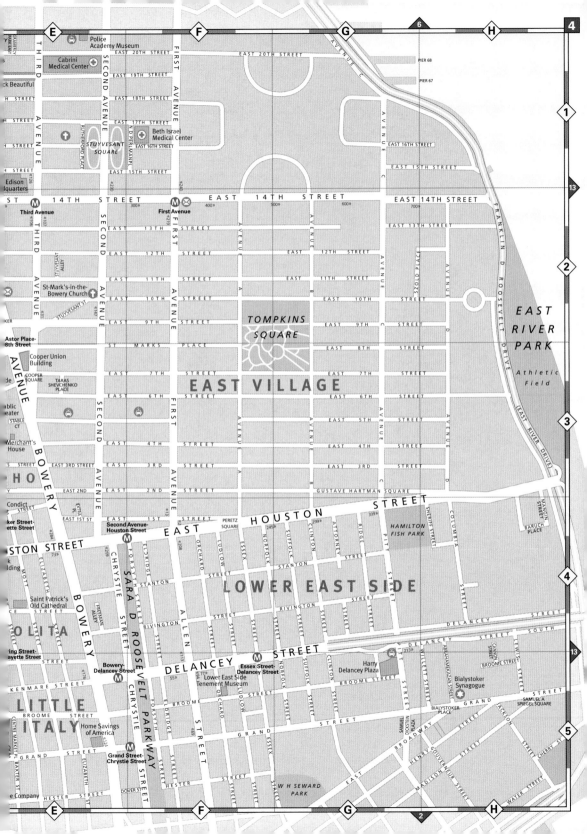

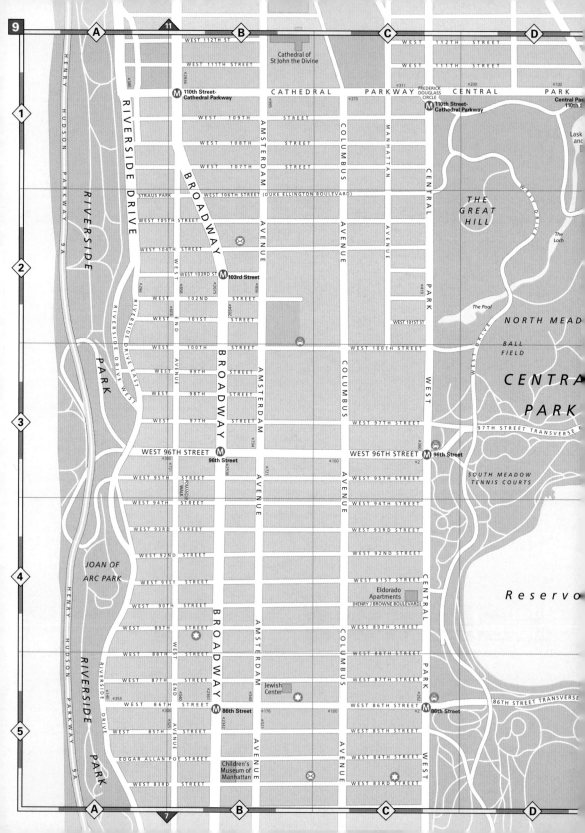

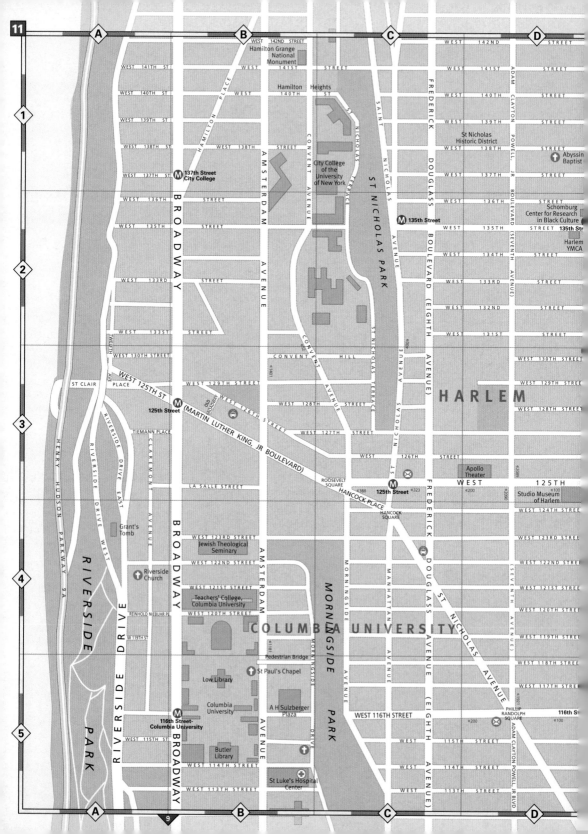

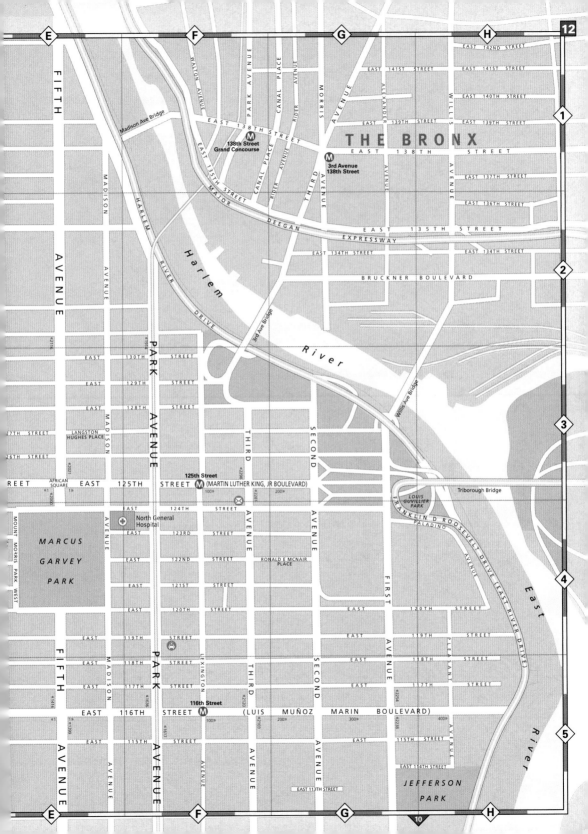

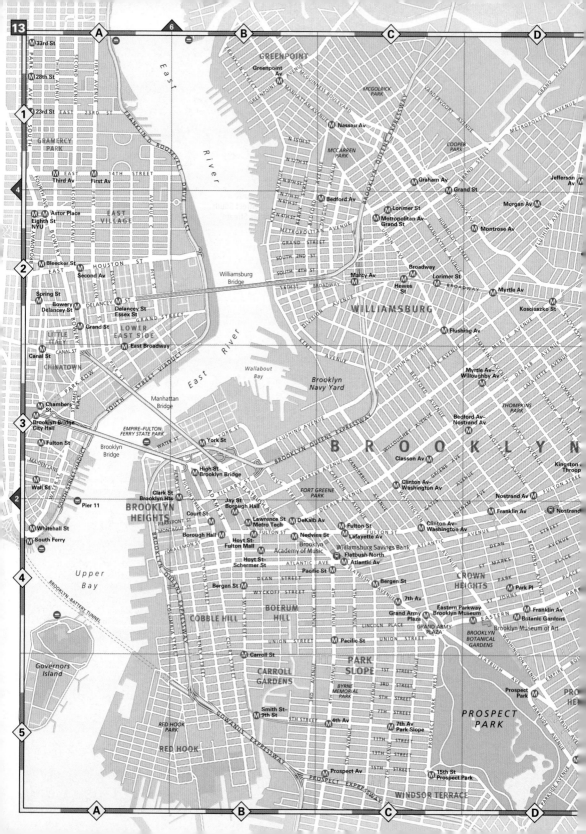

Street Finder Index

Street Finder Index

Index by Area

Downtown

Restaurants

Chinatown

Golden Unicorn (p33) $
18 East Broadway (Map 2 F1)
Chinese

Peking Duck House (p33) $$
28 Mott Street (Map 2 E1)
Chinese

HSF (p182) $$
46 Bowery (Map 2 E1)
Chinese

**Chinatown Ice Cream
Factory** (p182) $
65 Bayard Street (Map 2 E1)
Ice Cream Parlor

Great NY Noodle Town (p182) $
28½ Bowery at Bayard Street
(Map 2 E1)
Chinese

East Village

2nd Avenue Deli (p41) $$
156 2nd Avenue (Map 4 E2)
Deli

Angelica Kitchen (p40) $
300 East 12th St (Map 4 E2)
Vegetarian

Bao (p37) $
111 Avenue C (Map 4 G3)
Vietnamese

Crif Dogs (p44) $
113 St. Mark's Place (Map 4 F3)
American

Daily Chow (p38) $
2 East 2nd Street (Map 4 E3)
Asian

DT–UT (p184) $
41 Avenue B (Map 4 G2)
Café

The Elephant (p35) $$
58 East 1st Street (Map 4 F4)
French/Thai

Mermaid Inn (p39) $$
96 2nd Avenue (Map 4 E3)
Seafood

Mud Spot (p39) $
307 East 9th Street (Map 4 E2)
www.themudtruck.com
Café

Paul's Palace (p39) $
131 2nd Avenue (Map 4 E3)
American

Pommes Frites (p44) $
123 2nd Avenue (Map 4 E3)
Belgian

Pylos (p38) $$
128 East 7th Street (Map 4 F3)
Greek

Rue B (p184) $
188 Avenue B (Map 4 G2)
Café

Sobaya (p40) $/$$
229 East 9th Street (Map 4 E2)
Japanese

Le Souk (p37) $$
47 Avenue B (Map 4 G3)
North African

Le Tableau (p37) $$
511 East 5th Street (Map 4 F3)
French

Yaffa Cafe (p38) $
97 St. Mark's Place (Map 4 F3)
Middle Eastern

Lower East Side

Alias (p36) $$
76 Clinton Street (Map 4 G4)
American

Bereket (p35) $
187 East Houston St
(Map 4 F4)
Turkish

Cube 63 (p36) $$
63 Clinton Street (Map 4 G4)
Japanese

Fried Dumpling (p44) $
99 Allen Street (Map 4 F4)
Chinese

'inoteca (p36) $$
98 Rivington Street (Map 4 F4)
Italian

WD-50 (p36) $$$
50 Clinton Street (Map 4 G4)
American

Lower Manhattan

Amish Fine Food Market (p182)
17 Battery Place (Map 1 D5)
Deli/Sandwich Shop

Cosi Downtown (p182) $
55 Broad Street (Map 1 D4)
Deli/Sandwich Shop

Pret a Manger (p182) $
60 Broad Street (Map 1 D4)
Deli/Sandwich Shop

Meatpacking District

Bonsignour (p82)
35 Jane Street (Map 3 B2)
Bakery

Florent (pp46 & 183) $$
69 Gansevoort Street (Map 3 A2)
American/European

Pastis (p183)
9 Ninth Avenue (Map 3 A2)
French

Nolita

Cafe Gitane (p35) $
242 Mott Street (Map 4 E4)
North African

Cafe Habana (p35) $
229 Elizabeth St (Map 4 E4)
Cuban/Mexican

**Housing Works
Used Book Café** (p21) $
126 Crosby Street (Map 3 D5)
Café

SoHo

Balthazar (p33) $$
80 Spring Street (Map 3 D5)
French

Blue Ribbon Sushi (p41) $$
119 Sullivan Street (Map 3 C4)
Japanese

Dean & DeLuca (pp19, 75) $
560 Broadway (Map 3 D4)
Bakery/Deli

L'Ecole (p34) $/$$
462 Broadway (Map 3 D5)
French

Mercer Kitchen (p33) $/$$
99 Prince Street (Map 3 D5)
French/American

Tribeca

66 (p32) $$$
241 Church Street (Map 1 D1)
Chinese

Acappella (p32) $$$
1 Hudson Street (Map 1 C2)
Italian

Chanterelle (p46) $$$
2 Harrison Street (Map 1 C1)
www.chanterellenyc.com
French

Montrachet (p32) $$$
239 West Broadway
(Map 1 D1)
European

Nobu (p46) $$$
105 Hudson Street (Map 1 C1)
212 219 0500, www.myriad
restaurantgroup.com
Japanese

West Village

Babbo (p42) $$$
110 Waverly Place
(Map 3 C3)
Northern Italian

BB Sandwich Bar (p44) $
120 West 3rd Street (Map 3 C3)
Deli

Blue Ribbon $/$$$
Bakery (p41)
33 Downing Street (Map 3 C4)
European

Cones (p44) $
272 Bleecker Street (Map 3 C3)
Ice Cream Parlor

Deborah (p19) $
43 Carmine Street (Map 3 C4)
Brunch

Jane (p34) $$
100 West Houston Street
(Map 3 D4)
American

Joe (p39) $
141 Waverly Place
212 924 6750 (Map 3 C3)
Café

**John's of
Bleecker Street** (p43) $
278 Bleecker Street (Map 3 C3)
Pizzeria

Magnolia Bakery (p81) $
401 Bleeker Street (Map 3 B3)
Downtown/West Village

Mamoun's (p44) $
119 MacDougal St. (Map 3 C3)
Middle Eastern

Mary's Fish Camp (p45) $$
64 Charles Street (Map 3 B3)
Seafood

Mud Truck (p39) $
14th Street and Broadway
(Map 3 D2)
www.themudtruck.com
Café

NY Dosas (p45) $
West 4th Street & Sullivan
Street (Map 3 C3)
Vegetarian

Otto Enoteca $$
and Pizzeria (p42)
1 5th Avenue (Map 3 D3)
Italian

La Palapa Rockola (p42) $$
359 6th Avenue (Map 3 C3)
Mexican

Sumile (p46) $$$
154 West 13th Street (Map 3 C2)
Japanese

Paris Commune (p19) $
99 Bank Street (Map 3 A3)
Brunch

Pepe Rosso's (p44)
149 Sullivan Street (Map 3 C4)
Italian

Tartine (p46) $$
253 West 11th Street
(Map 3 B2)
French

Tea & Sympathy (p39)
108 Greenwich Ave. (Map 3 C2)
British

Tomoe Sushi (p41) $$
172 Thompson Street (Map 3 C4)
Japanese

Wallse (p45) $$$
344 West 11th Street
(Map 3A3)
Austrian

Shopping

East Village

Kiehl's (p77)
109 3rd Avenue (Map 4 E2)
Health & Beauty

St. Mark's Sounds (p78)
16 St. Mark's Place
(Map 4 E3)
Music

The Strand (p77)
828 Broadway (Map 3 D2)
Books

Little Italy

The Apartment (p76)
101 Crosby Street (Map 3 D4)
Interiors

Calypso (p77)
280 Mott Street (Map 4 E4)
Fashion

Hable Construction (p78)
230 Elizabeth St. (Map 4 E4)
Interiors

INA (p77)
21 Prince Street (Map 4 E4)
Fashion

Mayle (p78)
242 Elizabeth Street
(Map 4 E4)
Fashion

Rescue Nail Spa (p76)
21 Cleveland Place (Map 4 E5)
Health & Beauty

Lower East Side

ALife Rivington Club (p79)
158 Rivington Street (Map 4 G4)
Shoes & Accessories

Shop (p80)
105 Stanton Street (Map 4 F4)
Fashion

Teany (p80)
90 Rivington Street (Map 4 F4)
Food

TG-170 (p79)
170 Ludlow Street (Map 4 F4)
Fashion

Lower Manhattan

Century 21 (p70)
22 Cortlandt Street (Map 1 D3)
Fashion

Green Market (p182)
Farmer's market at Bowling
Green Park (Map 1 D4)
Food Market

Amish Market
Downtown (p182)
17 Battery Place (Map 1 D4)
Food Market

Meatpacking District

Alexander McQueen (p183)
417 West 14th Street (Map 3 A2)
Fashion

Bonsignour (p83)
35 Jane Street (Map 3 B2)
Food

Jeffrey (pp84 & 183)
449 West 14th St. (Map 3 A2)
Department Store

MXYPLYZYK (p83)
125 Greenwich Ave (Map 3 B2)
Interiors

Stella McCartney (p83)
429 West 14th St. (Map 3 A2)
Fashion

Vitra (p183)
29 9th Avenue (Map 3 A2)
Interiors

Nolita

Bond 07 By Selima (p78)
7 Bond Street (Map 3 D3)
Shoes & Accessories

LAFCO (p79)
285 Lafayette Street (Map 4 E4)
Health & Beauty

Rafe (p78)
1 Bleecker Street (Map 4 E4)
Shoes & Accessories

SoHo

Barney's Co-Op (p72)
116 Wooster Street (Map 3 D4)
Fashion

Clio (p73)
92 Thompson Street (Map 3 C4)
Interiors

Le Corset by Selima (p72)
80 Thompson Street
(Map 3 C5)
Lingerie

Costume National (p73)
108 Wooster Street (Map 3 D4)
Fashion

Dean & DeLuca (p75)
560 Broadway (Map 3 D4)
Food

Helmut Lang (p72)
80 Greene Street (Map 3 D5)
Fashion

Hotel Venus by
Patricia Field (p70)
382 W. Broadway (Map 3 D5)
Fashion

Kate Spade Travel (p70)
59 Thompson Street (Map 3 C5)
Shoes & Accessories

Kate's Paperie (p76)
561 Broadway (Map 3 D4)
Stationery

Keiko (p71)
62 Greene Street (Map 3 D5)
Fashion

Kirna Zabete (p73)
96 Greene Street (Map 3 D4)
Fashion

Miu Miu (p73)
100 Prince Street (Map 3 D4)
Fashion

Moss (p74)
146 Greene Street (Map 3 D4)
Interiors

Pearl River Mart (p71)
477 Broadway (Map 3 D5)
Department Store

Prada (p74)
575 Broadway (Map 3 D4)
Fashion

Scoop (p75)
532 Broadway (Map 3 D4)
Fashion

Chez es Saada (p161)
42 East 1st Street (Map 4 F4)
Bar

KGB (p162)
85 East 4th Street (Map 4 E3)
Bar

Korova Milk Bar (p165)
200 Avenue A (Map 4 F2)
Bar

Lansky Lounge (p159)
104 Norfolk Street (Map 4 G4)
Cocktail Lounge/DJ Bar

McSorley's Old
Ale House (p162)
15 East 7th Street (Map 4 E3)
Ale House

Nevada Smith's (p162)
74 3rd Avenue (Map 4 E2)
Bar

Parkside Lounge (p161)
317 East Houston Street
(Map 4 G4)
Bar

Rue B (p165)
188 Avenue B (Map 4 G2)
Bar

Swift (p162)
34 East 4th Street
(Map 4 E3)
Ale House

Uncle Ming's (p166)
225 Avenue B, 2nd Floor
(Map 4 G2)
DJ Bar

Little Italy

ñ (p158)
33 Crosby Street
(Map 3 D5)
Bar

Lower East Side

Arlene's Grocery (p137)
95 Stanton Street (Map 4 F4)
Bar & Music Venue

Barramundi (p160)
67 Clinton Street (Map 4 F4)
Bar

Slipper Room (p161)
167 Orchard Street (Map 4 F4)
Bar

Welcome to the
Johnson's (p160)
123 Rivington Street
(Map 4 F4)
Bar

Lower Manhattan

Pussycat Lounge (p156)
96 Greenwich Street
(Map 1 D4)
Bar

Meatpacking District

Cielo (pp168 & 183)
18 Little West 12th Street
(Map 3 A2)
Club

Cubbyhole (p168)
281 West 12th Street
(Map 3 B2)
Bar

Rhône (p168)
63 Gansevoort Street
(Map 3 A2)
Bar

Nolita

B-Bar & Grill (p163)
40 East 4th Street (Map 4 E3)
Bar

Pravda (p159)
281 Lafayette Street (Map 4 E4)
Cocktail Lounge

Temple Bar (p158)
332 Lafayette Street (Map 4 E4)
Cocktail Lounge

SoHo

Antarctica (p156)
287 Hudson Street (Map 3 C5)
Bar

THOM's Bar (p157)
60 Thompson Street (Map 3 C5)
Cocktail Lounge

West Village

Blind Tiger Ale House (p167)
518 Hudson Street (Map 3 B3)
Ale House

Chumley's (p166)
86 Bedford Street (Map 3 B3)
Bar

Lotus (p164)
409 West 14th Street
(Map 3 A2)
DJ Bar

Stonewall (p167)
53 Christopher Street
(Map 3 B3)
Bar

Sullivan Room (p166)
218 Sullivan Street (Map 3 C3)
DJ Bar

Vol de Nuit (p166)
148 West 4th Street (Map 3 C3)
Ale House

White Horse Tavern (p167)
567 Hudson Street
(Map 3 B3)
Ale House

Havens:
Parks & Gardens

Lower Manhattan

Battery Park (p182)
Battery Place & State Street
(Map 1 D4)
www.bpcparks.org

Havens:
Spas & Treatments

SoHo

Angel Feet (p192)
77 Perry Street (Map 3 B3)

Bliss SoHo (p192)
568 Broadway (Map 3 D4)

Jivamukti Yoga Center (p193)
404 Lafayette Street
(Map 4 E3)

Hotels

Meatpacking District

Abingdon $$
Guest House (p205)
13 8th Avenue (Map 3 B2)

SoHo House $$$
New York (p206)
29–35 9th Avenue (Map 3 A2)

SoHo

Bevy's SoHo Loft (p204) $$
70 Mercer Street (Map 3 D5)

60 Thompson (p204) $$$
60 Thompson Street (3 C5)

Mercer Hotel (p204) $$$
147 Mercer Street (Map 3 D4)

SoHo Grand Hotel (p204) $–$$
310 West Broadway (Map 3 D5)

Tribeca

Tribeca Grand $$$
Hotel (p205)
Two Avenue of the Americas
(Map 3 C5)

West Village

Washington Square $
Hotel (p205)
103 Waverly Place (Map 3 C3)

Midtown

Restaurants

Chelsea

Biltmore Room (p48) $$$
290 8th Avenue (Map 5 C5)
International

City Bakery (p47) $
3 West 18th Street (Map 3 C1)
Bakery

Grand Sichuan
International (p47) $
229 9th Avenue (Map 5 C5)
Chinese

Red Cat (p47) $$
227 10th Avenue (Map 5 B5)
International

Wild Lily Tea Room (p193)
511-a West 22nd Street
(Map 5 B5)
Tea Room

Flatiron

Tamarind (p49) $$
41–3 East 22nd Street
(Map 6 F5)
Indian

Bolo (p48) $$$
23 East 22nd Street (Map 6 E5)
Spanish

Museum of Television
and Radio (p115)
25 West 52nd Street
(Map 8 E5)
Museum

Rose Museum at
Carnegie Hall (p112)
154 West 57th Street, 2nd Floor
(Map 7 D5)
Museum

Performance

Chelsea

Hammerstein Ballroom (p141)
311 West 34th Street (Map 5 C3)
Music Venue

The Joyce Theater (p140)
175 8th Avenue (Map 3 B1)
Dance

The Kitchen (p140)
512 West 19th Street (Map 3 A1)
Combined Arts Center

Upright Citizen's
Brigade (p141)
307 West 26th Street (Map 5 C5)
Comedy

Flatiron

Gotham Comedy Club (p141)
34 West 22nd Street
(Map 6 E5)
Comedy

Kavehaz (p141)
37 West 26th Street (Map 6 E5)
Music Venue

Gramercy

Rodeo Bar (p142)
375 3rd Avenue (Map 6 F5)
Music Venue

Hell's Kitchen

The Soul Cafe (p142)
444 West 42nd St. (Map 5 B2)
Music Venue

Theater District

B.B. King Blues Club
& Grill (p142)
237 West 42nd St. (Map 5 C2)
Jazz & Blues Venue

City Center (p143)
131 West 55th Street (Map 7 D5)
Combined Arts Center

Don't Tell Mama (p143)
343 West 46th Street (Map 5 C1)
Cabaret

Ed Sullivan Theater (p144)
51 West 52nd Street (Map 7 D5)
TV Studio

NBC Studios (p144)
Main lobby, 49th St between
5th and 7th Avenues
(Map 6 E1)
TV Studio

Rainbow Room (p143)
30 Rockefeller Plaza, 65th Floor
(Map 6 E1)
Ball Room

Roundabout Theatre Company
@ The American Airlines
Theatre (p142)
227 West 42nd St. (Map 5 D2)
Theater

Swing 46 (p143)
349 West 46th Street (Map 5 C1)
Ball Room

Sports Arenas

Flatiron

Madison Square Garden (p151)
Map 6 E5
Sports Arena

Bars and Clubs

Chelsea

Avalon (p169)
47 West 20th Street (Map 3 C1)
DJ Bar

Bungalow 8 (p170)
515 West 27th Street (Map 5 B4)
Bar

Copacabana (p171)
560 West 34th Street (Map 5 B3)
Ball Room

Glass (p170)
287 10th Avenue (Map 5 B5)
Bar

Hiro (p170)
366 West 17th Street (Map 3 A1)
Bar

Plunge Bar (p175)
18 9th Avenue (Map 3 A1)
Bar

Roxy (p169)
515 West 18th Street (Map 3 A1)
Club

Serena (p169)
Chelsea Hotel, 222 West 23rd
Street (Map 5 C5)
Bar

Spirit (p170)
530 West 27th Street (Map 5 B4)
Bar

Flatiron

Eugene (p169)
27 West 24th Street (Map 6 E5)
Club

Sky Bar (p175)
17 W 32nd Street (Map 6 E4)
Bar

Hell's Kitchen

Rudy's Bar & Grill (p168)
627 9th Avenue (Map 5 C1)
Bar

Murray Hill

Campbell Apartment (p171)
15 Vanderbilt Ave., Southwest
Balcony, Grand Central Terminal
(Map 6 F2)
Bar

The Ginger Man (p171)
11 East 36th Street (Map 6 E3)
Bar

Métrazur (p172)
East Balcony, Grand Central
Station (Map 6 F2)
Cocktail Lounge

Theater District

Ava Lounge (p172)
210 West 55th Street (Map 7 D5)
Bar

Flûte (p172)
205 West 54th Street (Map 7 D5)
DJ Bar

Russian Vodka Room (p173)
265 West 52nd Street (Map 7 C5)
Bar

Single Room Occupancy (p172)
360 West 53rd Street (Map 7 C5)
Bar

Turtle Bay

Mica Bar (p168)
252 East 51st Street (Map 6 F1)
Bar

Top of the Tower @ Beekman
Tower Hotel (p194)
3 Mitchell Place at 49th Street &
First Avenue (Map 6 G1)
Bar

Havens:
Spas & Treatments

Theater District

The Spa at the Mandarin
Oriental (p194)
80 Columbus Circle at 60th
Street, 35th Floor (Map 7 C4)

Hotels

Chelsea

Chelsea Inn (p207) $
46 West 17th Street
(Map 3 C1)

Chelsea Lodge (p207) $
318 West 20th Street
(Map 3 B1)

Hotel Chelsea (p205) $$
222 West 23rd Street
(Map 5 C5)

Maritime Hotel (p207) $$
363 West 16th Street
(Map 3 A1)

Gramercy

W New York, $–$$
Union Square (p207)
201 Park Avenue South
(Map 3D1)

Murray Hill

Morgans (p209) $$$
237 Madison Avenue
(Map 6 E3)

Index by Area

Midtown

Hotels continued

Theater District

Bryant Park Hotel (p208) $$
40 West 40th Street
(Map 6 E2)

Four Seasons (p210) $$$
57 East 57th Street (Map 8 E5)

The Peninsula (p208) $$$
700 5th Avenue at 55th Street
(Map 8 E5)

The Plaza (p205) $$$
5th Avenue at Central Park
South (Map 8 E4)

Royalton (p208) $$
44 West 44th Street (Map 6 E2)

St. Regis (p208) $$$
2 East 55th Street (Map 8 E5)

Upper East Side

Restaurants

Annie's (p557) $
1381 3rd Avenue (Map 8 F1)
American

Atlantic Grill (p56) $$
1341 3rd Avenue (Map 8 F1)
Seafood

Candle 79 (p56) $$
154 East 79th Street (Map 8 F1)
Vegetarian/Vegan

Geisha (p54) $$$
33 East 61st Street (Map 8 E4)
Japanese

March (p55) $$$
405 East 58th Street (Map 8 G4)
Asian

Mezzaluna (p55) $$
1295 3rd Avenue (Map 8 F2)
Italian

Rotunda at the Pierre (p196)
The Pierre Hotel, 2 East 61st
Street (Map 8 E4)
Tea Room

Serendipity 3 (p55) $
225 East 60th Street (Map 8 F4)
American

Sushi of Gari (p57) $$$
402 East 78th Street (Map 8 G1)
Japanese

Via Quadronno (p39)
25 East 73rd Street (Map 8 F2)
www.viaquadronno.com
Italian

Shopping

ABH Designs (p94)
401 East 76th Street (Map 8 H1)
Interiors

Barney's New York (p92)
660 Madison Avenue
(Map 8 E4)
Department Store

Bra Smyth (p92)
905 Madison Avenue
(Map 8 E2)
Lingerie

Christian Louboutin (p93)
941 Madison Avenue
(Map 8 E2)
Shoes & Accessories

Clyde's (p93)
926 Madison Avenue
(Map 8 E2)
Heath & Beauty

Diane B (p93)
1414 3rd Avenue (Map 8 F2)
Fashion

Dylan's Candy Bar (p92)
1011 3rd Avenue
(Map 8 F4)
Food

Liliblue (p93)
955 Madison Avenue
(Map 8 E2)
Shoes & Accessories

La Perla (p92)
803 Madison Avenue
(Map 8 E3)
Lingerie

Searle (p94)
1124 Madison Avenue
(Map 10 E5)
Fashion

Art & Architecture

Asia Society (p115)
725 Park Avenue. at 70th Street
(Map 8 F2)
Gallery

Cooper-Hewitt National Design Museum (p117)
2 East 91st Street
(Map 10 E4)
Museum

Frick Collection (p114)
1 East 70th Street
(Map 8 E2)
Museum

Guggenheim Museum (p116)
1071 5th Avenue at 89th Street
(Map 10 E4)
Museum

The Jewish Museum (p117)
1109 5th Avenue at 92nd Street
(Map 10 E4)
Museum

Metropolitan Museum of Art (p115)
1000 5th Avenue (Map 8 E1)
Museum

El Museo del Barrio (p119)
1230 5th Avenue at 104th Street
(Map 10 E2)
Museum

Whitney Museum of American Art (p113)
945 Madison Avenue
(Map 8 E2)
Museum

Performance

92nd Street Y (p145)
1395 Lexington Avenue
(Map 10 F4)
Combined Arts Center

The Comic Strip (p145)
1568 2nd Avenue (Map 8 G1)
Comedy

Florence Gould Hall (p144)
55 East 59th Street (Map 8 F4)
Combined Arts Center

Bars

Baraonda (p173)
1439 2nd Avenue (Map 8 G2)
Bar

Bemelmans Bar (p173)
Carlyle Hotel, 35 East 76th
Street (Map 8 E1)
Bar

Havens: Parks & Gardens

Conservatory Gardens at Central Park (p195)
5th Avenue at 110th Street
(Map 10 E2)

The Iris and B. Gerald Cantor Roof Garden (p194)
Metropolitan Museum of Art,
1000 5th Avenue
(Map 8 E1)

The Ramble at Central Park (p195)
5th Avenue between 72nd and
80th streets (Map 7 D2)

Hotels

1871 House (p210) $$
130 East 62nd Street (Map 8 F4)

The Carlyle (p205) $$
Madison Avenue at 76th Street
(Map 8 E1)
www.thecarlyle.com

Hotel Wales (p212) $$
1295 Madison Avenue
(Map 10 E4)

The Lowell (p211) $$$
28 East 63rd Street
(Map 8 F4)

The Mark (p211) $$$
25 East 77th Street (Map 8 E1)

The Melrose (p211) $$
140 East 63rd Street
(Map 8 F4)

The Pierre (p211) $$$
5th Avenue at 61st Street
(Map 8 E4)

Upper West Side

Restaurants

Aix (p59) $$$
2398 Broadway (Map 9 B5)
French

El Malecón II (p58) $
764 Amsterdam Avenue (9 B3)
Caribbean

Ouest (p57) $$$
2315 Broadway (Map 9 B5)
American

Pasha (p58) $$
70 W. 71st Street (Map 7 C2)
Turkish

Picholine (p58) $$$
35 West 64th Street (Map 7 C3)
European

Tavern on the Green (p46)
Central Park West between 66th
and 67th sts. (Map 7 C3)
212 873 3200
www.tavernonthegreen.com
American

Shopping

Blades Board & Skate (p94)
120 West 72nd Street
(Map 7 B2)
Sporting Goods

**Housing Works
Thrift Shop** (p95)
306 Columbus Avenue
(Map 7 C2)
Thrift Store

Intermix (p94)
210 Columbus Avenue
(Map 7 C3)
Fashion

Super Runners (p95)
360 Amsterdam Avenue
(Map 7 B1)
Sporting Goods

Zabar's (p95)
2245 Broadway
(Map 7 B1)
Food

Performance

**Lincoln Center for the
Performing Arts** (p146)
Straddling Broadway and
Amsterdam Avenue between
62nd and 66th streets
(Map 7 B3)
Performing Arts Center

Makor (p147)
35 West 67th Street (Map 7 C3)
Combined Arts Center

Merkin Concert Hall (p145)
129 West 67th Street
(Map 7 B3)
Concert Hall

Smoke (p147)
2751 Broadway
(Map 9 B2)
Jazz Venue

Stand-Up NY (p147)
236 West 78th Street
(Map 7 B2)
Comedy

Symphony Space (p147)
2537 Broadway (Map 9 B3)
Combined Arts Center

Bars & Clubs

Boat Basin Café (p175)
West 79th St. at Henry Hudson
Parkway (Map 7 A1)
Bar

Library Bar (p168)
Hudson Hotel, 356 West 58th
Street (Map 7 B4)
Bar

Hotels

Hudson Hotel (p209) $$
356 West 58th Street
(Map 7 C4)

Above Central Park

Restaurants

Columbia University

Symposium (p59) $$
544 West 113th St. (Map 11 B5)
Greek

Fort Tryon

New Leaf Café (p59) $$
Fort Tryon Park
American

Harlem

Amy Ruth's (p185) $
113 West 116th St. (Map 11 D5)
212 280 8779
American

Shopping

Harlem

Demolition Depot (p96)
216 East 125th St. (Map 12 G3)
Interiors

Xukuma (p96)
183 Lenox Avenue (11 D4)
Fashion/Interiors

Art & Architecture

Fort Tryon

The Cloisters (p118)
Fort Tryon Park
Museum

Harlem

**Studio Museum in
Harlem** (p119)
144 West 125th Street
(Map 11 D3)
Museum

Performance

Harlem

Apollo Theater (p148)
253 West 125th Street
(Map 11 D3)
Music/Combined Arts Venue

Lenox Lounge (p149)
288 Lenox Avenue between
124th & 125th streets
(Map 11 D3)
Jazz Venue

Clubs

Harlem

Jimmy's Uptown (p174)
2207 Adam Clayton Powell, Jr.
Blvd. (Map 11 D3)
Club

Hotels

Harlem

**The Harlem
Flophouse** (p212) $
242 West 123rd Street
(Map 11 D4)

Brooklyn

Restaurants

Brooklyn Heights

**Brooklyn Ice Cream
Factory** (p186) $
Fulton Ferry Landing
(Map 13 A4)
Ice Cream Parlor

Connecticut Muffin (p186) $
115 Montague Street
(Map 13 A4)
Bakery

Noodle Pudding (p59) $$
38 Henry Street (Map 13 A3)
Italian

The River Café (p60) $$$
1 Water Street (Map 13 A3)
International

Teresa's (p186) $$
80 Montague St. (Map 13 A4)
Polish

Carroll Gardens

The Grocery (p60) $$
288 Smith Street (Map 13 B4)
American

Joya (p60) $
215 Court Street (Map 13 B4)
Thai

Coney Island

Café Arbat (p188)
306 Brighton Beach Avenue
Eastern European

Café Glechik (p188)
3159 Coney Island Avenue
Eastern European

**Nathan's Famous
Hotdogs** (p188) $
Corner of Surf & Stillwell avenues
American

Brooklyn

Restaurants *continued*

Fort Greene

Butta'Cup Lounge (p62) $$
271 Adelphi Street (Map 13 C3)
American

i-Shebeen Madiba (p62) $$
195 DeKalb Avenue
(Map 13 C3)
South African

LouLou (p61) $$
222 DeKalb Avenue
(Map 13 C3)
French

DiFara Pizzeria (p62) $
1424 Avenue J
Pizzeria

Park Slope

Al Di La (p61) $$
248 5th Avenue
(Map 13 C4)
Italian

Convivium Osteria (p61) $$
68 5th Avenue
(Map 13 C4)
Italian

Park Slope Chip Shop (p61) $
383 5th Avenue (Map 13 C4)
British

Williamsburg

Anna Maria's (p187) $
179 Bedford Avenue
(Map 13 C2)
Pizzeria

Bamonte's (p63) $$
32 Withers Street
(Map 13 C1)
Italian

Bliss Café (p187)
191 Bedford Avenue
(Map 13 C2)
Vegetarian

Cukiernia (p187) $
223 Bedford Avenue
(Map 13 B2)
Bakery

Peter Luger $$$
Steak House (p63)
178 Broadway (Map 13 B2)
American

Planet Thailand (p63) $
133 North 7th Street (Map 13 C2)
Thai/Japanese

Relish (p63) $$
225 Wythe Avenue (Map 13 B2)
American

S & B Polish Restaurant (p187)
194 Bedford Avenue
(Map 13 C2)
Restaurant

Verb Café (p187) $
218 Bedford Avenue
(Map 13 C2)
Café

Shopping

Boerum Hill

Bark (p97)
495 Atlantic Avenue
(Map 13 B4)
Interiors

Butter (p97)
405 Atlantic Avenue
(Map 13 B4)
Fashion

Brooklyn Heights

Heights Books (p186)
109 Montague Street
(Map 13 A4)
Books

Park Slope

Loom (p97)
115 7th Avenue (Map 13 C5)
Interiors

Nest (p98)
396A 7th Avenue (Map 13 C5)
Interiors

Williamsburg

Beacon's Closet (p99)
88 North 11th St. (Map 13 B1)
Thrift Store

Bedford Cheese Shop (p187)
218 Bedford Avenue
(Map 13 C2)
Food

Brooklyn Industries (p187)
162 Bedford Avenue
(Map 13 C2)
Shoes & Accessories

Brooklyn Lager Brewery (p187)
79 North 11th Street
(Map 13 C2)
Food

Earwax Records (p100)
218 Bedford Avenue
(Map 13 B2)
Music

Isa (p99)
88 North 6th Street
(Map 13 B2)
Fashion

Metaphors (p187)
195 Bedford Avenue
(Map 13 C2)
Fashion

Mini Minimarket (p98)
218 Bedford Avenue
(Map 13 B2)
Fashion

Moon River Chattel (p101)
62 Grand Street (Map 13 B2)
Interiors

Spacial (pp99 & 187)
199 Bedford Avenue
(Map 13 B2)
Interiors/Fashion

Spoonbill &
Sugartown (pp98 &187)
218 Bedford Avenue
(Map 13 C2)
Books

Two Jakes (p101)
320 Wythe Avenue (Map 13 B2)
Interiors

Art & Architecture

Boerum Hill

Brooklyn Historical
Society (p121)
128 Pierrepont Street (Map 2 H5)
Museum

Brooklyn Museum
of Art (p120)
200 Eastern Parkway
(Map 13 D4)
Museum

Williamsburg Savings Bank
Building (p121)
1 Hanson Place, corner of
Flatbush and Atlantic avenues
(Map 13 C4)
Modern Architecture

Park Slope

Prospect Park West (p119)
between Union and 15th streets
(Map 13 C5)
Historic Buildings

Williamsburg

Momenta Art (p120)
72 Berry Street (Map 13 B1)
Art Gallery

Pierogi 2000 (p120)
177 North 9th Street
(Map 13 B1)
www.pierogi2000.com
Art Gallery

Williamsburg Art & Historical
Center (p120)
135 Broadway at Bedford
Avenue (Map 13 B2)
Art Gallery

Performance

Brooklyn Heights

Barge Music (p140)
Fulton Ferry Landing
(Map 2 G3)
Concert Hall

Fort Green

Brooklyn Academy of Music
(BAM) (p149)
30 Lafayette Avenue
(Map 13 C4)
Performing Arts Center

Greenpoint

Warsaw (p150)
261 Driggs Avenue (Map 13 C1)
Music Venue

Bars & Clubs

Boerum Hill

Frank's Lounge (p174)
660 Fulton Street
(Map 13 B4)
DJ Bar

Zombie Hut (p174)
261 Smith Street
(Map 13 B4)
Cocktail Lounge

Gowanus Yacht Club (p175)
323 Smith Street
(Map 13 B4)
Bar

Coney Island

Ruby's (p175)
Coney Island Boardwalk
Bar

Greenpoint

Warsaw (p150)
261 Driggs Avenue
(Map 13 C1)
Bar/Music Venue

Park Slope

Buttermilk Bar (p176)
557 5th Avenue
(Map 13 C5)
Bar

Great Lakes (p175)
284 5th Avenue (Map 13 C4)
Bar

Williamsburg

Spuyten Duyvil (p176)
359 Metropolitan Avenue
(Map 13 C2)
Ale House

Larry Lawrence (p176)
295 Grand Street
(Map 13 C2)
Cocktail Lounge

Galapagos (p177)
70 North 6th Street
(Map 13 B2)
Bar/Music Venue

Trash (p176)
256 Grand Street
(Map 13 C2)
Bar

Havens: Parks & Gardens

Crown Heights

**Brooklyn Botanic
Garden** (p198)
1000 Washington Avenue
(Map 13 D4)

Jamaica Bay

**Jamaica Bay
Wildlife Refuge** (p198)
Crossbay Boulevard,
Broad Channel

Park Slope

Prospect Park (p197)
www.prospectpark.org
(Map 13 D5)

Hotels

Boerum Hill

Union Street B&B (p213) $
405 Union Street (Map 13 B4)

Park Slope

**Bed & Breakfast
on the Park** (p213) $$
113 Prospect Park West
(Map 13 C5)

Queens

Art & Architecture

**Noguchi Sculpture
Museum** (p199)
32–37 Vernon Boulevard,
Long Island City
Art Gallery/Garden

P.S.1 (p121)
22–5 Jackson Avenue
Art Gallery

Sports Arenas

Shea Stadium (p151)
123-01 Roosevelt Avenue
Queens/Flushing Meadows
Baseball Stadium

Bronx

Shopping

**Borgatti's Ravioli & Noodle
Company** (p189)
632 East 187th Street
Food

Egidio Pastry Shop (p189)
622 East 187th Street
Food

Sports Arenas

Yankee Stadium (p151)
161st Street & River Avenue
Baseball Stadium

Havens: Parks & Gardens

Wave Hill (p197)
675 West 252nd Street
Garden

New Jersey

Performance

**New Jersey Performing Arts
Center (NJPAC)** (p151)
1 Center Street, Newark
Performing Arts Center

Sports Arenas

Giants Stadium (p151)
50 State Route 120 (off map)
East Rutherford, New Jersey
Football and Soccer Stadium

EYEWITNESS TRAVEL

SPEAK LIKE A LOCAL

LEARN A LANGUAGE IN JUST
15 MINUTES A DAY

BOOKS £6.99

**BOOK & CD
PACK £12.99**

AVAILABLE NOW AT WHSmith

discover more at www.dk.com

Restaurants

Recommended places to eat, including cafés, tea rooms, and delicatessens

American

Alias (p36) $$
76 Clinton Street (Map 4 G4)
Downtown/Lower East Side

Amy Ruth's (p185) $
113 West 116th Street
(Map 11 D5)
212 280 8779
Above Central Park/Harlem

Annie's (p55) $
1381 3rd Avenue (Map 8 F1)
Upper East Side

Blue Smoke (p49) $$
116 East 27th Street (Map 6 F4)
Midtown/Gramercy

Butta'Cup Lounge (p62) $$
271 Adelphi Street (Map 13 C3)
Brooklyn/Fort Green

Crif Dogs (p44) $
113 St. Mark's Place (Map 4 F3)
Downtown/East Village

Florent (p46) $$
69 Gansevoort Street
(Map 3 A2)
Downtown/Meatpacking District

Four Seasons (p46) $$$
99 East 52nd Street (Map 7 D5)
www.fourseasons
restaurant.com
Midtown/Theater District

Gramercy Tavern (p46)
42 East 20th Street (Map 4 E1)
212 477 0777
Midtown/Gramercy

The Grocery (p60) $$
288 Smith Street (Map 13 B4)
Brooklyn/Carroll Gardens

Jackson Diner (p189)
37 74th Street
Queens/Jackson Heights

Jane (p34) $$
100 West Houston Street
(Map 3 D4)
Downtown/West Village

Mercer Kitchen (p33) $$
99 Prince Street (Map 3 D4)
Downtown/SoHo

**Nathan's Famous
Hotdogs** (p188) $
Corner of Surf &
Stillwell avenues
Brooklyn/Coney Island

New Leaf Café (p59) $$
Fort Tryon Park, One Margaret
Corbin Drive (off map)
*Above Central Park/Fort Tryon &
Inwood*

Ouest (p57) $$$
2315 Broadway (Map 9 B5)
Upper West Side

Paul's Palace (p39) $
131 2nd Avenue (Map 4 E3)
Downtown/East Village

Peter Luger $$$
Steak House (p63)
178 Broadway (Map 13 B2)
Brooklyn/Williamsburg

Relish (p63) $$
225 Wythe Avenue (Map 13 D2)
Brooklyn/Williamsburg

Serendipity 3 (p55) $
225 East 60th Street
(Map 8 F4)
Upper East Side

Tavern on the Green (p46)
Central Park West bet 66th and
67th streets (Map 7 C3)
212 873 3000
www.tavernonthegreen.com
Upper West Side

**Top of the Tower @ Beekman
Tower Hotel** (p195)
3 Mitchell Place at 49th Street
& 1st Avenue (Map 6 G1)
Midtown/Turtle Bay

Union Square Café (p47) $$$
21 East 16th Street (Map 3 D1)
Midtown/Gramercy

WD-50 (p36) $$$
50 Clinton Street (Map 4 G4)
Downtown/Lower East Side

Asian

Daily Chow (p38) $
2 East 2nd Street (Map 4 E3)
Downtown/East Village

March (p55) $$$
405 East 58th Street (Map 8 G4)
Upper East Side

Austrian

Wallse (p45) $$$
344 West 11th St. (Map 3 A3)
Downtown/West Village

Bakeries

*See also Cafés, Delis, and
Tea Rooms*

Bonsignour (p82) $
35 Jane Street (Map 3 B2)
*Downtown/Meatpacking
District*

Egidio Pastry Shop (p189) $
622 East 187th Street
Bronx

Ess-a-Bagel (p52) $
831 3rd Avenue (Map 6 F1)
Midtown/Murray Hill

City Bakery (p47) $
3 West 18th Street
(Map 3 C1)
Midtown/Chelsea

Cukiernia (p187) $
223 Bedford Avenue
(Map 13 B2)
Brooklyn/Williamsburg

Dean & DeLuca (pp19, 75) $
560 Broadway (Map 3 D4)
Downtown/SoHo

Magnolia Bakery (p81) $
401 Bleecker Street
(Map 3 B3)
Downtown/West Village

Belgian

Pommes Frites (p44) $
123 2nd Avenue (Map 4 E3)
Downtown/East Village

Breakfast/Brunch

Deborah (p19) $
43 Carmine Street
(Map 3 C4)
Downtown/West Village

Florent (p19, 46) $
69 Gansevoort Street
(Map 3 A2)
Downtown/West Village

Norma's (p54) $$
Le Parker Meridien Hotel, 118
W. 57th Street (Map 7 D5)
Midtown/Theater District

Paris Commune (p61)
411 Bleecker Street (Map 3 B3)
Downtown/West Village

British

Park Slope Chip Shop (p61) $
383 5th Avenue (Map 13 C4)
Brooklyn/Park Slope

Tea & Sympathy (p39)
108 Greenwich Ave. (Map 3 C2)
www.teaandsympathy
newyork.com
Downtown/West Village

Cafés

*See also Bakeries, Delis, and
Tea Rooms*

Bonsignour (p82)
35 Jane Street (Map 3 B2)
*Downtown/Meatpacking
District*

Connecticut Muffin (p186) $
115 Montague Street
(Map 13 A4)
Brooklyn/Brooklyn Heights

DT–UT (p184) $
41 Avenue B (Map 4 G2)
Downtown/East Village

Egidio Pastry Shop (p189) $
622 East 187th Street
Bronx

Housing Works Used Book $
Café (p21)
126 Crosby Street (Map 3 D5)
Downtown/Little Italy

Joe (p39) $
141 Waverly Place
212 924 6750 (Map 3 C3)
Downtown/West Village

Mud Spot (p39) $
307 East 9th Street (Map 4 E2)
www.themudtruck.com
Downtown/East Village

Mud Truck (p39) $
14th Street and Broadway
(Map 3 D2)
www.themudtruck.com
Downtown/West Village

Rue B (p184) $
188 Avenue B (Map 4 G2)
Downtown/East Village

Verb Café (p187) $
218 Bedford Avenue
(Map 13 C2)
www.verbcafe.com
Brooklyn/Williamsburg

Via Quadronno (p39)
25 East 73rd Street
212 650 9880
(Map 8 F2)
Upper East Side

Caribbean

El Malecón II (p58) $
764 Amsterdam Avenue
(9 B3)
Upper West Side

Chinese

66 (p24) $$$
241 Church Street
(Map 1 D1)
Downtown/Tribeca

Fried Dumpling (p44) $
99 Allen Street (Map 4 F4)
Downtown/Lower East Side

HSF (p182) $$
46 Bowery (Map 2 E1)
Downtown/Chinatown

Golden Unicorn (p33) $
18 East Broadway
(Map 2 F1)
Downtown/Chinatown

Grand Sichuan
International (p47) $
229 9th Avenue (Map 5 C5)
Midtown/Chelsea

Great NY Noodle Town (p182) $
28½ Bowery at Bayard Street
(Map 2 E1)
Downtown/Chinatown

Peking Duck House (p33) $$
28 Mott Street
(Map 2 E1)
Downtown/Chinatown

Cuban

Cafe Habana (p35) $
17 Prince Street
(Map 4 E4)
Downtown/Nolita

Delis/Sandwich Shops

*See also Bakeries, Cafés, and
Tea Rooms*

2nd Avenue Deli (p41) $$
156 2nd Avenue (Map 4 E2)
Downtown/East Village

Amish Fine Food Market (p182)
17 Battery Place (Map 1 D5)
Downtown/Lower Manhattan

BB Sandwich Bar (p44) $
120 West 3rd Street (Map 3 C3)
Downtown/West Village

Cosi (p182) $
55 Broad Street (Map 1 D4)
Downtown/Lower Manhattan

Dean & DeLuca (pp19, 75) $
560 Broadway (Map 3 D4)
Downtown/SoHo

Pret a Manger (p182) $
60 Broad Street (Map 1 D4)
Downtown/Lower Manhattan

Sandwich Planet (p51) $
534 9th Avenue (Map 5 C2)
Midtown/Hell's Kitchen

Zabar's (p95) $
2245 Broadway (Map 7 B1)
Upper West Side

Eastern European

Café Arbat (p188) $
306 Brighton Beach Avenue
Brooklyn/Coney Island

Café Glechik (p188) $
3159 Coney Island Avenue
Brooklyn/Coney Island

European

Artisanal (p50) $$
2 Park Avenue (Map 6 F4)
Midtown/Gramercy

Blue Ribbon
Bakery (p41) $–$$$
33 Downing Street (Map 3 C4)
Downtown/West Village

Four Seasons (p46) $$$
99 East 52nd Street
www.fourseasons
restaurant.com (Map 7 D5)
Midtown/Theater District

Montrachet (p32) $$$
239 West Broadway
(Map 1 C1)
Downtown/Tribeca

Picholine (p58) $$$
35 West 64th Street
(Map 7 C3)
Upper West Side

French

Aix (p59) $$$
2398 Broadway (Map 9 B5)
Upper West Side

Balthazar (p33) $$
80 Spring Street (Map 3 D5)
Downtown/SoHo

Chanterelle (p46) $$$
2 Harrison Street (Map 1 C1)
212 966 6960
www.chanterellenyc.com
Downtown/Tribeca

L'Ecole (p34) $
462 Broadway (Map 3 D5)
Downtown/SoHo

The Elephant (p35) $$
58 East 1st Street (Map 4 F4)
Downtown/East Village

LouLou (p61) $$
222 DeKalb Avenue
(Map 13 C3)
Brooklyn/Fort Greene

Mercer Kitchen (p33) $$
99 Prince Street (Map 3 D4)
Downtown/SoHo

Pastis (p183) $$
9 9th Avenue (Map 3 A2)
212 929 4844
www.pastisny.com
*Downtown/Meatpacking
District*

Le Tableau (p37) $$
511 East 5th Street (Map 4 F3)
Downtown/East Village

Tartine (p46) $
253 West 11th Street
(Map 3 B2)
Downtown/West Village

Greek

Pylos (p38) $$
128 East 7th Street (Map 4 F3)
Downtown/East Village

Symposium (p59) $$
544 West 113th Street
(Map 11 B5)
Above Central Park

Ice Cream Parlors

Brooklyn Ice Cream
Factory (p186) $
Fulton Ferry Landing
(Map 13 A4)
Brooklyn/Brooklyn Heights

Chinatown Ice Cream
Factory (p182) $
65 Bayard Street (Map 2 E1)
Downtown/Chinatown

Cones (p44) $
272 Bleecker Street (3 C3)
Downtown/West Village

Indian

Tabla (p48) $$$
11 Madison Avenue (Map 6 E5)
Midtown/Flatiron

Tamarind (p49) $$
41-43 East 22nd Street
(Map 6 F5)
Midtown/Flatiron

International

Biltmore Room (p48) $$$
290 8th Avenue (Map 5 C5)
Midtown/Chelsea

Red Cat (p47) $$
227 10th Avenue
(Map 5 B5)
Midtown/Chelsea

The River Café (p60) $$$
1 Water Street (Map 13 A3)
Brooklyn/Brooklyn Heights

Town (p54) $$$
Chambers Hotel, 15 West 56th
Street (Map 8 E5)
Midtown/Theater District

Italian

Acappella (p32) $$$
1 Hudson Street
(Map 1 C2)
Downtown/Tribeca

Acqua Pazza (p53) $$$
36 West 52nd Street
(Map 8 E5)
Midtown/Theater District

Index by Type

Restaurants

Italian *continued*

Al Di La (p61) $$
248 5th Avenue (Map 13 C4)
Brooklyn/Park Slope

Babbo (p42) $$$
110 Waverly Place (Map 3 C3)
Downtown/West Village

Bamonte's (p63) $$
32 Withers Street (Map 13 C1)
Brooklyn/Williamsburg

Convivium Osteria (p61) $$
68 5th Avenue (Map 13 C4)
Brooklyn/Park Slope

'inoteca (p36) $$
98 Rivington Street (Map 4 F4)
Downtown/Lower East Side

i Trulli (p50) $$
122 East 27th Street
(Map 6 F4)
Midtown/Gramercy

Mezzaluna (p55) $$
1295 3rd Avenue (Map 8 F2)
Upper East Side

Noodle Pudding (p59) $$
38 Henry Street (Map 13 A3)
Brooklyn/Brooklyn Heights

**Otto Enoteca and
Pizzeria** (p42) $$
1 5th Avenue (Map 3 D3)
Downtown/West Village

Pepe Rosso's (p44)
149 Sullivan Street
(Map 3 C4)
Downtown/West Village

Via Quadronno (p39)
25 East 73rd Street (Map 8 F2)
www.viaquadronno.com
Upper East Side

Japanese

Blue Ribbon Sushi (p41) $$
119 Sullivan Street
(Map 3 C4)
Downtown/SoHo

Cube 63 (p36) $$
63 Clinton Street
(Map 4 G4)
Downtown/Lower East Side

Geisha (p54) $$$
33 East 61st Street (Map 8 E4)
Upper East Side

Genki Sushi (p52) $
9 East 46th Street (Map 6 E1)
Midtown/Theater District

Nobu (p46) $$$
105 Hudson Street (Map 1 C2)
212 219 0500
www.myriadrestaurant
group.com
Downtown/Tribeca

Sobaya (p40) $/$$
229 East 9th Street (Map 4 E2)
Downtown/East Village

Sumile (p46) $$$
154 West 13th Street (Map 3 C2)
Downtown/West Village

Sushi of Gari (p57) $$$
402 East 78th Street (Map 8 G1)
Upper East Side

Tomoe Sushi (p41) $$
172 Thompson Street (Map 3 C4)
Downtown/SoHo

Korean

Cho Dang Gol (p51) $
55 West 35th Street (Map 6 E3)
Midtown/Murray Hill

Mandoo Bar (p50) $
2 West 32nd Street (Map 6 E4)
Midtown/Flatiron

Mexican

Dos Caminos (p49) $$
373 Park Ave. South (Map 6 F5)
Midtown/Gramercy

Itzocan Café (p184)
438 East 9th Street (Map 4 F2)
Downtown/East Village

Mi Nidito (p51) $$
852 8th Avenue (Map 5 C1)
Midtown/Theater District

La Palapa Rockola (p42) $$
359 6th Avenue (Map 3 C3)
Downtown/West Village

Middle Eastern

Mamoun's (p44)
119 MacDougal St. (Map 3 C3)
Downtown/West Village

Yaffa Cafe (p38) $
97 St. Mark's Place (Map 4 F3)
Downtown/East Village

North African

Cafe Gitane (p35) $
242 Mott Street (Map 4 E4)
Downtown/Nolita

Le Souk (p37) $$
47 Avenue B (Map 4 G3)
Downtown/East Village

Pizzerias

Anna Maria's (p187) $
179 Bedford Avenue
718 559 4550 (Map 13 C2)
Brooklyn/Williamsburg

DiFara Pizzeria (p62) $
1424 Avenue J
Brooklyn/Midwood

Joe's Pizza (p25) $
233 Bleecker Street
212 366 1182 (Map 3 C4)
Downtown/West Village

**John's of Bleecker
Street** (p43) $
278 Bleecker Street
(Map 3 C3)
Downtown/West Village

Polish

S & B Polish Restaurant (p187)
194 Bedford Avenue
718 963 1536 (Map 13 C2)
Brooklyn/Williamsburg

Theresa's (p186)
80 Montague Street
718 797 3996 (Map 13 A4)
Brooklyn/Brooklyn Heights

Seafood

Atlantic Grill (p56) $$
1341 3rd Avenue (Map 8 F1)
Upper East Side

Mary's Fish Camp (p45) $$
64 Charles Street
(Map 3 B3)
Downtown/West Village

Mermaid Inn (p39) $$
96 2nd Avenue
(Map 4 E3)
Downtown/East Village

South African

i-Shebeen Madiba (p62) $$
195 DeKalb Avenue (Map 13 C3)
Brooklyn/Fort Greene

South American

**Churrascaria
Plataforma** (p52) $$$
316 West 49th Street (Map 5 C1)
Midtown/Theater District

Spanish

Bolo (p48) $$$
23 East 22nd Street
(Map 6 E5)
Midtown/Flatiron

Swedish

Aquavit (p53) $$$
65 East 55th Street
(Map 8 F5)
Midtown/Theater District

Tea Rooms

*See also Bakeries, Cafés, and
Delis*

Lady Mendl's Tea Room (p39)
56 Irving Place
(Map 4 E1)
www.innatirving.com
Midtown/Gramercy

Palm Court Tea Room (p39)
Plaza Hotel, 768 5th Avenue
(Map 8 E4)
Midtown/Theater District

Rotunda at the Pierre (p196)
The Pierre Hotel, 2 East 61st
Street (Map 8 E4)
Upper East Side

Tea & Sympathy (p39)
108 Greenwich Avenue
(Map 3 C2)
www.teaandsympathy
newyork.com
Downtown/West Village

Teany (p80)
90 Rivington Street
(Map 4 F4)
Downtown/Lower East Side

Wild Lily Tea Room (p193)
511-a West 22nd Street
(Map 5 B5)
Midtown/Chelsea

Thai

The Elephant (p35) $$
58 East 1st Street
(Map 4 F4)
Downtown/East Village

Joya (p60) $
215 Court Street
(Map 13 B4)
Brooklyn/Carroll Gardens

Planet Thailand (p63) $
133 North 7th Street
(Map 13 B2)
Brooklyn/Williamsburg

Turkish

Bereket (p35) $
187 East Houston Street
(Map 4 F4)
Downtown/Lower East Side

Pasha (p58) $$
70 W. 71st Street
(Map 7 C2
Upper West Side

Ukrainian

Veselka (p25) $
144 2nd Avenue
(Map 4 E2)
Downtown/East Village

Vegetarian

Angelica Kitchen (p40) $
300 East 12th Street
(Map 4 E2)
Downtown/East Village

Bliss Café (p187)
191 Bedford Avenue
718 599 2547 (Map 13 C2)
Brooklyn/Williamsburg

Candle 79 (p56) $$
154 East 79th Street
(Map 8 F1)
Upper East Side

NY Dosas (p45) $
West 4th Street & Sullivan
Street (Map 3 C3)
Downtown/West Village

Vietnamese

Bao (p37) $
111 Avenue C (Map 4 G3)
Downtown/East Village

Shopping

Books

Heights Books (p186)
109 Montague Street
(Map 13 A4)
Brooklyn/Brooklyn Heights

**Spoonbill & Sugartown
Booksellers** (pp98, 187)
218 Bedford Avenue
(Map 13 B2)
Brooklyn/Williamsburg

The Strand (p87)
828 Broadway (Map 3 D2)
Downtown/East Village

Department Stores

Barney's New York (p92)
660 Madison Avenue
(Map 8 E4)
Upper East Side

Bergdorf Goodman (p91)
754 5th Avenue (Map 8 E4)
Midtown/Theater District

Bloomingdale's (p86)
1000 3rd Avenue (Map 8 F4)
212 705 2000
www.bloomingdales.com
Upper East Side

Henri Bendel (p86)
712 5th Avenue at 56th Street
(Map 8 E5)
212 247 1100
Midtown/Theater District

Jeffrey (p84)
449 West 14th Street (Map 3 A2)
*Downtown/Meatpacking
District*

Macy's (p86)
151 West 34th Street
(Map 5 D3)
www.macys.com
Midtown/Chelsea

Pearl River Mart (p71)
477 Broadway (Map 3 D5)
Downtown/SoHo

Saks 5th Avenue (p86)
611 5th Avenue
(Map 6 E1)
212 753 4000
www.saksfifthavenue.com
Midtown/Flatiron

Takashimaya (p89)
693 5th Avenue (Map 8 E5)
Midtown/Theater District

Fashion

Alexander McQueen (p183)
417 West 14th Street
(Map 3 A2)
www.alexandermcqueen.com
*Downtown/Meatpacking
District*

Banana Republic (p80)
1136 Madison Avenue between
84th and 85th streets (Map 10
E5) 212 570 2465
www.bananarepublic.com
Upper East Side/Yorkville

Barney's CO-OP (p72)
116 Wooster Street (Map 3 D4)
Downtown/SoHo

Brooklyn Industries (p187)
162 Bedford Ave. (Map 13 C2)
www.brooklynindustries.com
Brooklyn/Williamsburg

Butter (p97)
389 Atlantic Avenue (Map 13 B4)
Brooklyn/Boerum Hill

Calypso (p77)
280 Mott Street (Map 4 E4)
Downtown/Nolita

Century 21 (p70)
22 Cortlandt Street (Map 1 D3)
Downtown/Lower Manhattan

Costume National (p73)
108 Wooster Street (Map 3 D4)
Downtown/SoHo

Diane B (p93)
1414 3rd Avenue (Map 8 F2)
Upper East Side

Gap (p80)
60 West 34th Street
(Map 5 D3)
212 760 1268
www.gap.com
Midtown/Chelsea

Helmut Lang (p72)
80 Greene Street (Map 3 D5)
Downtown/SoHo

**Hotel Venus by
Patricia Field** (p70)
382 W. Broadway (Map 3 D5)
Downtown/SoHo

INA (p77)
21 Prince Street (Map 4 E4)
Downtown/Little Italy

Intermix (p94)
210 Columbus Avenue
(Map 7 C3)
Upper West Side

Isa (p99)
88 North 6th Street (Map 13 B2)
Brooklyn/Williamsburg

J. Crew (p80)
347 Madison Ave. (Map 6 E3)
212 949 0570
www.jcrew.com
Midtown/Theater District

Keiko (p71)
62 Greene Street (Map 3 D5)
Downtown/SoHo

Kirna Zabete (p73)
96 Greene Street (Map 3 D4)
Downtown/SoHo

Marc by Marc Jacobs (p82)
403–405 Bleecker Street
(Map 3 B4)
Downtown/West Village

Marc Jacobs (p74)
163 Mercer Street
(Map 3 D4)
Downtown/West Village

Mayle (p78)
242 Elizabeth Street
(Map 4 E4)
Downtown/Little Italy

Metaphors (p187)
195 Bedford Avenue
(Map 13 C2)
Brooklyn/Williamsburg

Mini Minimarket (p98)
218 Bedford Avenue
(Map 13 B2)
Brooklyn/Williamsburg

Miu Miu (p73)
100 Prince Street (Map 3 D4)
Downtown/SoHo

Prada (p74)
575 Broadway (Map 3 D4)
Downtown/SoHo

Sahil Sari Palace (p189)
37–55 74th Street
Queens/Jackson Heights

Jazz Record Center (p88)
236 West 26th Street,
8th floor (Map 5 C5)
Midtown/Chelsea

St. Mark's Sounds (p88)
16 St. Mark's Place (Map 4 E3)
Downtown/East Village

Subterranean Records (p81)
5 Cornelia Street (Map 3 C3)
Downtown/West Village

Shoes & Accessories

ALife Rivington Club (p79)
158 Rivington Street (Map 4 G4)
Downtown/Lower East Side

Bond 07 By Selima (p78)
7 Bond Street (Map 3 D3)
Downtown/Nolita

Christian Louboutin (p93)
941 Madison Avenue
(Map 8 E2)
Upper East Side

Flight 001 (p82)
96 Greenwich Avenue
(Map 3 B2)
Downtown/West Village

Jimmy Choo (p88)
645 5th Avenue (Map 8 E5)
Midtown/Theater District

Kate Spade Travel (p70)
59 Thompson Street
(Map 3 C5)
Downtown/SoHo

Liliblue (p93)
955 Madison Avenue (Map 8 E2)
Upper East Side

Manolo Blahnik (p88)
31 West 54th Street
(Map 8 E5)
Midtown/Theater District

Niketown (p90)
6 East 57th Street (Map 8 E5)
Midtown/Theater District

Rafe (p78)
1 Bleecker Street (Map 4 E4)
Downtown/Nolita

Sporting Goods

Blades Board & Skate (p94)
120 West 72nd St. (Map 7 B2)
Upper West Side

Paragon Sporting Goods (p86)
867 Broadway (Map 3 D1)
Midtown/Gramercy

Super Runners (p95)
360 Amsterdam Avenue
(Map 7 B1)
Upper West Side

Stationery

Kate's Paperie (p76)
561 Broadway (Map 3 D4)
Downtown/SoHo

Thrift Stores

Beacon's Closet (p989)
88 North 11th Street
(Map 13 B1)
Brooklyn/Williamsburg

**Housing Works
Thrift Shop** (p95)
306 Columbus Avenue
(Map 7 C2)
Upper West Side

Art & Architecture

Art Galleries

Asia Society (p115)
725 Park Avenue at 70th Street
(Map 8 F2)
Upper East Side

Deitch Projects (p108)
18 Wooster Street
(Map 3 D5)
212 941 9475
Downtown/SoHo

Forbes Magazine Gallery (p110)
60 5th Avenue at West 12th
Street (Map 3 D2)
Downtown/West Village

Gagosian (p108)
555 West 24th Street
(Map 5 B5)
www.gagosian.com
Midtown/Chelsea

**International Center of
Photography** (p112)
1133 Ave. of the America
(Map 5 D2)
Midtown/Theater District

Leo Koenig (p108)
249 Centre Street (Map 2 E2)
212 334 9255
Downtown/Chinatown

Mary Boone (p108)
541 West 24th Street
(Map 5 B5)
www.maryboone.com
Midtown/Chelsea

Momenta Art (p120)
72 Berry Street
(Map 13 B1)
www.momentaart.org
Brooklyn/Williamsburg

Pace Wildenstein (p108)
534 West 25th Street
(Map 5 B5)
www.pacewildenstein.com
Midtown/Chelsea

Pierogi 2000 (p120)
177 North 9th Street
(Map 13 B1)
www.pierogi2000.com
Brooklyn/Williamsburg

P.S.1 (p121)
22–5 Jackson Avenue
www.ps1.org
Queens

**Williamsburg Art & Historical
Center** (p120)
135 Broadway at Bedford
Avenue (Map 13 B2)
718 486 7372
Brooklyn/Williamsburg

Historic Buildings

Block Beautiful (p110)
East 19th Street, between Irving
Place & 3rd Avenue
(Map 4 E1)
Midtown/Gramercy

**Jefferson Market
Courthouse** (p110)
425 6th Avenue
(Map 3 C2)
Downtown/West Village

Prospect Park West (p119)
between Union and 15th streets
(Map 13 C5)
Brooklyn/Park Slope

U.S. Custom House (p106)
1 Bowling Green (Map 1 D5)
Downtown/Lower Manhattan

Woolworth Building (p108)
233 Broadway at Barclay Street
(Map 1 D2)
Downtown/Lower Manhattan

Installations

Broken Kilometer (p108)
393 West Broadway
(Map 3 D5)
Downtown/SoHo

Earth Room (p108)
141 Wooster Street
(Map 3 D4)
Downtown/SoHo

Modern Architecture

*See also Museums:
Guggenheim and The Whitney*

Chanin Building (p111)
122 East 42nd Street at
Lexington Avenue
(Map 6 F2)
Midtown/Murray Hill

Chrysler Building (p111)
405 Lexington Avenue
(Map 6 F2)
Midtown/Murray Hill

Daily News Building (p111)
220 East 42nd Street
(Map 6 G2)
Midtown/Murray Hill

General Electric Building (p111)
570 Lexington Avenue at 51st
Street (Map 6 F1)
Midtown/Murray Hill

Ground Zero (p107)
(Map 1 C3)
Downtown/Lower Manhattan

**Williamsburg Savings Bank
Building** (p121)
1 Hanson Place, corner of
Flatbush and Atlantic avenues
(Map 13 C4)
Brooklyn/Boerum Hill

Art & Architecture

Museums

Brooklyn Historical Society (p121)
128 Pierrepont Street
(Map 2 H%)
Brooklyn/Boerum Hill

Brooklyn Museum of Art (p120)
200 Eastern Parkway (13 D4)
Brooklyn/Crown Heights

The Cloisters (p118)
Fort Tryon Park (off map)
Above Central Park/Fort Tryon & Inwood

Cooper-Hewitt National Design Museum (p117)
2 East 91st Street
(Map 10 E4)
Upper East Side/Yorkville

Frick Collection (p114)
1 East 70th Street (Map 8 E2)
Upper East Side

Guggenheim Museum (p116)
1071 5th Avenue at 89th Street
(Map 10 E4)
Upper East Side/Yorkville

The Jewish Museum (p117)
1109 5th Avenue at 92nd Street
(Map 10 E4)
Upper East Side/Yorkville

Lower East Side Tenement Museum (p104)
90 Orchard Street
(Map 4 F5)
Downtown/Lower East Side

Merchant's House Museum (p109)
29 East 4th Street (Map 4 E3)
Downtown/Nolita

Metropolitan Museum of Art (p115)
1000 5th Avenue (Map 8 E1)
Upper East Side

El Museo del Barrio (p119)
1230 5th Avenue at 104th Street
(Map 10 E2)
Upper East Side/Spanish Harlem

Museum at the Fashion Institute of Technology (p110)
7th Avenue at 27th Street
(Map 5 D4)
Midtown/Chelsea

Museum of Chinese in the Americas (p182)
70 Mulberry Street, 2nd Floor
(Map 2 E1)
212 619 4785
Downtown/Chinatown

Museum of Modern Art (p113)
11 West 53rd Street (Map 8 E5)
Midtown/Theater District

Museum of Television and Radio (p115)
25 West 52nd Street
(Map 8 E5)
Midtown/Theater District

Rose Museum at Carnegie Hall (p112)
154 West 57th Street, 2nd Floor
(Map 7 D5)
Midtown/Theater District

Skyscraper Museum (p107)
39 Battery Place (Map 1 D5)
Downtown/Lower Manhattan

Studio Museum in Harlem (p119)
144 West 125th Street
(Map 11 D3)
Above Central Park/Harlem

Whitney Museum of American Art (p113)
945 Madison Avenue
(Map 8 E2)
Upper East Side

Whitney Museum of American Art at Altria (p112)
120 Park Avenue at 42nd Street
(Map 6 F2)
Midtown/Murray Hill

Religious Buildings

Cathedral Church of St. John the Divine (p196)
1047 Amsterdam Avenue at
112th Street (Map 9 B1)
Upper West Side

Mahayana Buddhist Temple (p182)
133 Canal Street (Map 2 E1)
Downtown/Chinatown

St. Paul's Chapel (p106)
209 Broadway between
Fulton & Vesey streets
(Map 1 D3)
Downtown/Lower Manhattan

Walking Tours

Big Apple Jazz Tours (p185)
www.bigapplejazz.com
718 606 8442
Above Central Park/Harlem

Harlem Spirituals (p185)
www.harlemspirituals.com
212 391 0900
Above Central Park/Harlem

Radical Walking Tours (p185)
718 492 0069
Above Central Park/Harlem

Performance

Ballrooms

Rainbow Room (p143)
30 Rockefeller Plaza, 65th Floor
(Map 6 E1)
Midtown/Theater District

Swing 46 (p143)
349 West 46th Street
(Map 5 C1)
Midtown/Theater District

Cabaret

Don't Tell Mama (p143)
343 West 46th Street
(Map 5 C1)
Midtown/Theater District

Duplex (p136)
61 Christopher Street
(Map 3 B3)
Downtown/West Village

Combined Arts

92nd Street Y (p145)
1395 Lexington Avenue
(Map 10 F4)
Upper East Side/Yorkville

Apollo Theater (p148)
253 West 125th Street
(Map 11 D3)
Above Central Park/Harlem

City Center (p143)
131 West 55th Street (Map 7 D5)
Midtown/Theater District

The Florence Gould Hall (p144)
55 East 59th Street (Map 8 F4)
Upper East Side

The Kitchen (p140)
512 West 19th Street (Map 3 A1)
Midtown/Chelsea

Makor (p147)
35 West 67th Street (Map 7 C3)
Upper West Side

P.S.122 (p140)
150 1st Avenue (Map 4 F2)
Downtown/East Village

Symphony Space (p147)
2537 Broadway (Map 9 B3)
Upper West Side

Comedy

The Comedy Cellar (p135)
117 MacDougal Street
(Map 3 C3)
Downtown/West Village

The Comic Strip (p145)
1568 2nd Avenue
(Map 8 G1)
Upper East Side

Gotham Comedy Club (p141)
34 West 22nd Street
(Map 6 E5)
Midtown/Flatiron

Stand-Up NY (p147)
236 West 78th Street
(Map 7 B2)
Upper West Side

Upright Citizen's Brigade (p141)
307 West 26th Street (Map 5 C5)
Midtown/Chelsea

Concert Halls

See also Music Venues

Barge Music (p150)
Fulton Ferry Landing (Map 2G3)
Brooklyn/Brooklyn Heights

Brooklyn Academy of Music (p149)
30 Lafayette Avenue
(Map 13 C4)
Brooklyn/Fort Greene

Carnegie Hall (p145)
881 7th Avenue at 57th Street
(Map 7 D5)
Midtown/Theater District

**Lincoln Center for the
Performing Arts (p146)**
Straddling Broadway and
Amsterdam between 62nd and
66th streets (Map 7 B3)
Upper West Side

Merkin Concert Hall (p145)
129 West 67th Street
(Map 7 B3)
Upper West Side

**New Jersey Performing Arts
Center (p151)**
One Center Street
New Jersey/Newark

Dance

The Joyce Theater (p140)
175 8th Avenue (Map 3 B1)
Midtown/Chelsea

Film Theaters

Film Forum (p134)
209 West Houston Street
(Map 3 C4)
Downtown/SoHo

**Landmark's Sunshine
Theater (p138)**
143 East Houston Street
(Map 4 F4)
Downtown/East Village

Jazz & Blues

55 Bar (p136)
55 Christopher Street
(Map 3 C3)
Downtown/West Village

B.B. King Blues Club (p142)
237 West 42nd Street
(Map 5 C2)
Midtown/Theater District

Blue Note (p135)
131 West 3rd Street
(Map 3 C3)
Downtown/West Village

Lenox Lounge (p149)
288 Lenox Avenue between
124th & 125th streets
(Map 11 D3)
Above Central Park/Harlem

Smoke (p147)
2751 Broadway (Map 9 B2)
Upper West Side

Village Vanguard (p136)
178 7th Avenue South
(Map 3 B2)
Downtown/West Village

Music Venues

Apollo Theater (p148)
253 West 125th Street
(Map 11 D3)
Above Central Park/Harlem

Arlene's Grocery (p137)
95 Stanton Street (Map 4 F4)
Downtown/Lower East Side

Bowery Ballroom (p137)
6 Delancey Street (Map 4 E5)
Downtown/Lower East Side

CBGB (p138)
315 Bowery (Map 4 E4)
Downtown/East Village

C-Note (p139)
157 Avenue C (Map 4 G2)
Downtown/East Village

Galapagos (p177)
70 North 6th Street
(Map 13 B2)
Brooklyn/Williamsburg

Hammerstein Ballroom (p141)
311 West 34th Street (Map 5 C3)
Midtown/Chelsea

Kavehaz (p141)
37 West 26th Street
(Map 6 E5)
Midtown/Flatiron

Knitting Factory (p134)
74 Leonard Street (Map 1 D1)
Downtown/Tribeca

Mercury Lounge (p136)
217 East Houston Street
(Map 4 F4)
Downtown/Lower East Side

Rodeo Bar (p142)
375 3rd Avenue (Map 6 F5)
Midtown/Gramercy

S.O.B.'s (p134)
204 Varick Street (Map 3 C4)
Downtown/SoHo

The Soul Cafe (p142)
444 West 42nd St. (Map 5 B2)
Midtown/Hell's Kitchen

Tonic (p137)
107 Norfolk Street (Map 4 G4)
Downtown/Lower East Side

Warsaw (p150)
261 Driggs Avenue (Map 13 C1)
Brooklyn/Greenpoint

Performing Arts

**Brooklyn Academy
of Music (p149)**
30 Lafayette Avenue
(Map 13 C4)
Brooklyn/Fort Green

**Lincoln Center for the
Performing Arts (p146)**
Straddling Broadway and
Amsterdam between 62nd and
66th streets (Map 7 B3)
Upper West Side

**New Jersey Performing
Arts Center (p151)**
1 Center Street, Newark
New Jersey

Poetry

Bowery Poetry Club (p138)
308 Bowery (Map 4 E4)
Downtown/East Village

Cornelia Street Cafe (p135)
29 Cornelia Street (Map 3 C3)
Downtown/West Village

Nuyorican Poets Cafe (p139)
236 East 3rd Street (Map 4 G3)
Downtown/East Village

Sports Arenas

Giants Stadium (p151)
50 State Route 120,
East Rutherford (special
buses from the Port Authority
Terminal at 8th Ave. & 41st St.)
www.giants.com
New Jersey

**Madison Square
Garden (pp23 & 151)**
Map 6 E5
Midtown/Flatiron

Shea Stadium (p151)
123 Roosevelt Avenue, Flushing
(7 IRT Flushing Line Subway

from Times Sq., 5th Ave., and
Grand Central)
www.mets.com
Queens/Flushing Meadows

Yankee Stadium (p151)
161st Street & River Avenue
(4, B, D subway trains from
Manhattan), www.yankees.com
Bronx

Theater

The Public Theater (p139)
425 Lafayette Street (Map 4 E3)
Downtown/Nolita

**Roundabout Theatre Company
at the American Airlines
Theatre (p142)**
227 West 42nd Street
(Map 5 D2)
Midtown/Theater District

TV Studios

Ed Sullivan Theater (p144)
1697 Broadway,
at 52nd Street (Map 7 D5)
Midtown/Theater District

NBC Studios (p144)
Between 5th Avenue & 7th
Avenue from 47th to 51st streets
(Map 6 E1)
Midtown/Theater District

Bars & Clubs

Ale Houses

Blind Tiger Ale House (p167)
518 Hudson Street
(Map 3 B3)
Downtown/West Village

The Ginger Man (p171)
11 East 36th Street (Map 6 E3)
Midtown/Murray Hill

**McSorley's Old
Ale House (p162)**
15 East 7th Street (Map 4 E3)
Downtown/East Village

Spuyten Duyvil (p176)
359 Metropolitan Ave. (13 C2)
Brooklyn/Williamsburg

Index by Type

Bars & Clubs

Ale Houses *continued*

Swift (p162)
34 East 4th Street (Map 4 E3)
Downtown/East Village

Vol de Nuit (p166)
148 West 4th Street (Map 3 C3)
Downtown/West Village

White Horse Tavern (p167)
567 Hudson Street (Map 3 B3)
Downtown/West Village

Bars

2A (p161)
25 Avenue A (Map 4 F3)
Downtown/East Village

Antarctica (p156)
287 Hudson Street (Map 3 C5)
Downtown/SoHo

Arlene's Grocery (p137)
95 Stanton Street (Map 4 F4)
Downtown/Lower East Side

Baraonda (p173)
1439 2nd Avenue (Map 8 G2)
Upper East Side

Barramundi (p160)
67 Clinton Street (Map 4 F4)
Downtown/Lower East Side

Bar Veloce (p164)
175 2nd Avenue (Map 4 E2)
Downtown/East Village

B-Bar & Grill (p163)
40 East 4th Street (Map 4 E3)
Downtown/Nolita

Boat Basin Café (p175)
West 79th St. at Henry Hudson
Parkway (Map 7 A1)
Upper West Side

Bungalow 8 (p170)
515 West 27th Street (Map 5 B4)
Midtown/Chelsea

Buttermilk Bar (p176)
577 5th Avenue (Map 13 C5)
Brooklyn/Park Slope

**Cabin Club at Pine
Tree Lodge** (p168)
326 East 35th St. (Map 6 G3)
Midtown/Murray Hill

Campbell Apartment (p171)
15 Vanderbilt Ave., Southwest
Balcony, Grand Central Terminal
(Map 6 F2)
Midtown/Murray Hill

Chez es Saada (p161)
42 East 1st Street (Map 4 F4)
Downtown/East Village

Chumley's (p166)
86 Bedford Street (Map 3 B3)
Downtown/West Village

Cubbyhole (p168)
281 West 12th Street (Map 3 B2)
Downtown/Meatpacking District

Galapagos (p177)
70 North 6th Street (Map 13 B2)
Brooklyn/Williamsburg

Glass (p170)
287 10th Avenue (Map 5 B5)
Midtown/Chelsea

Gowanus Yacht Club (p175)
323 Smith Street (Map 13 B4)
Brooklyn/Boerum Hill

Great Lakes (p175)
284 5th Avenue (Map 13 C4)
Brooklyn/Park Slope

Hiro (p170)
366 West 17th Street
(Map 3 A1)
Midtown/Chelsea

KGB (p162)
85 East 4th Street (Map 4 E3)
Downtown/East Village

Korova Milk Bar (p165)
200 Avenue A (Map 4 F2)
Downtown/East Village

Library Bar (p168)
Hudson Hotel, 356 West 58th
Street (Map 7 B4)
Upper West Side

Mica Bar (p168)
252 East 51st Street (Map 6 F1)
Midtown/Turtle Bay

ñ (p158)
33 Crosby Street (Map 3 D5)
Downtown/Little Italy

Nevada Smith's (p162)
74 3rd Avenue (Map 4 E2)
Downtown/East Village

Parkside Lounge (p161)
317 E. Houston St. (Map 4 G4)
Downtown/East Village

Plunge Bar (p175)
18 9th Avenue (Map 3 A1)
Midtown/Chelsea

Pussycat Lounge (p156)
96 Greenwich Street (Map 1 D4)
Downtown/Lower Manhattan

Rhône (p168)
63 Gansevoort Street (Map 3 A2)
Downtown/Meatpacking District

Ruby's (p175)
Coney Island Boardwalk
(F, D, Q subway trains to Coney
Island/Stillwell Avenue)
Brooklyn

Rudy's Bar & Grill (p168)
627 9th Avenue (Map 5 C1)
Midtown/Hell's Kitchen

Rue B (p165)
188 Avenue B (Map 4 G2)
Downtown/East Village

Russian Vodka Room (p173)
265 West 52nd Street
(Map 7 C5)
Midtown/Theater District

Serena (p169)
Chelsea Hotel, 222 West 23rd
Street (Map 5 C5)
Midtown/Chelsea

Single Room Occupancy (p172)
360 West 53rd Street (Map 7 C5)
Midtown/Theater District

Sky Bar (p175)
17 West 32nd Street (Map 6 E4)
Midtown/Flatiron

Slipper Room (p161)
167 Orchard Street (Map 4 F4)
Downtown/Lower East Side

Stonewall (p167)
53 Christopher Street (Map 3 B3)
Downtown/West Village

Trash (p176)
256 Grand Street (Map 13 C2)
Brooklyn/Williamsburg

**Welcome to the
Johnson's** (p160)
123 Rivington Street (Map 4 F4)
Downtown/Lower East Side

Winnie's (p156)
104 Bayard Street (Map 2 E1)
Downtown/Chinatown

Clubs

Avalon (p169)
47 West 20th Street (Map 3 C1)
Midtown/Chelsea

Cielo (p168)
18 Little West 12th Street
(Map 3 A2)
*Downtown/Meatpacking
District*

Copacabana (p171)
560 West 34th Street (Map 5 B3)
Midtown/Chelsea

Eugene (p169)
27 West 24th Street (Map 6 E5)
Midtown/Flatiron

Jimmy's Uptown (p174)
2207 Adam Clayton Powell, Jr.
Blvd. (Map 11 D3)
Above Central Park/Harlem

Roxy (p169)
515 West 18th Street
(Map 3 A1)
Midtown/Chelsea

Spirit (p170)
530 West 27th Street
(Map 5 B4)
Midtown/Chelsea

Cocktail Lounges

Angel's Share (p162)
8 Stuyvesant Street (Map 4 E2)
Downtown/East Village

Ava Lounge (p172)
210 West 55th Street
(Map 7 D5)
Midtown/Theater District

Beauty Bar (p164)
231 East 14th Street
(Map 4 E2)
Downtown/East Village

Bemelmans Bar (p173)
Carlyle Hotel, 35 East 76th
Street (Map 8 E1)
Upper East Side

Lansky Lounge (p159)
104 Norfolk Street (Map 4 G4)
Downtown/Lower East Side

Larry Lawrence (p176)
295 Grand Street (Map 13 C2)
Brooklyn/Williamsburg

Métrazur (p172)
East Balcony, Grand Central
Terminal (Map 6 F2)
Midtown/Murray Hill

Pravda (p159)
281 Lafayette Street (Map 4 E4)
Downtown/Nolita

Temple Bar (p158)
332 Lafayette Street (Map 4 E4)
Downtown/Nolita

THOM's Bar (p157)
60 Thompson Street
(Map 3 C5)
Downtown/SoHo

**Top of the Tower @ Beekman
Tower Hotel** (p194)
3 Mitchell Place at 49th Street
& 1st Avenue (Map 6 G1)
Midtown/Turtle Bay

Zombie Hut (p174)
261 Smith Street (Map 13 B4)
Brooklyn/Boerum Hill

DJ Bars

Beauty Bar (p164)
231 East 14th Street (Map 4 E2)
Downtown/East Village

Flûte (p172)
205 West 54th Street (Map 7 D5)
Midtown/Theater District

Frank's Lounge (p174)
660 Fulton Street (Map 13 B4)
Brooklyn/Boerum Hill

Lansky Lounge (p159)
104 Norfolk Street (Map 4 G4)
Downtown/Lower East Side

Lotus (p164)
409 West 14th Street
(Map 3 A2)
*Downtown/Meatpacking
District*

Sullivan Room (p166)
218 Sullivan Street (Map 3 C3)
Downtown/West Village

Uncle Ming's (p166)
225 Avenue B, 2nd Floor
(Map 4 G2)
Downtown/East Village

Warsaw (p150)
261 Driggs Avenue (Map 13 C1)
Brooklyn/Greenpoint

Hotels

Expensive

60 Thompson (p204)
60 Thompson Street
(Map 3 C5)
Downtown/SoHo

Carlyle (p205)
Madison Avenue at 76th Street
Upper East Side

Four Seasons (p210)
57 East 57th Street (Map 8 E5)
Midtown/Theater District

The Lowell (p211)
28 East 63rd Street (Map 8 F4)
Upper East Side

The Mark (p211)
25 East 77th Street (Map 8 E1)
Upper East Side

Mercer Hotel (p204)
147 Mercer Street (Map 3 D4)
Downtown/SoHo

Morgans (p209)
237 Madison Avenue
(Map 6 E3)
Midtown/Murray Hill

The Peninsula (p208)
700 5th Avenue at
55th Street (Map 8 E5)
Midtown/Theater District

The Pierre (p211)
5th Avenue at 61st Street
(Map 8 E4)
Upper East Side

Plaza (p205)
5th Avenue at Central Park
South (Map 8 E4)
Midtown/Theater District

Soho House New York (p206)
29–35 9th Avenue
(Map 3 A2)
Downtown/Meatpacking District

The Stanhope (p212)
995 5th Avenue at 81st Street
(Map 8 E1)
Upper East Side

St. Regis (p208)
2 East 55th Street (Map 8 E5)
Midtown/Theater District

Tribeca Grand Hotel (p205)
2 Avenue of the Americas
(Map 3 C5)
Downtown/SoHo

Moderate

1871 House (p210)
East 62nd Street (Map 8 F4)
Upper East Side

Abingdon Guest House (p205)
13 8th Avenue (Map 3 B2)
Downtown/Meatpacking District

**Bed & Breakfast
on the Park** (p213)
113 Prospect Park West
(Map 13 C5)
Brooklyn/Park Slope

Bevy's SoHo Loft (p204)
70 Mercer Street (Map 3 D5)
Downtown/SoHo

Bryant Park Hotel (p208)
40 West 40th Street (Map 6 E2)
Midtown/Theater District

Hotel Chelsea (p205)
222 West 23rd Street
(Map 5 C5)
Midtown/Chelsea

Hotel Wales (p213)
1295 Madison Avenue
(Map 10 E4)
Upper East Side/Yorkville

Hudson Hotel (p209)
356 West 58th Street
(Map 7 C4)
Upper West Side

Maritime Hotel (p207)
363 West 16th Street (Map 3 A1)
Midtown/Chelsea

Melrose (p211)
140 East 63rd Street
(Map 8 F4)
Upper East Side

Royalton (p208)
44 West 44th Street
(Map 6 E2)
Midtown/Theater District

SoHo Grand Hotel (p204)
310 West Broadway (Map 3 D5)
Downtown/SoHo

Cheap

Chelsea Inn (p207)
46 West 17th Street (Map 3 C1)
Midtown/Flatiron

Chelsea Lodge (p207)
318 West 20th Street
(Map 3 B1)
Midtown/Chelsea

**The Harlem
Flophouse** (p212)
242 West 123rd Street
(Map 11 D4)
Above Central Park/Harlem

Union Street B&B (p213)
405 Union Street (Map 13 B4)
Brooklyn/Boerum Hill

**Washington Square
Hotel** (p205)
103 Waverly Place
(Map 3 C3)
Downtown/West Village

**W New York,
Union Square** (p207)
201 Park Avenue South
(Map 3 D1)
Midtown/Gramercy

General Index

General Index

Acknowledgements

Contributors

Dahlia Devkota's love of travel has taken her to many parts of the globe, from Nepal to Cuba. As well as writing for travel publications, she has been Beauty Editor at W fashion magazine, covering beauty and fitness trends, and spas around the world. For this guide, she wrote the Shopping chapter.

Rachel F. Freeman, native New Yorker and committed foodie and nightowl, loves finding the spice in food, people, and destinations. She's lived in Scotland and Poland and has written for publications including *The Unofficial Guidebook to New York City* and *Voyage* magazine. She wrote the **Hotels, Havens, Performance,** and **Streetlife** chapters of this guide, as well as part of the **Restaurants** chapter.

Jonathan Schultz, a New England native, co-authored DK's *Top 10 Boston* guide. Despite a profound love for his adopted home of Brooklyn, Jonathan remains an ardent Boston Red Sox fan. For this guide, he wrote the **Art & Architecture, Bars & Clubs, Seasonal,** and **Top Choices** chapters, as well as part of **Restaurants.**

Andrew Holigan combines commercial travel-based photography and art photography. Since the 1980s he has lived and worked in New York, London, Sydney, and Melbourne. His works have been exhibited at galleries in the UK, and he has also worked on DK's guides to the *USA* and *France.*

Susannah Sayler is a New York-based photographer and artist. She has worked on more than 20 guidebooks, as well as *Metropolis* and *Planet* magazines. While shooting for this guide, Sayler reported that she had discovered many great spots that she hadn't known about, despite having lived in New York for eight years!

Acknowledgements

PHOTOGRAPHY PERMISSIONS

The publishers would like to thank all the museums, hotels, restaurants, bars, clubs, shops, galleries and other sights for their assistance and kind permission to photograph at their establishments.

Placement Key: t = top; tc = top centre; tca = top centre above; tcb = top centre below; tl = top left; tr = top right; c = centre; ca = centre above; cl = centre left; cla = centre left above; clc = centre left centre;
cr = centre right; crb = centre right below; crc = centre right centre; b = bottom; bl = bottom left; br = bottom right; l = left; r = right.

The publishers would like to thank the following companies and picture libraries for permission to reproduce their photographs:

ADDITIONAL PHOTOGRAPHY: Nelson Hancock, Edward Hueber, Tim Knox, Norman McGrath, Susannah Sayler, Chris Stevens, Robert Wright

1871 HOUSE: 210br; 66: 30tc, 32tl.

AKWAABA MANSION: 212tl; AMERICAN AIRLINES: 227cr; ASIA SOCIETY: Frank Oudeman 115bl.

BLACK BETTY: Mareike Voss 176br; BLACK STAR: 123cra; /H. Matsumoto 232cr, 235tr. BLISS SOHO: 150ca/cbl/cbr; BROKEN KILOMETER: Walter de Maria 108cl; THE BROOKLYN MUSEUM OF ART, NEW YORK: Adam Husted 120tl/tc; BROOKLYN ACADEMY OF MUSIC: 149br; BROOKLYN BOTANIC GARDENS: 16bl; BROOKLYN HISTORICAL SOCIETY: 121tl.; BUNGALOW 8: 170cla.

CAMERA PRESS: Gamma/Frank Gysenbergh 231tl; CAMPBELL APARTMENT: 171br; THE J. ALLAN CASH PHOTOLIBRARY: 226cr; CHELSEA LODGE: 207tl; CITY CENTER: 143br; A. CLINTON: 237cl; CORBIS: Bettmann 17cr, 122cb, 123crb, 123b, 124cra, 126bl, 127cl, 231b; Todd Gipstein 125tl; Vivian Moore 16tr; Bill Ross 226bl; Adam Woolfitt 17bl; Michael S. Yamashita 226t; CULVER PICTURES INC: 124cb, 125cra, 125crb, 127cr.

EARTH ROOM: Walter De Maria 108br; ELLIS ISLAND NATIONAL MONUMENT, NATIONAL PARK SERVICE: 122tl, 122ca, 122br.

CHRIS FAIRCLOUGH COLOUR LIBRARY: 233bla; FOUR SEASONS: 10br, 200-1, 203tc, 210tl; THE FRICK COLLECTION, NEW YORK: John Bigelow Tayler 114tr/bl/br.

GETTY IMAGES: Imagebank/Mitchell Funk 128-9.

HERITAGE IMAGE PARTNERSHIP: Spectrum Colour Library 240b.

© 1993 K-III MAGAZINE CORP: all rights reserved reprinted with permission of New York magazine 217tr.

LOTUS: 164br.

MANDARIAN ORIENTAL: 194tl; PATTI MCCONVILLE: 241c; MERCER HOTEL: 10cra, 202bl, 204crb; MICHAEL MELFORD: 241b; METROPOLITAN TRANSPORTATION AUTHORITY: 238tl, 239tc/cla/cc: P. MILLER:231tr; MORGANS: 209clb; COURTESY OF MUSEUM OF THE CITY OF NEW YORK: 117tl; THE MUSEUM OF MODERN ART, NEW YORK: © 2005 Photo Elizabeth Felicella, architectural rendering Kohn Pedersen Fox Associates, digital composite Robert Bowen 113tr;

NEW JERSEY PERFORMING ARTS CENTER: 151tl/tr; NEW YORK STATE DEPARTMENT OF MOTOR VEHICLES: 234b; NEW YORK CITY FIRE DEPARTMENT: 221bl; NEW YORK POLICE DEPARTMENT: Photo Dept 220cl.

RAINBOW ROOM: 143crb; REX FEATURES: 240cl; ROYALTON HOTEL: 208cla.

SATTERWHITE PRODUCTIONS: 125br; SKYSCRAPER MUSEUM: Robert Polidori 107bl; SOHO GRAND HOTEL: 204cl; SOHO HOUSE NEW YORK: 202tc, 206tr. STATUE OF LIBERTY NATIONAL MONUMENT, NATIONAL PARK SERVICE: 124cl, 125clb; THE STRAND BOOKSTORE: 87bl.

TURNER ENTERTAINMENT: © 1933 RKO Pictures All Rights Reserved 127br.

© US POSTAL SERVICE: 225tc/ca/cb.

WHITNEY MUSEUM OF AMERICAN ART: 16bl, 113bl; WHITNEY MUSEUM OF AMERICAN ART AT ALTRIA:112cl.

COVER IMAGE: CORBIS/James Leynse.